Michael Harrington was nominated for the National Book Award for *The Vast Majority*, his last book. He is the distinguished author of *The Other America*, a classic work on poverty in the United States, *The Accidental Century* and *The Twilight of Capitalism*. An activist in social movements for more than 25 years, he is currently the National Chairman of the Democratic Socialist Organizing Committee, the main successor organization to the Socialist Party of Eugene Debs and Norman Thomas.

The Crisis of
the American System

Also by Michael Harrington

The Vast Majority
The Twilight of Capitalism
The Accidental Century
Fragments of the Century
The Other America: Poverty in the United States
Retail Clerks
Socialism
Toward a Democratic Left

DECADE
OF
DECISION

MICHAEL HARRINGTON

SIMON AND SCHUSTER
NEW YORK

Copyright © 1980 by Michael Harrington
All rights reserved
including the right of reproduction
in whole or in part in any form
Published by Simon and Schuster
A Division of Gulf & Western Corporation
Simon & Schuster Building
Rockefeller Center
1230 Avenue of the Americas
New York, New York 10020

Designed by Stanley S. Drate
Manufactured in the United States of America
Printed and bound by Fairfield Graphics, Inc.
1 2 3 4 5 6 7 8 9 10

Library of Congress Cataloging in Publication Data
Harrington, Michael.
  Decade of decision.

  Bibliography: p.
  Includes index.
  1. United States—Social policy. 2. United
States—Economic conditions—1961–
3. United States—Economic policy—1961–
I. Title
HN65.H368   309.1'73'092   79-24716
ISBN 0-671-24112-5

To the members and friends of the
Democratic Socialist Organizing Committee:
With gratitude and hope

Contents

1. Decade of Decision   11
2. Stagflation   40
3. The Dinosaur Returns   80
4. The Corporate Ideology: Triumph of Illusion   108
5. The Dirty Little Secret   148
6. The United States of Appalachia   178
7. The Nonpeople   222
8. Revolution Without Change   256
9. To the Left, Right and Center   285
10. Turning Point   318
     Bibliography   329
     Index   337

1

Decade of
Decision

America has entered a decade of decision. For better or for worse, the 1980s will change our lives at least as profoundly as the 1930s. The structural contradictions of this society are no longer the speculative province of futurists, philosophers and radical social critics. They are the immediate problems of policy makers and people in the streets. The long run is here again.

In 1969, the Council of Economic Advisers* said that prosperity had become the "normal state" of the American economy. In 1979, many established economists were appalled because of a strong growth rate in the last quarter of 1978. That success, they feared, was a portent of even more inflation and a new recession. "The higher you rise, the further you fall," said a Mellon Bank vice-president. But if full employment is no longer possible because prosperity is inherently unstable, then none of the social goals of the past generation—racial and sexual equality, recon-

---

* The notes are grouped in numbered sections for each chapter. Thus all the references for the next several pages will be found in note 1 for chapter 1.

struction of ruined cities, protection of the environment, national health and all the rest—can be achieved. So it was that, as the seventies ended, a Democratic president, elected by a revived version of the New Deal coalition, actually proposed what his Republican predecessors had threatened but never carried out: the unraveling of New Deal programs.

One can evoke the quality of this historic moment by comparing it to the recent past. In the Cold War fifties, liberals and conservatives celebrated the superior productivity, as well as the democratic political institutions, of the West as against the East. In the socially conscious sixties, at least until Vietnam destroyed the Great Society, the White House proclaimed that a fine-tuned affluence under conditions of price stability would create fiscal dividends sufficient to make justice not only possible but profitable. But as the eighties begin, these same people, now chastened, insist that the essential point is what the system cannot do. They promise the nation limits, austerity; they boldly envision an end to all generous and humane visions.

So the old theories and the old policies don't work anymore, which everyone knows; there are not yet new theories and policies, which almost everyone tries to ignore. This book does not. It focuses precisely on the unprecedented nature of our plight and shows how it is grounded in the very organization of wealth and power in this country. It therefore proposes solutions which will be as bold in the eighties and nineties as the New Deal reforms were in the thirties. It is not "the" answer, for there is no "the" answer to these complexities. It is merely, but emphatically, a contribution to a desperately needed collective effort which will enable this nation to understand, and master, what is now happening to it.

But then, let me be more frank, and therefore immodest: this analysis is a contribution from the democratic Left to a discussion which, thus far, has been dominated by conservatives, some calling themselves liberals, and which has consequently been either irrelevant or reactionary or both. If it does not claim to resolve all of our problems, it is written from unique perspective as far as the recent public debate is concerned. And it asserts, not the omniscience, but the special value of that perspective.

The immediate and obvious source of our confusion is a phenomenon which cannot be understood on the basis of the conventional Keynesian wisdom of the last half century: stagflation, the simultaneous coexistence of high unemployment and high prices. This juncture, *The New York Times* said in 1977, marks "the bankruptcy of modern theory," adding that "the resulting intellectual vacuum has pushed economic policy to the right, by default." And Senator William Proxmire of the Joint Economic Committee of the Congress commented ruefully at about the same time, "Economists may not know the answer to stagflation. Perhaps there is no answer."

Indeed, there is a consensus of perplexity. Herbert Stein, who had been Nixon's chairman of the Council of Economic Advisers, held that "we are running out of the time when it seemed we could have everything—spending without taxes, rapid expansion without controls and controls without compulsion. Choices will have to be made and the choices are fundamental." Walter Heller, who had chaired the Economic Advisers for John F Kennedy and Lyndon Johnson, noted that economists used to say that there were "no roses without thorns," that there was a cost to every pleasure. But now, Heller noted, we seem to have grown thorns without roses. In 1978, Hyman Minsky, an economist from Washington University, attacked all the mainstream theorists, liberal or conservative. He told the Joint Economic Committee that "the years since the mid-sixties are littered with the errors of establishment economists" who, he added, seemed to get larger fees and more political influence after each flawed prediction. As a *Business Week* headline made that point in 1979: "Right or Wrong, Forecasts Pay."

In the summer of 1979 long lines of automobiles appeared at dawn outside of filling stations in some areas of the country. At that point, the rank-and-file citizen became suddenly and dramatically aware of how extraordinary and trying these times are. They responded, as the next chapter will show, with superficial conspiracy theories which contained a profound truth. The shortage, they said, was consciously contrived by the oil companies in order to bid up prices and there were bursting tanks of fuel which were being deliberately withheld from the market. That was simplistic. But the basic insight in those fantasies was quite right as we will see shortly: that multinational energy companies were, and have been for half a century, using their enormous power over both the market and the government to the detriment of individual consumers and of the society as a whole. That development, important as it is, is only a piece in a larger pattern. The same structures which made it difficult, or impossible, for the United States to deal with the energy crisis were also at work in the perplexing phenomenon of simultaneous unemployment and inflation.

These bewilderments of stagflation are the starting point of this book, but only the starting point. For that problem interacts with our culture, our schools, our social classes, our attitudes toward the poor of the globe, to cite only a few of the important relationships. More to the point, an analysis of this phenomenon must deal with underlying structures of the economy and society. When the long run suddenly becomes the short run, as it now has, the cause is precisely a breakdown in seemingly settled institutional patterns. That, it will be demonstrated, is what is taking place now.

This is not to say that the focus will be on an epochal development like that complex process which led from feudalism to capitalism. Rather, it will deal with changes which transform the structure of the system which then survives in a radically altered form. In the late nineteenth century, for instance, roughly twenty years of economic crisis were the background of a shift from entrepreneurial to monopoly capitalism; the Depression of the thirties saw the emergence of welfare capitalism committed to—but almost never in this country achieving—full employment.

The eighties, I suggest, are likely to witness, not the end of American capitalism, but a deep-going alteration in its structures comparable to those earlier changes.

There are rhythms in these changes and one such pattern, the periodic realignments of the American party system, will be examined in some detail in chapter 9. At this point, however, I want to allude to an extremely imaginative attempt to explain the historic transitions within the system. It is associated with the names of two economists, N. D. Kondratiev and Joseph Schumpeter. If one treats their concept as a strict "law," then there is not enough evidence to corroborate it and it is certainly too imprecise to help us cope with the next ten or twenty years. But if one takes it, as I do, as a stimulating intuition, it casts a fascinating light upon the more prosaic analyses which will follow.

Kondratiev was a Russian who eventually died, under unknown circumstances, at the hands of Stalinism. There were, he said, long cycles in the history of capitalism, periodic collapses which prepared the way for new advances. This was not the pattern of boom-and-bust which Marx had discovered, for each Kondratiev cycle contained several such crises and recoveries. Rather, his long cycles stretched over half a century. On the upswing, recessions still occurred but they were brief and not very deep; on the downswing they were chronic and lingering. That projection became involved in the Bolshevik debates of the twenties over whether capitalism was in its death throes (Trotsky was one of Kondratiev's critics), and it probably would have been known to only a few specialists had Joseph Schumpeter not taken up the idea.

Schumpeter was one of the greatest economists of the twentieth century, a procapitalist who predicted the end of capitalism for utterly un-Marxian reasons. Indeed, in the work in which he immortalized Kondratiev, he insisted that the Great Depression of the thirties "was a proof of the vigor of capitalist evolution to which it was— substantially—the reaction." There were, Schumpeter said, "junctures" in which the system is dominated by "scrapping and rearranging." In some cases, "adjustments to long-range and more fundamental . . . changes" prevail and even coincide with short-run crises.

Schumpeter explained these long cycles in the light of one of his own key terms, innovation. That did not necessarily mean invention but rather "doing things differently," even on the basis of the same technology. The long cycles—which Schumpeter baptized "Kondratievs"—occurred because innovation regularly disturbed the normal equilibrium, then a new equilibrium was worked out only to be disturbed in its turn. From 1843 to 1897 railroads were the decisive innovation; from 1898 to 1913, electricity played the innovating role. In the 1920s, there was a Kondratiev downswing, as the economy first worked through previous innovations, like the automobile and chemicals, and then spectacularly sputtered to a halt in the thirties.

Schumpeter's book appeared in 1939 and he died in 1950, but one can speculate in his terms about the postwar period. Is it possible that the period 1945–67 was a gigantic Kondratiev upswing powered by electronics, petrochemicals and the restoration of war-ravaged economies? From the late forties to the late sixties, the Council of Economic Advisers said in 1978, there was "one of the most successful periods of modern world economic history." And could it be that the years since the late sixties have seen a long-term downswing? What are the striking inventions and new markets of the recent past? The pocket calculator, semi-conductors and not much else.

I do not want to insist too hard upon the point. One economist, Jay W. Forrester of MIT, believes that we have entered a Kondratiev downswing in which there is no real need for additional capital plant during the next ten years. Therefore, he concludes, "the real tradeoff of activist policies will not be between unemployment and inflation but between temporary and long-run solutions." On the other hand, W. W. Rostow, an economist and a major figure in the Johnson administration, also invoking Kondratiev, argues that the nation is on the eve of an upswing in which "it will take a great lack of skill and wisdom to produce chronic unemployment." Rostow sees a capital boom in the future.

I clearly incline more toward Forrester's view but the issue is not decisive for my analysis. The roots of the present crisis are profoundly structural and mark a historic turning point whether they fit into a pattern of long cycles or not. Still, I find at least two aspects of the Kondratiev-Schumpeter theory quite relevant. First, there are times of basic readjustment, dominated by "scrapping and rearranging." The seventies and eighties, it will be shown, are one of them. And second, such periods require a methodology which does not apply in calmer times. There is, Schumpeter said, a distinction between the genesis of a species, and its operation after its genesis, which is borrowed from physiology and zoology and "is at the threshold of all clear thinking about economic matters."

In the sixties, economists were concerned about the operation of the system and they were able to make some relatively solid predictions because each year was more or less a continuation of its predecessor. Keynesianism, which had helped in the creation of the welfare state, adequately described its operations. But in the late sixties, and then most unmistakably in the seventies, there was a new time of genesis, and the old rules ceased to apply. A first approximation of two central points in this book should begin to make this point clear: the meaning of a "structural" crisis; the roots of that crisis in a system of corporate power whose priorities pervade government policy.[1]

I

The worldwide crisis of the steel industry at the end of the seventies is both an excellent illustration of a structural contradiction in the system and a marvelous case in point of some of the sources of stagflation in the entire economy.

Steel was, of course, at the very center of the dramatic

expansion of capitalism in the mid-nineteenth century. Between 1850 and 1870, Peter Drucker has pointed out, the Western economies shifted from coal to steel and electricity, organic chemicals and the internal-combustion engine (the second industrial revolution). Indeed, that technological shift was both prelude and cause of the trend toward monopolies and trusts at the end of the century, a process which created U.S. Steel and other giant corporations. It was at that time—in 1890—that this country became the major steel producer in the world.

From that moment until the last decade, steel was a key product in the American economy. But then in recent years it became apparent that there was not a periodic crisis but a fundamental and long-range crisis. "Steel industries throughout the world," the Council of Economic Advisers said in 1978, "have been especially hard hit by the protracted weakness of economic activity in the industrialized countries. Even under moderately optimistic assumptions about the growth of demand, excess steel-making capacity is likely to persist through 1980."

More dramatically, the Chairman of the U.S. Steel Corporation himself talked in 1979 of the "insidious liquidation of the steel industry." *Business Week* editorialized that this trend could cause the United States to become dependent on foreign steel makers much as it has subjected itself to the power of the Organization of Petroleum Exporting Countries (OPEC). "Sometimes," the magazine said, "it is possible to see a disaster in the making a decade before it occurs."

Helmut Schmidt, perhaps the most successful economic manager of the seventies, was equally pessimistic: ". . . you have a structural crisis involving industrial capacity and invested capacity because of the build-up of shipbuilding and steel capacity during the Vietnam war. Capacity in those industries all over the world is too big for peaceful uses now. At the same time, ships and steel can be made cheaper in low-wage countries." This development was part of a larger process: "It's not just a downward business cycle, it's something much more important."

So the problem is global and will even affect the relations of the advanced countries with the Third World. At the end of 1978, Representative John Murtha, a Democrat from Pennsylvania and member of the House Steel Caucus, was very explicit on the last point. "Since 1945," he said, "the U.S. has invested, either directly or indirectly, $4.5 billion to develop steel in 46 countries. Obviously those people are competing with us." There are, however, even more threatening competitors in Japan and Western Europe. That, as will be seen in a moment, was the basis for introducing an inflationary "trigger price" system for steel in the United States in the middle of a campaign against inflation.

At home, the crisis in steel resulted in massive layoffs and mergers which increased the concentration in the industry, and devastated an entire region in the Middle West —the Mahoning River Valley, often called the American Ruhr. In this last aspect, this development is part of the urban crisis described in chapter 6. Steel also shows how inflationary tendencies are built into a system of concentrated corporate power in major American industries, a point which will be developed in a moment.

Even this partial list of the consequences of the situation in the steel industry makes it possible to begin to focus on what is meant by a "structural" crisis. When long-range disruptions occur in a key sector and continue, in good times and bad, over a long period, ramifying throughout the entire national and international economy, that is a structural crisis. And when those events occur in an industry which has been basic to the very existence and progress of the system for a century, that suggests that we are approaching one of those critical turning points described earlier.

But there is more than this generality in the case of steel. There is also material for anticipating themes which will become important later on in the book.

To begin with, even though the steel crisis is obviously structural it is not simply so. Economic "forces," "trends" and "contradictions" are abstractions which permit one to understand developments in the real world; they are not a depiction of that world which is always more complex and sloppy than the abstractions. This is particularly obvious in this case. The industry gave considerable—though not decisive—aid and comfort to its own woes. As Henrick Houthakker, a member of the Nixon Council of Economic Advisers, told the Joint Economic Committee in 1978, ". . . I want to submit that the steel industry is not a well managed industry, and one of the best contributions the steel industry executives could make is a rash of resignations by the top executives." The reason for Houthakker's contempt was that those executives had allowed the industry to become technologically backward.

The basic oxygen furnace, a process which enormously increased steel efficiency and output, was introduced in Europe and Japan in the mid-fifties, but did not reach the United States until the mid-sixties. This lag is one of the reasons why Merrill Lynch, the brokerage house, reported in 1978 that the average Japanese steelworker produces 400 tons of steel per year compared to 250 tons in the United States. At the most modern American mills, workers average 600 tons a year, which is comparable to the Japanese in like facilities. But even when the American plants did finally adopt the new technology (which they actually improved in some cases), they did so on a spotty basis. In 1978, 63 percent of American steel was fired in basic oxygen furnaces as compared to 80 percent in Japan and 72 percent in West Germany. In continuous casting, another innovation, America was even further behind.

The industry, the *London Economist* commented, was "geriatric." That magazine could make such a judgment with reason since it had followed steel's policy of high prices and inefficiency for some time. In 1970 it had editorialized, "With its usual lack of political sense, the American steel industry, presumably managed almost entirely by Republicans, is celebrating a year with yet another round of price increases." That price insensitivity had a long history, going back to the "Gary dinners" where Judge Gary of U.S. Steel used to entertain his competitors for the purpose of price collusion. But now, it takes a specifically contemporary form which is quite relevant to the analysis of stagflation. Steel, Houthakker rightly notes, is "just an extreme example . . . of manufacturing industry generally . . . when there is an increase in aggregate demand, then all the firms raise their prices. There has not been a decrease in steel list prices for 10 years."

The technologically backward industry tried to blame its troubles on unfair foreign competition and high wages in the industry. (In recent years the wages of Japanese steelworkers have been rising faster than those of Americans.) And it fought back by mergers on the theory that bringing together badly managed corporations would give them a "synergistic" power from the mere fact of combination. So it was that LTV bought Jones and Laughlin and Lykes purchased Youngstown Sheet and Tube in the late sixties. They didn't have the internal profits to finance such a move given the poor performance of the industry. So they went into debt to merge and had to sacrifice their cash flow to the creditors rather than being able to put it into modernizing. Lykes was the owner of the Youngstown plant which was dramatically shut down in 1977 with the sudden announcement of five thousand dismissals. In that year, sixty thousand steelworkers lost their jobs in places like Youngstown, Buffalo, Middletown, Johnstown.

Then LTV and Lykes, both the product of failed mergers, proposed to deal with their problems by merging. When the Department of Justice agreed to their plan, Senator Edward Kennedy pointed out that no provision had been made for the workers or the members of the communities who might be hurt, or even ruined, by this "rationalizing" of production. What was involved in all this was precisely one of those radical periods of "scrapping and rearranging" that Schumpeter had described as a symptom of a critical point in the long cycle.

Edward Kelly, a public-interest activist, told Kennedy's committee an incredible story of how irresponsibly capital acted in this situation. "A number of major banks," Kelly said, "Chemical Bank, Citibank, Chase Manhattan and some other major banks, loaned Lykes a tremendous amount of money in 1968 in order to accomplish the takeover. Yet, soon afterward, even though they had helped to create this tremendous need for a continuing debt, and to service that debt, they began to withdraw credit from Lykes. At the same time, they were making tremendous investments in Japanese steel companies. In fact, overall, American banks have been making large investments in Japanese industry, but the largest one of these industries in Japan that they have been investing in is the steel industry." In short, not only steel management, but the pillars of the American financial establishment, helped to make the worst out of the structural crisis in the Mahoning Valley.

The *London Economist* summarized the issue with its usual candor: "The time is needed to allow the obsolete plants of established steel, notably in the United States and Western Europe, to be run down at a socially acceptable rate." But then the *Economist* said, with excessive optimism, "Not even the American government is willing to withstand the political odium of standing by and watching market forces at work." That, however, is more or less what is being done. The workers are being scapegoated for the specific incompetence of the American steel executives, the greed of the banks and the structural crisis of the industry on a global scale. The bill for the "scrapping and rearranging" is being paid by the most vulnerable people in terms of high unemployment and the destruction of living communities and areas.

Meanwhile, the companies are demanding that they get welfare. They hold that they are the victims of "dumping" carried out by "foreign steelmakers . . . [with] preferential access to capital through governmental loans, grants, interest subsidies and target industry programs. This means that foreign producers can operate at a loss and still maintain investment programs. They can set prices unprofitably low in order to maintain operating rates (and employment) or to capture a large market share."

There are a number of things to be said about this plea.

First, the industry conveniently forgets its own inefficiency and backwardness, blaming everything on the foreigners. Second, it wildly exaggerates the phenomenon. Steelmakers in Japan and the Common Market have actually *cut* their prices, an economic tactic which has not occurred to their American counterparts in ten years. And, the Federal Trade Commission found, those subsidies add up to 46 cents a ton in Japan and 44 cents in West Germany—and an average ton costs $300.

But there is also a rather subtle point hidden in that industry statement. The foreigners were accused of using subsidies "to maintain operating rates (and employment) . . . " To an American executive, the crucial point is the operating rates; the employment policy gets a parenthesis. And yet, in at least some European countries, the government take-overs were designed with precisely that job-maintenance point in mind. As a result of the structural crisis of the industry, there have been a rash of nationalizations: in Sweden, Belgium and France. And in Italy and Britain, this sector was already government owned. In some cases—France—the state ownership is a means of rationalization paid for in considerable measure by unemployment. But in Sweden, the government stepped in to maintain employment. The idea that it is sensible to run a plant at a loss in order to avoid the greater human distress and financial deficits which would be incurred if it were closed down is slow to penetrate the American steel mind. In social thought as in basic oxygen furnaces, our industry is backward.

But if the industry's arguments for protectionism are largely specious, the government support it has won is quite real. "Trigger prices" were introduced in July 1978. These are based on the cost of the most efficient steel producers in the world—and include an 8 percent profit rate. Any imports which go below that price will be presumed to come under the federal prohibition against dumping and will be investigated. That is, of course, an inflationary policy initiated by a government which, at the same time, was declaring that inflation was the main enemy. Late in 1978, that situation became even more ironic. The Treasury Department decreed a bigger than usual hike in the trigger price—and the industry, after receiving this inflationary present, was in the forefront of those praising President Carter's anti-inflation package.

The immediate results were gratifying from the steel corporation's point of view. In 1979, after these protectionist measures, capacity utilization and profits went up. Of course, American society paid for that happy outcome by facing higher prices in all of the myriad products with a steel component. And even though U.S. Steel proclaimed in the spring of 1979 that it had a full order book, at the very same time it announced that it would further reduce its capacity over the next five to ten years. While all this was happening, the Economic Development Administration in Washington rejected a proposal for long-term federal loan guarantees to permit a community- and worker-owned cooperative to take over the Campbell Works in Youngstown, one of the plants shut down as steel "rationalized" its situation. The workers were turned down; the companies were given handsome aid.

But steel is not satisfied with such indirect subsidies. Like all of big business in America it wants Washington to provide it "risk" capital by following tax policies which will promote investment, i.e., legislate an increase in the profit rate to the detriment of ordinary taxpayers. So it was that the American Iron and Steel Institute statement which inveighed against foreign government's subsidizing their steel industries approvingly cited a Brookings Institution study asking "a significant role for the government as financial intermediary to ensure that adequate amounts of both personal and governmental savings [flow] to the favored kinds of investment." Needless to say, steel wanted to be "favored."

At the same time, the industry was also carrying on its fight against environmental regulation, another case where inept management managed to inflict wounds upon itself. Steel, *Business Week* reported in 1979, had been "vigorously fighting government efforts to clean up its operations" for years. To be sure, the federal government—which had refused loan guarantees to the community in Youngstown—gave $500 million of such guarantees to help the corporations deal with pollution. But even so, *Business Week* editorialized, the industry "had increased its costs substantially by postponing compliance at a time of rising prices." It can be confidently predicted that steel, in addition to getting protectionist measures and guaranteed loans, will also piously battle against environmental regulations in the name of "productivity."

This is a key theme of the new corporate ideology which will be treated at length in chapter 4. Wages and government spending must be held down to fight inflation, the environment must be sacrificed—but profits and the incomes of wealthy investors must be increased in order to encourage productivity and modernization. And yet, as a very important Joint Economic Committee study noted, even as the steel industry demanded federal aid in raising billions for modernization, it raised prices and did not mention all of the analyses pointing to a decline in the need for steel.

More broadly, the Joint Economic Committee study generalized its findings on the steel industry. Traditionally, it said, declining industries and their workers "have had to make their own adjustments by reallocating resources and writing off their loss." The companies, it added, get a tax write-off for their loss; the workers, I would note, do not. Moreover, "declining sectors have been replaced in the past by other new and growing sectors. *If such a decline is now to effect a broad array of industries of strategic importance, however, a more active government role in the adjustment will be called for. The time-honored device of tax incentives to stimulate investment will probably not suffice. A national or international plan for phasing out excess capacity may be needed*" (emphasis added).

That statement with its italicized conclusion can stand as a summary of this brief analysis of a spectacular case of structural crisis in the American economy. Giant corporations with market power to set prices and maintain them in spite of declining demand contribute to inflation and unemployment at the same time as they try to cope with a situation in which basic, century-old capitalist patterns are being shattered. Workers and the public are the victims, but the companies blithely ask for societal aid which, in this particular case, would subsidize a manifestly inefficient and backward industry, exacerbate the maldistribution of wealth through tax handouts for the rich and almost certainly not solve the problem. Steel writes these contradictions very large—but they are the contradictions of the entire American economy in this time of "scrapping and rearranging."

Indeed, this example points toward a central theme of this book, which is why it is explored in the first chapter: that the basic source of the crisis of stagflation is the continuing domination of corporate priorities in American society.

In three previous books—*Toward a Democratic Left* (1968), *Socialism* (1972) and *The Twilight of Capitalism* (1976)—I showed how corporate priorities permeate the society, including government policy under liberal administrations. In this volume, I will deepen and extend that analysis to bring it to bear on the phenomenon of stagflation. At this point, however, I will merely outline it in summary form.

The United States is increasingly a corporate collectivist nation. The commanding heights of the economy are dominated by multinational oligopolies with a sense of social responsibility like that of the banks which helped Japanese steelmakers destroy American jobs. The government, which is essential to the operation of the system, favors the corporations no matter who is in power. It creates trigger prices, as in the case of steel, to protect an industry from the capitalist competition which the society officially exalts; it builds an enormous public infrastructure for private cars and not so incidentally sponsors both waste and pollution; it provides tens of billions in tax expenditures for the rich on the grounds that this will make them kind to the poor; etc.

This convergence of corporate and governmental priorities is often the result of the fact that the social upper class, i.e., the owners of those multinationals, play a disproportionate role in public policy making. And yet, it would be wrong to explain the procorporate outcomes as mainly, or primarily, the result of a conscious conspiracy on the part of those who benefit from them. For even when honest and sincere critics of corporate power win office including the presidency—the very structure of economic power forces them to adapt to, and serve, their enemies in the boardroom.

The executives control the investment process. They decide on what technology will be developed, where it will be located and what price will be charged for it. If they call a strike of capital, which can be done without raising a picket sign or, for that matter, without the public even noticing, the system will not work. There are thus severe, institutional limits to reform so long as that decisive investment function is monopolized by a corporate elite. The elected representatives of the people must defer to the minority in the boardroom more than to the majority at the ballot box. But this relationship between economic and political power is not simple and straightforward. Indeed, it often works behind the backs of those who act it out. A good part of this book will be devoted to unraveling some of these intricate patterns.

These trends have been developing for some time. In the post–World War II period, they accelerated. For instance, the one hundred largest firms control about the same share of the nation's assets in 1978 as the two hundred largest firms did thirty years earlier. In and of itself, that evolution did not, however, create the current crisis. It only did so when the economy turned that corner somewhere in the late sixties. At that point, increasingly concentrated corporate power sought relief from its problems in governmentally induced recessions, which is a classic capitalist strategy under the welfare state, *and* had enough power over the market to raise prices at the same time, which was something new. This is the basic cause of our plight and its consequences ramify through the entire society, as we will see.

In order to avoid such a radical truth, the appropriate scapegoats were summoned for public vilification. Our woes, it was and is said, are due to high wages, or to government intervention, or to excessive liberality toward the poor and the minorities. Robert Solow summarized the quintessence of this thesis in an interview with *The Wall Street Journal* in 1979. "The single most important reason for inflation is that we are a society that has tried to prevent deep recessions, to provide income security for people and to help those who suffer," Solow said. In short, a leading liberal economist finds that the basic source of our woes is liberalism.

If that is taken to mean that liberalism has been too radical, or that its social commitments are the cause of stagflation, it is, this book will show in documented detail, not true. Indeed, the truth lies in precisely the opposite direction. If this nation is to deal with the crises of the 1980s it will have to go far beyond the New Deal, which was not at all radical in its stance toward corporate power, rather than, as so many now argue, retreating back toward Herbert Hoover.

The New Deal was an ambiguous event. On the one hand it was a reform pushed through by a gigantic popular movement of working people, blacks, liberals and others. Those constituencies did indeed change significant aspects of their lives: it is better to be an old person today than it was before Social Security or to belong to the United Auto Workers rather than to work in a nonunion plant. But on the other hand, the structural changes took place within the system and, once the tumult and social energy of the Great Depression abated, the system shaped and co-opted the very reforms which most of the corporate rich had abominated. Thus, I disagree with Arthur Schlesinger, Jr.'s, judgment that Roosevelt "rejecting the platonic distinction between 'capitalism' and 'socialism,' he led the way toward a new society which took elements from each and rendered both obsolescent." That "platonic distinction" is, I think, crucial to understanding what is happening in the America of the eighties.

The New Deal assumed that the basic corporate infrastructure of the society was sound and good and that most investment decisions should be made in corporate boardrooms. It was the government's function to follow fiscal and monetary policies which would permit the private sector to carry out its Adam Smithian mission. Here, for example, is Gardner Ackley, one of the leading liberal economists of the Great Society, in 1967: "If one were to examine all of the thousands of decisions made daily by the managers of the modern corporations, I think he would be struck by the relatively small number in which significant questions of conflict between public and private interest arise. In the vast majority of these decisions, business need not explicitly master the 'public interest'; nor does government have any cause for concern. What sources of material are cheapest, what products sell best, what production method is more efficient—these are questions to which answers that maximize private profit in most cases also maximize public welfare."

This book will suggest that Ackley—and the majority of the theorists and policy makers in this country who agree with him—are wrong.

It is precisely the private corporate domination of the investment process which is the source of stagflation. In the case of steel we have seen how monopoly pricing and protectionism made a major contribution to simultaneous unemployment and rising prices. In the chapters that follow, the same basic phenomenon will be explored throughout the American economy. And this analysis obviously has important policy implications: the solution of the structural crisis of the seventies and eighties requires subjecting that corporate power to democratic social control in hundreds of different ways. That is not, let me be clear once again, to argue that a basic transformation of capitalism is on the immediate agenda. I do not believe that it is. But we will not emerge from our present dilemmas without innovations as bold as Roosevelt's were in his days—which is to say, innovations which go in the opposite direction of most conventional thinking in the United States.

It was thought in the 1960s that this country could have a social revolution without the inconvenience of changing any basic institutions. Uninterrupted economic growth with stable prices would guarantee sufficient funds to do away with all injustices and the educational system would move the society in the direction of class-lessness by making everyone middle class. In the 1970s, it turned out that the business cycle had not been mastered and that new demons had appeared so that there was little growth and tremendously unstable prices. The initial response to this new situation—on the part of all conservatives and many liberals—was to sound retreat. The problem is, as this book will document, that the rightward drift offered no real solutions but did function to make corporate power, which is at the very core of the problem, all the stronger. In the not so long run, then, such politics would exacerbate our woes.

In short, this book will show that the answers to the structural crisis of these times will be structural in character or else they will fail.[2]

II

The analysis will focus primarily on the domestic economic basis of the structural crisis of the seventies and eighties. Before outlining that project, it is important to specify its limits. The task I have set myself is quite ambitious but it is not all-embracing.

There will, of course, be a discussion of the international dimensions of the American crisis. Our problem, it has already been shown in the case of steel, is global in character and cannot be solved by an isolated nation. But I will not deal exhaustively, or even at great length, with this particular aspect of our situation. For one thing, it requires book-length treatment in its own right. For another, domestic structures shape our international involvements, a point which applies with special force to the United States, a country with a vast internal market and domestic forms of "imperialism" (the Northern exploitation of the South) which made it, until quite recently, less dependent upon the world market than any advanced power. And finally, I have treated at least some of the international ramifications of American policy in a recent book, *The Vast Majority*, and see no reason to go over that ground again at this time.

Second, there are moral, psychological and social consequences to this crisis which will not be analyzed in any detail. Chapter 9 will show how the moods and attitudes of an unsolved stagflation contribute mightily to the fragmentation and nastiness of our politics, but that is only a peripheral exploration of an extremely important theme. I am convinced that, as Christopher Lasch has pointed out in *The Culture of Narcissism*, there are social sources of the self-centered hedonism so characteristic of these times. I find much of Lasch's analysis compelling and brilliant, yet I have certain disagreements about the way the connections are drawn between the societal and the psychological. Here, again, it would take another book to deal with such matters adequately so I will not even attempt to do so.[9]

Third, I do not discuss the military dimensions of our plight. That is hardly because they are unimportant: thermonuclear war still threatens the very existence of humanity and disarmament is therefore the precondition of survival. But I do not think that the arms sector is the key to understanding our economic problems or that a reduction in defense spending—desirable as that is—is the way to solve all of our woes. There is a facile theory which asserts that America should be seen as necessarily dependent on the Cold War for domestic economic survival. Seymour Melman, a longtime peace activist, has shown that, far from guaranteeing our prosperity, armament expenditures have made a significant contribution to undermining American productivity and therefore to the genesis of stagflation. So I feel justified in not taking up a subject which is, in some respects, more important than the one with which I have decided to deal.

These disclaimers, however, do not mean that the focus of this book is unrelated to weightier themes about the world economy, social psychology and the arms race. Clearly each one of those topics cannot be analyzed unless it is related to the underlying structural crisis which pervades American society today. Indeed, I believe that the structures which I will analyze are critical—if complex— determinants of those other spheres. And I am struck, not by the modesty of my subject matter, but by its intricate vastness.

I will begin with an examination of the phenomenon of stagflation itself. In this chapter many of the points which were merely alluded to in the discussion of the steel industry, like the impact of industrial concentration upon administered prices and unemployment, will be examined in greater detail. That does not mean that the reader will find a full, worked-out theory of stagflation and a program which will miraculously resolve that economic plague. There will be many loose ends and inadequacies precisely because the problem is new, unprecedented and exceedingly complex. Yet I do unhesitatingly claim that my analysis, whatever its flaws, is infinitely more realistic than most of what passes for the conventional wisdom in this area. To use a cliché which nevertheless accurately conveys my meaning, the emperors of our theory and practice wear no clothes these days.

The inability to cope with inflation then leads to the rationalization of intolerably high levels of unemployment. That historic retreat, chapter 3 will show, makes it impossible to win effectively *any* social and economic gains in the foreseeable future: it does not simply strike at the poor, the minorities and women; it also grievously wounds employed workers, the people of the Third World and the hopes for a livable environment. So it is that I regard a full employment program as at least as important as an anti-inflation program. But then, the two are intertwined in political reality as well as in the economic fact of stagflation. Inflation is used as the decisive argument against a genuine full employment policy. In part that is because, as these two chapters will show, policy makers arc complctcly unwilling to cmbark on thc radical structural change required to solve the twin evils of soaring prices and high joblessness.

Instead of actually facing up to that situation, to an extraordinary degree the discussion and policy proposals have focused on nonsolutions which have the effect of increasing the maldistribution of income and wealth in the United States. That is the corporate ideology of the seventies which will be the subject of chapter 4. It is also the reason why Washington follows antisocial priorities— and why geniuses in economic and social theory, wearing these blinkers, are often blind. The result, which chapter 5 documents, is not simply a basically unjust allocation of the riches of the society, but an allocation that also contributes to institutionalizing stagflation. It is an economic, as well as an ethical, evil.

Those four chapters describe the structural foundations of the American system—and the radical transformations which are necessary if the crisis of the eighties is to be resolved. The next three chapters outline some of the most dramatic consequences which are inherent in that structure. Chapter 6 deals with the decay of the great cities of the Northeast and industrial Middle West—and the deterioration which is already beginning to afflict a far from idyllic "Sun Belt." The problem posed by the ruin of the original centers of American capitalism is so profound that many Establishment policy makers literally want to ignore it, claiming that this cruel process will ultimately effect a benign, and economically beneficial, "shrinkage" of overly large metropolitan areas. All they leave out is the shrinkage of human life potential which occurs at the same time.

All of this strikes most disastrously at the poor, of course. Given the soaring commitments to end poverty in the sixties, this comes as a distinct embarrassment. Therefore, as chapter 7 will detail, there is a strong movement within both academe and the government to define this agony out of existence. But it should not be thought that "only" the poor and the minorities are the victims of this process. Another casualty is the middle-class hope for an educational panacea that would solve all social problems and not require any institutional change. The fact of the eighties, chapter 8 will show, is that, even if one assumes the return of full employment and price stability, the society will still systematically waste the talent and disappoint the expectations of the young in every social class.

Solutions will be proposed in each of these chapters since my proposals obviously follow from the analysis. But a fundamental issue will be put into parenthesis upon chapter 9: However desirable my program may be, is it politically possible? The structural crisis of the economy and social structure has clearly already had a major impact upon politics. The old coalitions seem to be breaking down but there are no new coalitions to replace them— much as the Keynesian theory and practice shatter but are not succeeded by another theory and practice. Indeed, it is conceivable that this nation is entering a time of unprecedented change with a party system which is increasingly incapable of any kind of progressive response. That grim eventuality will also be considered in chapter 9.

But another possibility will be considered, too: that a new coalition can be assembled around the program urged here, that the eighties will, like the period before World War I or the Depression, produce both new solutions and a political instrument capable of introducing them into the nation. I assume it is obvious that I do not contemplate these radically divergent alternatives with the serene calm of a disinterested scholar. I write this book, not simply to observe and record social reality, but to help to change it.

For that to happen, the United States needs a new vision in several meanings of that term.

First, I have already alluded to the way in which society's ability to see is conditioned by social structures and historic moments. Let me be more specific on that count. In recent years, statisticians—who gain a certain authority since they deal in "facts," in "hard" numbers, not merely in opinions—have been busy defining certain critical problems out of existence. Three examples, all of which will be developed at greater length later on, should illustrate what I mean. First, there has been feverish activity to change the definition of riches, including something called "Social Security wealth" in our computations and, on the basis of this ingenious and completely questionable technique, to reduce the inequities in the society radically while in fact leaving them very much intact.

Second, the experts have been busy refashioning the definition of full employment. The amount of "necessary" joblessness has been increased and the "full employment unemployment rate"—for, curiously, we define full employment as a certain level of tolerable unemployment—has been raised. The innocent bystander might not realize that every 1 percent upward shift in that definition involves misery for almost one million citizens. That is the fact. Here again, a worsening of the reality is camouflaged by the statisticians' art.

Third, and most cruelly, new definitions of poverty have been developed which prove that there are no more poor people in this country. The scholars who work out this remarkable insight must be careful not to wander into the ruined slums of the great cities for one of the social problems they have proved nonexistent might mug them. But then this is a way of dealing with our structural turmoil which is designed for theorists and policy makers who keep a careful distance from our sordid social reality. Moreover, since these numbers act as triggers in various social programs, redefining them is a way of reducing the funds available to the most vulnerable people in the land.

These three redefinitions are not unrelated. It is not that there is an intellectual conspiracy in America to hide our miseries from our eyes, though that might seem to be the case. Rather, historic periods tend to have ideological moods and those specify what thinkers are to spotlight and what they are to shove into the shadows. In the Cold War fifties, for instance, it was considered an act of disloyalty, of subversion, to criticize the United States. Therefore those scholars were acclaimed who celebrated this society and discovered virtues which had long been hidden. In the sixties, the emergence of a militant nonviolent black movement under the leadership of Martin Luther King, Jr., the rebirth of student activism and the Kennedy-Johnson presidency made social criticism fashionable. Writers, as I well know, were rewarded for pointing out what was wrong with America.

The seventies, precisely because of the confusion attendant upon a structural crisis which was neither understood nor mastered, did not have the coherence of those earlier decades. But as time went on disillusionment, cynicism and a new conservatism appeared. Some of the most enthusiastic antienthusiasts were repentant activists from the sixties. Now a thinker or a politician was cheered if he or she made some new revelation of what the society could not do.

In the process myths emerged. The sixties, one was told, had innovated boldly and radically and failed. Therefore the seventies and the eighties must be chastened and uninnovative. The misleading specifics of that indictment will be exposed in chapter 7. For now, I merely want to suggest the social roots of its hold upon the American imagination, which, lacking both a realistic analysis and program for dealing with our structural crisis, accepted illusions—which often took the form of disillusionment. Thus one task of this book is to demythologize, to penetrate beneath the surface of our society to the actual sources of our troubles. If it succeeds in this, it will help give America its eyes back.

That, however, is not a romantic undertaking, for one cannot counter the formidable statistical apparatus of the new naysayers with random, journalistic observations. So it is that even though I address myself to a general audience, I will take great care to explore complicated statistical issues. In this technological age, with its excessive reverence for the artful "facts" of the experts, that is the only way to proceed. Even so, I must confess that a walk down a ghetto street or a drive through a rural backwater is a more persuasive experience for me than reams of computer printouts.

There is yet another way in which America needs to get back its vision. It is difficult to imagine and utterly necessary.

One of the consequences of the present crisis is a decline in intellectual coherence. There are ad hoc explanations of our plight but no theory which comprehends it. At the same time, stagflation pits against one another constituencies which should be together. Broadly speaking, those at the bottom and middle of the society fight with one another in such a period instead of uniting against the corporate rich at the top of the system who are responsible for our woes. And even within constituencies there are suspicion and anger. Workers, one leading American trade unionist told me in 1977, think that other workers are responsible for inflation. In such times of confusion and fragmentation it is difficult to achieve a social unity when everyone regards everyone else as part of their problem.

We live in a time, Samuel Beer has suggested, without a "public philosophy." The New Deal was not simply a political or an economic program, it was a way of making sense of societal life, a purpose, a vision. Now the New Deal—and all of its heirs up to the Great Society—no longer provides a framework for policy. Beer much too optimistically thinks that we have stumbled into an "equilibrium without a purpose" which will fulfill some of the functions of the old public philosophy. I disagree. We are in for a period of continuous, nerve-wracking disequilibria, and so long as we do not know how to cope with that fact, the society will be pervaded by a certain kind of social meanness.

But, then, it would be silly to think that new public philosophies—new visions—are easily created. Roosevelt, to continue with that example, did not even hint at a new philosophy in the campaign of 1932 and the New Deal itself was never a coherent plan but rather an ad hoc and innovative response to problems and politics. Indeed, it is doubtful whether Roosevelt understood the Keynesian theories he sometimes applied, a judgment attested to by his commitment to conventional fiscal policy in the campaign of 1936.

So I have no illusion that a single book, or an individual, can reverse the massive trends I describe here. But even with that chastened awareness, I must admit that my ultimate purpose is even more radical than I have as yet hinted. America is not simply in the midst of an economic and political crisis; it suffers from that bewilderment of the spirit I mentioned earlier. And if, as I said at that point, this book will not undertake an analysis of that problem, it will, I hope, make at least some contribution to its resolution. For in a complex way which I cannot begin to describe, the private and interior anxieties and woes of these times are conditioned, and sometimes even caused, by the public failures which will be my subject. When a society cannot understand and master its own environment, its individual members can despair about their own ability to cope with such an utterly uncertain world.

I do not claim that the ideas in this book are social therapy which will make all those individuals whole. That is preposterous. What I am saying is similar to a famous toast made by John Maynard Keynes. To the economists, he said; not the trustees of civilization, but the trustees of the possibility of civilization. In that spirit, it is my conviction that if the policies urged here are adopted, then that would not simply mean lower prices and more useful work and an end to discrimination and all the rest, but also the possibility that in a structurally transformed environment, more and more people might—just, but emphatically, might—find their own best selves.

_____ Notes _____

1. Council of Economic Advisers (hereafter CEA) 1969, p. 94. Mellon: Clyde Farnsworth, _The New York Times_, January 19, 1977. _The New York Times_ editorial: "Paralyzed Economists, Stagnant Economy," September 24, 1977. Proxmire: Joint Economic Committee (hereafter JEC), _Midyear Review of the Economy_, 1977, p. 96. Stein: "The Class of '79," _The Wall Street Journal_, January 20, 1977. Heller: "The Realities of Inflation," _The Wall Street Journal_, January 19, 1978. Minsky: JEC, _Special Study on Economic Change_, pt. 3, pp. 841–42. Kondratiev: Joseph Schumpeter, _Business Cycles;_ also Richard Day, "Trostky versus Kondratiev." Schumpeter on Depression: Ibid., vol. II, p. 908. Structures: Ibid., vol II, p. 907. Innovation: Ibid., vol. I, pp. 84 ff. Cycles: Ibid., vol I, 303, 397; vol II, 753–54. CEA, 1978: p. 97. Forrester: "Are We Headed for Another Recession." Rostow: "It Will Take Skill to Avoid a Boom." Genesis and operation: Schumpeter, vol. I, p. 37.

2. Drucker: _The Age of Discontinuity_, pp. 11–12. CEA on steel: 1978 Report, p. 136. _Business Week_, September 17, 1979: "Big Steel's Liquidations"; Editorial: "Disaster in the Making." Schmidt: Interview, _Business Week_, June 28, 1978. Murtha: "Steel Like Oil," _New York Post_, AP dispatch, December 26, 1978. Houthakker: JEC, _Special Study_, pt. 3, p. 807. Steel production: Bogdanich, "Steel Mill Blues"; Bensman and Carpenter, "Steel Industry Woes." _London Economist:_ "Enough, No More," June 3, 1978, _London Economist_ in 1970. January 31, 1970. Houthakker: Op. cit. supra, p. 825. Wages: Bogdanich. Mergers: Walter Adams, "Merging Sick Steel Giants," _The New York Times_, August 8, 1978; U.S. Senate Subcommittee on Antitrust and Monopoly, p. 5. Layoffs: "Steel Trap," _The New Republic_, July 22, 1978. _London Economist:_ "From Free Trade to Adjustment," December 31, 1977. Dumping: U.S., Senate, Subcommittee on International Economics, _The Trade Deficit_, p. 90; "Steel Trap." Triggers: Leonard Silk, "Inflation, Trade Protectionism and Rising Steel Prices," _The New York Times_, May 11, 1978. JEC: _U.S. Long Term Economic Growth Prospects_, p. 58. Concentration: _The Trade Deficit_, p. 1. U.S. Steel reductions: _The Wall Street Journal_, May 8, 1979. _Business Week:_ "EPA Puts Heat on Steel," May 7, 1979. Loan guarantees: Robert Howard, "Going Bust in Youngstown." Robert Solow: Quoted in Richard J. Levine, "Price of Progress," _The Wall Street Journal_, June 19, 1979. Schlesinger: _The Politics of Upheaval_, p. 651. Ackley: _The Wall Street Journal_, May 1, 1967.

3. Lasch: _The Culture of Narcissism_, passim. Melman: _The Permanent War Economy_, passim. Beer: in Anthony King, ed., _New American Political System_, pp. 5–6.

2

Stagflation

During the 1976 presidential campaign, Jimmy Carter proclaimed unemployment to be the critical domestic problem for American society. In 1978 and 1979 Carter dramatically announced his conversion to a conservative theme: inflation was now the decisive challenge.

The problem is, as the Carter administration itself understood in its more thoughtful moments, that neither full employment nor price stability can be achieved independently of one another. Put another way, inflation has become an excuse for high unemployment; and high unemployment, contrary to the established wisdom, is clearly a source of inflation. Once upon a time it was thought that these two evils could be "traded off" against each other, that economic managers could induce a mild dose of joblessness to bring down high prices, or a gentle case of inflation to get full employment. Now that is no longer the case—or more precisely, the level and duration of joblessness required to bring prices down is politically unacceptable even to conservatives—which is why both the theorists and the policy makers are so confused.

This chapter will focus on the inflation aspect of the

dilemma; the next chapter, on full employment. In each case, I will be concerned, not so much with exploring the intricacies of short periods in the economy, but with the underlying and structural forces which have brought about this unprecedented situation. As I write, in 1979, the president is pursuing a program of traditional budget-cutting remedies to a totally untraditional problem. By the time this book appears, it is conceivable that the failure of that tactic will have caused a lurch to the Left similar to Richard Nixon's conversion to Keynesianism, i.e., to his own reelection, in August 1971. Such developments are unpredictable; the deep trends they refract are not.

This does not mean, let me be quick to add, that I claim to present a new synthesis on the order of Keynes's *General Theory of Employment Interest and Money*. That would be an absurdly arrogant undertaking which is totally beyond my competence—and indeed beyond the competence of people much more trained in the mechanics of economic analysis than I am. What I will do is deal with familiar facts within an unfamiliar framework: the knowledge that the American system, for all of its reforms, remains crisis ridden and contradictory, producing stagflation as normally as it makes cars and computers. That intellectual vantage point, I suggested in the last chapter, offers insights denied authentic geniuses wearing blinkers. The fact that almost everyone was surprised by the current crisis is an excellent case in point.

In the 1960s, extraordinarily gifted and talented thinkers, experienced in practical politics as well as in academic theory, became euphoric and visionary. So did elected leaders. There had been, they well knew, twenty-six recessions between 1854 and their own day. But now, those problems of boom-and-bust were over and finished. "No longer do we view our economic life as a relentless tide of ups and downs," Lyndon Johnson told the Congress in his last economic message in 1969. "No longer do we fear that automation and technical progress will rob workers of jobs rather than help us to achieve greater abundance. No longer do we consider poverty and unemployment permanent landmarks on our economic scene."

There were still, to be sure, nagging problems which came with success: as the Phillips Curve demonstrated, full employment brought inflationary tendencies. That theory held that when the labor market is tight, wages rise and so do prices; if that market slackens, wages and prices fall. The Council of Economic Advisers illustrated that well-known theory—"One of the most important concepts of our time," the Nobel Laureate in economics, Paul Samuelson, had called it—in the report sent along to Congress with Johnson's message. But there was more concern about how to cope with the prodigies the American economy was going to perform with relentless regularity. There was much fear of "fiscal drag"—of the enormous federal revenues which a perpetually growing gross national product (GNP) would automatically produce and which would have to be spent quickly lest that deduction become deflationary. America, Walter Heller said in 1966, could afford guns and butter and might have to take expansionary steps in 1970 even if it were still fighting in Vietnam. Daniel Patrick Moynihan, who was to become a senator some years later, spoke in a similar vein in 1969 of "a situation utterly without parallel in modern government: administrations that must be constantly on the lookout for new ways to expend public funds in the public interest."

The theorists were not alone in their giddy confidence. In the late sixties and early seventies, the corporations broke with sound capitalist practice and turned more and more to short-term debt as a source of finance. In the traditional view, such funds should only be used for current expenses. But if every year was going to be better than the last, the traditional restraints were as inapplicable to business as they were to government. In 1969 and again in 1973, the short-term borrowing almost equaled long-term, a fact which was to fuel the corporate panic when the stagflation of 1973–74 broke out (and which was to provide the real-world basis for fantasies about a capital shortage which appeared at that time).

How did such people—executives, theorists, policy makers—come to believe in an economic fairy tale? Because, I would suggest, mainstream—which is to say, nonradical—thinkers always implicitly assume that the system is fundamentally sound and benign and honestly ignore contrary evidence. In bad times, like the present, one can argue—and I anticipate remarks by leading citizens which will be treated later on—that the economy is simply "wringing" inflation out, or that it is the victim of "one-time shocks" like the Organization of Petroleum Exporting Countries' (OPEC) price increase. In good times, like the sixties, one can mistake a temporary juncture for a permanent trend and assume that skillful manipulation of the budget and money supply suffice to put an end, once and for all, to the business cycle.

In contrast to such analysts, I take the inherent instability of the capitalist economy as my point of departure. That is not to say that the stagflation of 1973–74 was simply a replay of the crisis of 1873. Obviously, our recent woes occur within the context of a welfare state which only dates back to the thirties, and that makes an enormous difference. And yet, that welfare state cannot be understood apart from the cycle of boom-and-boost to which it was a response. Moreover, in the present situation one will see that the solutions of the past generations are part of our problem, that the old instabilities were not banished but have taken on new forms and are still an inevitable structural consequence of the system.

These questions can only be confronted in the framework of the postwar evolution of the American economy. So in dealing with stagflation in this chapter, I will begin with a brief history which emphasizes the structural sources of our crisis. That will lead to what may at first seem an exactly contrary analysis in which the role of individuals and political choices will be stressed. But even though human error and ambition do indeed play a role in all of this, it will be seen that basic institutions set the limits in which they operate. Once this underlying context is outlined, it will then be possible to examine three theories of our plight: that government spending is the root evil; that administered prices are to blame; that the sectoral problems of food and fuel, housing and health, are the source of our contradictions.

The emphasis here, and throughout the book, will be on the structural and the systemic. Those factors, as I will make clear when dealing with the particulars, are by no means the only cause of our troubles. They are merely decisive.[1]

I

A brief structural history introduces, and prepares the way for, an account of the present and immediate future in which the long run is crucial.

There is a fundamental imbalance between the tendency of the American economy to expand capacity in the search for profit and the constricted ability of the people to buy that increased output. That imbalance is structural because it is a precondition of production under all variants of capitalism, from Adam Smith to the late welfare state. Private wealth is assigned the social function of making and financing investment decisions which means that the possessors of private wealth must have much more money than anyone else. Inequality is thus built into the system. But that same inequality is also one of the sources of periodic breakdowns in a structure which favors, and increases, production and profits as against consumption and the satisfaction of needs. Keynesian policies did not alter those basic structures, i.e., they did not call for the public planning of investment or the radical redistribution of wealth. Rather, the government was to engage in the debt financing of sufficient effective demand to make the private, corporate economy work again.

In effect, John Maynard Keynes argued for a gentle, controlled inflation as a means of achieving full employment. Workers, he argued, would rightly resist any reduction in their money wages and on this count they were "instinctively more reasonable economists than the classical school . . ." But they would not resist a decline in real wages which brought more jobs. So when the government intervened to stimulate that effective demand, part of the new money would raise output and part would be translated into higher costs. It was only when such policy would not induce an increase in output that it would become merely inflationary. As long as the deficits would put unused people and capacity to work, that would not happen. Keynes's followers, the economist Ben Seligman pointed out, held "that inflation in the ordinary sense was no longer the heinous affair that the conservative mood made it out to be [and] they insisted that a secular rise in prices could be a pleasant and respectable experience."

In the thirties, it must be strongly emphasized, that strategy did not work. In 1940, Keynes commented on the "comparative failure of New Deal expenditure out of borrowed funds to produce even an approach to full employment in the United States." The reason, he said, was that the modern powers of production had become gigantic, making it "politically impossible for a capitalist democracy to organize expenditures on the scale necessary to make the grand experiments which would prove my case." The war, he understood, would do what the peace could not accomplish. He predicted, accurately as it turned out, that the United States had the resources to fight in a global conflict and expand domestic consumption at the same time.

The period of 1945 to 1970 was the time of the Keynesian euphoria. The Depression of the thirties did not return with the peace as many, including most businessmen, had feared. There were, to be sure, recessions in 1949, 1953 and 1958. But they were much milder than the Crash of the late twenties and their severity was clearly mitigated, politically as well as economically, by the "built-in" stabilizers, like unemployment compensation. Then came the sixties, with the longest peacetime boom in American history. It seemed that the business cycle had been conquered. True enough, the society continued to "overproduce," i.e., to create new capacity faster than maldistributed income. But experience now seemed to have proved what Keynes hypothesized: that planning and redistribution on a grand scale were neither necessary nor desirable. The judicious "fine-tuning" of the fiscal and monetary aggregates was all that was required.

After all, the early sixties were characterized by economic growth, declining unemployment and low rates of inflation. The beginning of the end of that idyll, we now know, was the unconscionable American intervention in Vietnam. The escalation of the war in 1965 was, as the Council of Economic Advisers admitted in 1979, the historic origin of the current inflation. Prices had increased by 2 percent in 1965 and 6 percent in 1969. In between, the Johnson administration had made its famous, and wildly optimistic, assumptions about imminent victory in Southeast Asia—and more to the point, constructed budgets on the basis of those projections. The result was a classic case of inflation, something we have not seen since. Abundant money, in conformity with the old formula, chased after scarce goods in a time of high production. That is the "demand-pull" inflation celebrated in the textbooks. It is, we shall see, irrelevant to almost everything that came afterward.

Are we then faced with a "political business cycle" rather than a structural crisis of the system? Before responding to that question, it is important to survey some data which seem to make a more compelling case for answering yes.

In 1969, Richard Nixon decided to deal with the Vietnam-induced inflation according to time-honored theories. The economy would be "cooled off" and, in accordance with the Phillips Curve, a moderate increase in joblessness—moderate, i.e., for those who did not suffer it—would bring prices down. The 1969 budget showed a surplus, the 1970 budget a very slight deficit—and when computed as a percentage of full employment GNP, both were in surplus. But—and now the thunder of stagflation is heard—prices did not fall as they were supposed to but rose at a rate of almost 6 percent a year even though the gross national product declined in 1970.

Richard Nixon had good reason to appreciate the political power of economic trends since it is quite likely that a sluggish economy in 1959–60 cost him the presidency. Indeed, Nixon and Arthur Burns had proposed to stimulate the economy at the time precisely in order to aid the presidential campaign—and had been turned down by Eisenhower, a man of principled, even suicidal, commitment to the old truths (who also probably did not like Nixon). In 1971, however, Nixon was his own master and he proceeded to orchestrate the entire American economy with one overriding purpose in mind: to ensure his own reelection. The Watergate affair was shocking evidence of deceit and criminality in the highest office in the land—but this economic Watergate was, in terms of its consequences, even more momentous.

The climactic moment in that fateful process took place on August 15, 1971. "The time has come," the president told the people, "for a new economic policy for the United States." There were not simply price controls but tax deductions for individuals and corporations, investment incentives, funds for research and development. Actually, as Nixon himself noted, the shift had begun in 1970 when budgetary policy became more expansionary and the money supply surged forward. That last point is of some importance. Arthur Burns, then chairman of the Federal Reserve System, has been a public symbol of prudent money management for a generation. Yet he had joined with Nixon in 1960 to seek a politically motivated expansion of the economy and in the seventies there is strong evidence that he carried out his friend's policy.

As a governor of the Federal Reserve at the time remembered 1971–72, "It was . . . clear to the White House where new expansionary pressures ought to be generated.

The finger pointed right at the Federal Reserve. Because of the independent position of the Fed, no direct orders could be issued, but the White House made its views plain." Arthur Burns, I believe, went along with enthusiasm. The game plan worked. Between the fourth quarter of 1971 and the first quarter of 1973, the economy grew in real terms at an incredible rate of 7¾ percent. In the fourth quarter of 1972—which included the presidential election—GNP was advancing at an 11.5 percent rate.

The liberal economist Arthur Okun sees the excessive monetary and fiscal stimulus of 1972 as a major source of the double-digit inflation of 1973–74. And *Business Week* was later to talk of Nixon's "unprincipled use of the power of governmnent to orchestrate the greatest electoral victory ever in 1972." Safely reelected, Nixon reverted to type and attempted to contain the gigantic economic forces he had set in motion. But with controls removed, the inflationary tendencies which he had cynically stimulated for personal advantage surged forward. The OPEC embargo did not occur until the fall of 1973, yet by the third quarter of that year the inflation rate hit 7.5 percent (and 9.5 percent in the fourth quarter). This bears very much on the theory that our problems today result from the lagging consequences of "onetime shocks."

Those "shocks" include the OPEC price hike, the bad harvest in Russia which created a tremendous demand for American food exports and the impact of Nixon's devaluation of the dollar in a world in which all advanced nations were expanding at the same time. In this perspective, the underlying situation in the United States is sound and it is only necessary to live through a series of unfortunate, converging, but nonsystemic, accidents. This analysis was, for example, offered by the Congressional Budget Office (CBO) in 1977.

There is clearly some truth to this thesis, and it would be foolish to insist that only structural factors were, and are, at work in the economy (a point emphasized earlier in the description of the steel crisis). The system can hardly be blamed for poor harvests in the Soviet Union—though it was certainly responsible for the incredible mismanagement of the American grain sale to the Russians that resulted. And, it might be said, corporations cannot be faulted because there are huge oil deposits in the Middle East or a war broke out there in 1973. But, then, I would respond that the American dependence on Middle Eastern oil was the outcome of political policies subordinated to the priorities of oil multinationals for over a generation and that the "accidents" of 1973 and 1974 in this area were not totally accidental.

I documented this view at chapter length in *The Twilight of Capitalism,* but the energy crisis is so paradigmatic of the crisis as a whole for the people that it is worthwhile briefly summarizing the facts and argument contained in that book. America has paid *hundreds of billions* in direct and indirect subsidies to giant oil companies and thereby financed a wasteful energy infrastructure which made it prone and vulnerable to the shortages occasioned by the original OPEC boycott of 1973-74 and the fall of the Shah of Iran in 1979. The simple plot theories of angry motorists lining up for gas are wrong but their fundamental intuition—that corporations and the government policies they inspired are the root cause of the problem—is quite correct. And the whole process illustrates the central theme of this book: that it is Washington's subordination to the priorities determined in the boardroom which, interacting with a major turn in the economy, is responsible for the crisis of the 1980s.

In the 1920s, the oil companies of the world met at a grouse hunt in Scotland and divided up the globe to suit their purposes. From that date to this writing, the American corporations among them were granted effective immunity from antitrust prosecution. When, during the waning days of the Truman administration in the fifties, the Department of Justice was finally allowed to act upon the mountain of evidence proving this illegal collusion, the criminal suit was withdrawn almost as soon as it was filed and the civil procedure did not even result in a tap on the corporate wrist. Government lawyers at the time complained that the company lawyers knew more about federal policy decisions, supposedly taken in secret, than they did.

But then the industry, which often pays large sums of money to disseminate the ideas of Adam Smith, has always been statist in its practice. In the thirties, the legislatures in states like Texas mandated controlled production output and Washington happily joined in by making it a federal crime to buy any oil in intrastate commerce which had been produced in violation of the state quotas. Even more to the present point, Texaco and Standard of California persuaded the government to take on the real enemy during World War II: the British oil men who threatened to take over the Saudi fields. Indeed, the private sector was so convincing in demonstrating that Saudi oil was crucial to national defense that Franklin Roosevelt and his crusty secretary of the interior, Harold Ickes, decided to create a publicly owned Petroleum Reserve Corporation to protect the American stake in that country. The industry denounced the move as "fascism" and, in effect, threatened to go on strike if the decision were not reversed. It was, the United States officially determined that aid to the Saudis was in the national interest, and the private companies were the beneficiaries of the public largesse.

After World War II, federal planners became worried that some of America's despotic, inefficient and corrupt friends in the Middle East might be overthrown by Communists because of their inability to deal with festering social problems. Washington did not, however, commit itself to deal with these problems or to help unseat the regimes that allowed them to persist. Instead, a secret way was found to channel monies to those shaky, unjust governments. The oil corporations were permitted to deduct taxes paid to foreign powers, not as a business expense (the rule for other companies), but as a credit against its American taxes. This meant that the energy multinationals from this country were willing to pay unlimited taxes to the Saudis and like regimes because the burden was effectively borne by the taxpayers. So it was accurately said that these companies became collectors for foreign governments which were given the right to tax American consumers at the gasoline pump.

That was ethically outrageous on the face of it but it also had profound economic consequences which ramify to the present day. The government was paying the corporations to make the nation more dependent on Middle Eastern oil. Since those companies also controlled all other forms of energy—dominating the natural gas, coal and nuclear industries, owning rights to oil shale—they were subsidized for not developing alternate technologies. On two occasions during this history, conservative presidents—Herbert Hoover and Dwight Eisenhower—formally ruled against extracting the oil from shale.

However, federal support did not go only to the international companies. In the 1950s, Eisenhower introduced an oil import quota program which kept some of the cheap, American-subsidized, foreign oil out of the country so that American consumers could be forced to buy expensive American oil. This, it should be noted, was done at a time when the cheap oil did not come with political (anti-Israel) strings attached to it. It was, as one wit put it, a "drain America first" program which, in violation of the law of supply and demand but in keeping with the fact of corporate power, wasted energy which might have made America much less vulnerable to the OPEC pressures of the seventies.

The nation also purchased wastefulness in other ways, most notably through a federal highway program costing more than $100 billion. The impact of that commitment will be examined in chapter 6 where its ruinous effect upon the cities of the Northeast and Middle West will be chronicled. For now it should be simply noted that the resultant infrastructure was a precondition of the energy crisis of the seventies. The situation could become as acute as it did only because Washington's loyalty to corporate priorities created a prodigal energy system that could be manipulated by OPEC. The "one-time" shock in this case was made possible by a generation of federal policy and the expenditure of hundreds of billions of dollars.

It should come as no surprise that when the crisis did occur the government, under both Democrats and Republicans, turned to the companies which had done so much to create it and asked them to solve it. It was like hiring the cattle rustlers to board up the empty barn door. Gerald Ford, at the urging of Nelson Rockefeller, came out for $100 billion in cheap governmental credit to pay the corporate malefactors to clean up the mess they had so profitably made. And Jimmy Carter in 1979 proposed more than $140 billion, most of it to finance synthetic fuels which were environmentally threatening and economically dubious.

The free enterprise ideologues of *The Wall Street Journal* editorial page and a good number of conservative Republicans regarded this massive intervention of the government as left-wing. But the more sophisticated organs of the corporate world understood that this huge subsidy would, like all those which went before it (and helped to buy the crisis), benefit the private sector. The Congress, *Business Week* editorialized, "should be prepared to underwrite the creation of a synthetic fuel industry big enough to be an effective weapon against the oil ministers of OPEC—in the same way that the nation created a synthetic rubber industry almost overnight during World War II."

That precedent, on closer examination, turns out to be quite revealing. The company which was supposed to spearhead that synthetic rubber program during World War II, New Jersey Standard Oil (later to be Exxon), had secret, monopoly agreements with I. G. Farben, the German company then under Nazi control, and the American war effort was set back because of that deal. That is one more example of how the common good can be subverted by corporate priorities even in the midst of a war. However, even without that reminder the facts are plain enough in the present case: a Democratic president is proposing a multibillion-dollar handout to those who did so much to create the energy crisis. And that, as chapter 10 will show, opens up the probability that the forthcoming corporate "solution" will once again be the source of yet another crisis. Technology, we will see, is designed by politicians and executives more than by engineers.

For my present purpose, however, the central point is already clear. One cannot explain stagflation away by reference to "one-time shocks." There were, to be sure, unpredictable events. Who would have thought that the Shah of Iran, armed to the teeth with American weapons, would be overthrown, thus cutting back on the amount of oil on the world market? But the impact of those surprises in the United States was determined by structural factors which were the work of more than half a century of conscious public policy which almost always followed the priorities of the oil multinationals. As the seventies were ending, the result was high prices, layoffs in the automobile and allied industries, exacerbated inflation and unemployment, i.e., stagflation.

In 1979, the Harvard Business School Report, "Energy Future," corroborated the basic point which I have just summarized. In the aftermath of the OPEC embargo, it said, "It became fashionable to discuss the crisis as though it were a unique event, a freak storm that had been weathered. We have completely disagreed, viewing it instead as a warning of a fundamental and dangerous disorder, for the basic conditions that have allowed the first shock [OPEC in 1973] and now the second [the interruption in supplies after the fall of the Shah of Iran] have continued to prevail." To be sure, the Harvard study does not share my analysis, but on this critical point it does arrive at my conclusion.

But then, doesn't the political dimension of this brief history subvert my basic thesis? Shouldn't stagflation be blamed on Lyndon Johnson and Richard Nixon and all the presidents who worked with the oil companies, rather than the system? Again, there is no question that the political calculations of those men made a difference and that their decisions were not predetermined. But they are not irrelevant to the system either. One of the structural consequences of the New Deal response to the cycle of boom-and-bust is that presidents can now rig the economy to suit their own purposes. That politicalization of economic decisions is hardly external to the system. Indeed, in the sixties it was regularly seen as one of its glories. Furthermore, Nixon and Johnson were not the automatons of fate but neither were they men from Mars. They were products of social classes and ideologies as well as unique individuals. It is, for example, of some moment that practically the entire *haute bourgeoisie* supported Nixon against the "irresponsible" George McGovern in 1972 at the very moment when Nixon was recklessly directing the entire national economy in order to maximize his personal political advantage.

Moreover, it should be carefully noted that the two events which triggered—but did not cause—the tendencies toward stagflation were not the result of liberal domestic programs but of Vietnam and Richard Nixon's ferocious opportunism. But above all, this brief history shows how the evolution of structures limits, and even predetermines, the choices made in the White House. Policies which didn't work in the thirties were so effective in the sixties that statesmen and scholars believed in their own fairy tales—which then shattered on the realities of the seventies. What were the glacial and systemic changes which underlay, and shaped, those erratic events?

Let a coconspirator in Nixon's economic Watergate, Arthur Burns, introduce one of the most popular answers to that question: *Government spending is the cause of the contemporary stagflation.*[2]

II

In 1978, Burns told the American Enterprise Institute that the "persistence of substantial deficits in Federal finance is mainly responsible for the serious inflation that got under way in our country in the mid-sixties. When the government runs a budget deficit, it pumps more money into the pocketbooks of the people than it takes out of their pocketbooks. This is the way a serious inflation is typically started and later nourished." In January 1979, Jerry Brown, the apostle of national austerity, declared in his inaugural address as governor of California that "people know that something is wrong when the Federal government stimulates inflation . . ."

It is easy enough to refute Burns's simplistic assertion of Washington setting off demand-pull inflation by putting too much money into people's pockets or Brown's equally simplistic assertions about the one-to-one relation between federal deficit and inflation. That will be done shortly—but it does not begin to dispose of the problem which is much more complex than the Burns-Brown formulations suggest. Part of the answer relates to one of the main themes of the structural history of the last section: that the impact of government spending varies in different periods. Moreover, there are various forms of government spending. There are outlays for social needs which, chapter 7 will show, have been much more moderate than the current mythology pretends and thus cannot possibly explain the economic tumult of the last ten years. There is private spending subsidized and facilitated by Washington, which is of enormous importance and often not even mentioned. And there is federally mandated spending, e.g., for environmental protection, which is the most popular demon in the corporate boardroom.

I will try to sort out some of these complexities, emphasizing how the inherent contradictions of a corporate-dominated economy are, much more often than not, the cause rather than the effect of federal policy.

To begin with, there is a fundamental divide in postwar American history, and the truth of propositions about the relation between government spending and inflation depends on which side of that line is being considered. And that, in turn, implies that the underlying causes are the ones which explain why that divide exists and that the government-inflation relationship is derived from that fact rather than creating it.

With the exception of one year during the Korean War and two years during the Vietnam War, the United States experienced moderate inflation rates between 1950 and 1970. It was only in 1969 that the annual rate went over 6 percent and that was probably an aftereffect of the Vietnam budgetary "mistake" of 1967–68. Even including the war years, the average rate of inflation for those two decades was about 2.4 percent. One reason for that trend was the scandalous record of intolerable unemployment during this period: in thirteen of those twenty years the job level was below its potential. Since the Phillips Curve worked relatively well on that side of the divide, it is quite likely that joblessness played a role in holding down prices.

More to the point, the stimulative years of Kennedy-Johnson policy prior to Vietnam were not particularly more inflationary than the pinchpenny years under Eisenhower. Moreover, the Great Society expeditures of the sixties, even when they were accompanied by the huge investments in the Southeast Asian carnage, did not set off an inflation comparable to the double-digit increases in peacetime 1974. We spent almost $29 billion on the war in 1969 and only $3.1 billion in 1974, yet the inflation rate in the latter year was about double the former. And, one should add, in 1974 there was soaring unemployment, in 1969 a relatively tight labor market. Clearly, then, one is dealing with a radical break in American economic continuity, and algebraic propositions about generalized interrelationships between federal spending and inflation are useless—or else must be adjusted when they pass over the great divide in 1970.

That suggests, as I have indicated, that a structural explanation is in order. To begin somewhat speculatively, perhaps that Schumpeter-Kondratiev theory about long cycles has something to do with our situation. The 1930s were clearly a dramatic low point on the Kondratiev graph and, as Keynes himself acknowledged, New Deal deficit spending programs were unable to even bring about a semblance of full employment at that time. The period from 1945 to the late sixties was the greatest boom in the history of world capitalism. Within the environment, it was possible for government to combat mild recessions through moderate deficits and to achieve rapid growth with price stability. The one problem with this idyll is that the American (but not the European) version of it included intolerably high rates of unemployment.

Is it possible that Washington's planners merely nurtured, but did not at all cause, the advance of those years? I think so. And is it possible that, just as Schumpeter suggested, the dramatic change in the economic weather at the end of the sixties was a conjuncture of long-wave factors (the end of a time of innovation and new markets) and more immediate causes (the loss of American dominance on the world market as a revived Europe and Japan became much more competitive)? If the answer to these questions is yes, then the underlying basis of the present problem is the inherent, cyclic character of the capitalist economy itself.

That Kondratiev insight agrees with, but is not necessary to, a further explanation of stagflation and the Great Divide in the economy. In his attempt to show why the New Deal failed, Keynes, it will be remembered, said that the productive capacity of the system had grown so much that capitalist democracies would not be politically capable of making the expenditures required to put the system to work again. But why, then, were those same countries able to do so much better in the postwar period? Why did the same Keynesian policies prove adequate then? Because there was a fundamentally different—ascendant— economic environment. But by the same token the successes of 1945–69 also laid the basis for the difficulties in 1970 and after.

Tens of millions of new workers have been brought into the labor force (indeed, as the next chapter will show, the women among them are often blamed for our problems). The industrial plant has been expanded. Living standards have risen. But that meant that a deep recession in the seventies would involve much greater losses than the milder downturns of the fifties and sixties. Using the computations of the Brookings' economist, George L. Perry, the potential GNP not produced due to inadequate economic performance between 1957 and 1964 totaled $256.6 billion over eight years. But between 1970 and 1976, in a mere six years, the American economy wasted $381.6 billion in production. (The figures are given in constant dollars.)

The federal experts gave a sort of backhanded recognition of that change but they did so in such a technical manner that it escaped the attention of almost the entire nation. Potential GNP, the outgoing Ford Council of Economic Advisers said in January 1977, is now lower than it used to be. For one thing, inflation now begins to threaten at a much higher rate of unemployment; for another, the optimum capacity in an American industrial system with more than a little obsolete plant is now lower. In a typical reaction of the seventies, the council did not propose ways to deal with the joblessness and the factories but simply altered the measure of economic potential in the American economy. The Carter council then endorsed this "conceptual" change. Our best, the official statisticians are telling us, is no longer as good as it used to be.

But if this is the case, then one of the reasons why federal expenditures rise is that recessions have now become much more costly to the government. The House Budget Committee published a chronology of stabilization policy for the period 1960–77. It quite usefully reminds us that in 1972—the period leading up to the great stagflation of 1974–75—the White House under Nixon was locked in a bitter struggle with Congress over spending. Typically, Nixon had stimulated the economy to ensure his reelection by means of easy money and an export boom, not by social innovation. The one exception to this statement was a major rise in Social Security benefits which was imposed upon the president (and for which he then took credit).

The huge and unprecedented deficits of the seventies, then, came *after* stagflation and as a result of it, not before. In the four years, 1970–73, the deficits totaled $58.1 billion; in the five years, 1974–78, they were $212.6 billion. It would thus seem to be truer to say that stagflation causes government spending rather than the other way around. During the 1974–78 period, federal revenues went down as a result of high unemployment, but federal responsibilities went up. This was a particularly acute problem for the Social Security system which faced an intense crisis because those jobless workers no longer paid in but the indexed benefits were increased because of inflation.

So the relative success of Keynesian fiscal and monetary policy in an ascendant economic period created problems for that policy when the economy found itself in deep trouble. Actually, however, this tendency has been understated thus far because of a definition. I have been talking about "government spending"; now let us look at governmentally induced spending as well.

It has long been conservative theory and practice to stimulate the economy by "trickle-down" incentives given to those at the very top. The Democrats disagreed on this point, but not in principle. So it was, for instance, the Kennedy-Johnson policies included investment tax credits, accelerated depreciation and the like. In 1960, corporate income taxes were 23.2 percent of federal budget receipts; in 1975, they were estimated at 13.8 percent. That huge decrease comes from government actions designed to increase profits and thereby investment and jobs. The Democratic administration had reduced the corporate levies from 23.2 percent to 18.7 percent of federal revenues; the Republicans, from 18.7 percent to 13.8 percent. Then, as part of its general conservative turn, the Carter administration in 1979 announced principled agreement with the conservatives on the issue.

"Over the long term . . .," Carter's economic advisers said in 1979, "opportunities for further general tax reductions will emerge. As they do, reductions carefully designed to strengthen incentives for investment should be given high priority." Treasury Secretary W. Michael Blumenthal was more forthright, telling the Senate Budget Committee that "this administration is determined to restrain the growth of federal expenses and to rely principally on the private sector as the source of economic growth." The full implications of all this will be analyzed in chapter 4. For now, let us focus on how this impinges on the relation between federal spending and stagflation.

In theory, taxes, both personal and corporate, are assigned in this country on the basis of ability to pay. However, there are huge exceptions made when the government decides to encourage an activity by reducing the taxes on those who invest in it. Such decisions are rightly called "tax expenditures" since, all other things being equal, cutting someone's taxes is a way of increasing their income and putting a greater burden on those who do not engage in the favored activity. So government spending should include the huge sums made available to the private sector in this way. And we should at least take account of the monies that become available when the Federal Reserve loosens up the money market as it obligingly did during Nixon's reelection campaign in 1971–72.

On this last count, it is not generally realized that corporations—whose executives delight in lecturing the nation on fiscal responsibility—are much more deeply involved in deficit financing than the government. In 1946, public debt as a percentage of GNP was 129.4 percent; private debt as a similar percentage was 73.6 percent. In 1974, the public debt had *declined* to 46 percent of GNP; the private debt had risen to 152.8 percent. That was why there was a genuine fear during the stagflation of 1974–75 that there would be spectacular bank failures on the model of the twenties and early thirties. That did not happen, primarily because the Federal Reserve functioned as a lender of last resort. But it is a measure of the extent of the phenomenon that the fears were both real and widespread. On the basis of these data the Marxist, Ernest Mandel, has argued that "the prime cause of infla-

tion is the swelling of credit in the *private* sector . . ."
(emphasis added).

Walter Heller, the liberal Keynesian, has provided data
similar to Mandel's. In arguing that federal deficits were
not the cause of inflation, Heller pointed out in 1979 that,
since 1950, federal debt has gone up less than three times,
while consumer debt has risen fourteen times, mortgage
debt sixteen times, corporate debt fourteen times and
state and local debt thirteen times. All of that private debt,
I would add, did not just happen. At every point, the federal government had to intervene, in many ways, to facilitate this borrowing. Yet this prodigality is rarely noted by
conservatives like Arthur Burns (who, since he was one of
the prodigals, does not dwell on the fact in speeches attacking prodigality). Here again, it is not an accident that
the issues are framed in a way which guarantees reactionary answers. The inflationary potential of government policies which, through fiscal and monetary channels,
subsidize corporations is not even mentioned in the debate, yet these were of much greater moment than the
meager funds allocated to social goals.

This shoddy, but functional, way of defining the issues
is evident in still another area of the discussion of the
government's responsibility for inflation: environmental
regulation.

Corporate anger during the seventies was extremely
intense when it came to expenses imposed by federal-
rules-mandated environmental and occupational safety
standards. There, some relatively shrewd analysts said, is
a major source of our difficulties. In a period when there
was growing disenchantment with government at all levels, the argument had a considerable resonance, which is
one of the reasons why it was made. But this attack is also
a marvelous example of how problems can be conceptual-
ized so as to make conservative responses inevitable—and
how statistics can be designed to conceal the reactionary,
and value-laden, premises upon which they rest.

Within the late capitalist economy, industry produces
social costs almost as massively as goods and services.

This is an inherent tendency of a profit-oriented technology created without a thought to social cost. Given that fact—which is not a fact but a choice—there is no way of avoiding the bill. The only question at issue is, Who pays? There are three possibilities; the corporations, which cause and benefit from the social costs, could be required to internalize them, paying for them out of profits and/or by a burst of ingenuity to reduce those externalities; the workers can pay them by being forced to tolerate occupational conditions which will bring premature death from cancer or from mine cave-ins and similar tragedies; the consumers can be made to pay them through administered prices. The "anti-inflation" argument in this case is a shrewd way of making workers and consumers pay corporate costs.

Murray Weidenbaum, a conservative economist, is the main management advocate on this count. In fiscal 1979, he warned in 1978, the compliance cost for Federal regulation—i.e., the money business has to spend to stay within the law—was estimated at $97.9 billion. "This practice," Weidenbaum writes, "apparently costs the government little and represents no direct burden on the taxpayer. But the public does not escape paying the cost. Every time, for example, the Environmental Protection Agency imposes a more costly (albeit less polluting) method of production of any form the cost of the firm's product to the consumer will tend to rise. Similar effects flow from the other regulatory efforts, including those involving product safety, job health, and hiring and promotion policies." So the allegedly inflationary impact of clean air and safe factories is cited as a reason for reducing standards.

There are a number of fascinating aspects to this rationale. First, as is so often the case in this area, the statistics are not quite what they seem to be. Weidenbaum rightly distinguishes between the older federal agencies, mandated to deal with a single industry, like the Interstate Commerce Commission, and the new departments dealing with a problem in many industries, like the Environmental Protection Agency. But he does not linger over the fact that the compliance costs of the latter agencies are much less than those of the former. In 1976, Steven Kelman has pointed out, the environmental and occupational standards resulted in roughly $11 billion of expenditures—which were only 16⅔ percent of the total. The other costs came from federal regulations favoring business, e.g., by those limiting access to the trucking industry and imposing inefficiencies upon it. Weidenbaum does not, of course, bother to make this crucial distinction, for it suggests that monopolists, not environmentalists, are the problem.

Robert Eisner of Northwestern has compiled a useful, but only partial, list of the inflationary regulations that subsidize corporations and add to inflation: "price supports for milk as dairy prices skyrocket; trigger prices to 'protect' the steel industry from foreign competition as the profits of our steel industry soar; licensing arrangements and route restrictions that drastically cut competition in the trucking industry, laying the ground for repeated increases in prices and wages while truckers suffer from idle capacity and small trucking firms go out of business; sugar quotas and price supports to maintain and raise sugar prices; acreage restrictions that reduce agricultural supply; import quotas, tariffs and 'orderly marketing agreements' that limit the import of cheaper and frequently better automobiles, television sets and textiles; and Federal, state and local restrictions in countless occupations and industries that reduce competition and raise prices."

If Washington acts to protect the lungs of workers, or the public in general, business cries out—but it fails to mention the tremendous profits it makes from these other restrictions. Then, if such regulations are challenged, it is never the executives who pay the cost of deregulation, but the workers in the industry. Heads, the executive suite wins; tails, everybody else loses.

Second, there is an implicit assumption in this argument which deserves to be brought out into the open. Weidenbaum assumes that industry can pass the regulatory costs on to the consumer. In short, he recognizes a reality of administered pricing which is indeed one of the major sources of stagflation (as will be seen shortly). But it is the ability of industry to force the people to pay for controlling its malignant technology which is the problem, not society's determination to refuse to tolerate such malignancy. And third, Weidenbaum does not view pollution as a cost; only the elimination of pollution is treated in that way. Thus, he talks about "a more costly (albeit less polluting) method of production." Pollution is a parenthetical phenomenon in this view, having nothing to do with tough economic calculations.

That, alas, is the conceptual basis of the official statistics as well as of Weidenbaum's argument. The Council of Economic Advisers was candid about this point in its 1979 Report: "The gain from social regulation—in such forms as reduced pollution and greater safety—are generally not included in measured output. When an increasing fraction of society's labor and capital resources is diverted to producing these gains, measured productivity growth is reduced." But in fact there are quantifiable economic benefits from reducing pollution and increasing safety. The waste of human life in the form of premature death is, among many other things, a reckless expenditure of human capital which subtracts from our productivity. More prosaically, the paint on houses and cars will last longer in a clean environment. I hasten to add that I am primarily moved by thinking of the intrinsic value of worker's limbs or people's lungs.

For example, the *London Economist* noted in 1979 that mining productivity on the official figures went up by 4 percent a year between 1950 and 1965, but declined by 6 percent a year since 1973—which was precisely when new safety laws went into effect. Underground deaths averaged 225 a year in the sixties and 130 a year in the seventies, "but such gains are not recorded." If that trend were to persist, then the "lowered" productivity would have yielded almost a thousand fewer deaths in the matter of a decade. More to the present point, the current statistic about a 6 percent decline in mining productivity assumes a callous indifference to human life.

So one must be aware that when the council talks about "diverting" society's resources to the care of the environment and to safety it is using a value-laden term. And the very statistics in which these problems are calculated are profoundly biased since they assign a zero benefit to dealing with enormous evils while a new, non-nutritional and unnecessary breakfast food would be given a positive weight. Using such numbers, it is hardly surprising that economists come to reactionary conclusions, since those conclusions were contained in the numbers in the first place. In short, the very way in which we conceptualize these federally mandated expenditures refracts the corporate interest rather than that of the worker or the consumer. (This point will be explored in more detail in chapter 4.)

Small wonder, then, that this particular "anti-inflation" argument results in a demand for federal subsidies for pollution. We must, we are told, reduce, or eliminate, environmental and safety standards to fight inflation. At the same time, as chapter 4 will detail, the government is supposed to channel more money, in the form of lowered taxes and increased depreciation allowances, to the private sector in order to spur investment. But note that the government subsidies will then be going to investments which impose huge social costs—and in some instances life-and-death costs—upon the society. The people of the United States are thus being asked, not simply to allow, but also to fund, the degradation of their environment and indeed of their very lives.

All of this is not to suggest that the existing regulatory system is perfect. If, as Henry Aaron, the Brookings' scholar, has pointed out, we now have cleaner air and water and more safety, it is also true that there have been mistakes and contradictions in the federal intervention. And yet, if one even begins to compute true costs *and* benefits, the antienvironmental and occupational safety arguments come unstuck. They are based on statistical artifacts, not upon facts.

In summary, then, the relationship between the federal government and inflation is quite complex and not at all as most people imagine it. It is not true that Washington's deficits have created a demand-pull inflation, as Arthur Burns and Jerry Brown think. However, it is true that government has facilitated an enormous increase in private debt in order to deal with the structural imbalances of a corporate-dominated economy which, for all of the changes of the past generation, is still crisis prone. Moreover, it is also true that, on this side of the divide that appeared in American economic life around 1970, those traditional anticrisis policies no longer work, or, more precisely, work to create simultaneous inflation and recession. It is now time to look at one of the structural changes that helped create this new, and unprecedented, situation. I refer to the power of giant corporations to dictate prices to the market, rather than the other way around.[3]

III

Earlier, in discussing the idea that federal environmental regulations are at the root of many of the nation's problems, I noted in passing that it was assumed that corporations would pass those costs along to the public. They would be paid for out of prices, not from profits. But if that is the case, then the very structure of American capitalism has changed, the system is dominated by giant oligopolies and that fact, rather than the protection of human beings and our natural heritage, is a cause of stagflation.

In the bad old days of the 1930s, unemployment went from 3.2 percent in 1929 to 24.9 percent in 1933—and, at the same time and for the same reason, the price index (based on 1967 as 100) fell from 51.3 to 38.8. But in 1974, when joblessness rose to the highest rate since the Great Depression, General Motors raised the sticker price of its cars even as it laid off thousands of workers and demand fell radically. The consumer price index soared over 12 percent even as unemployment reached almost 10 percent. Is the ability of giant corporations to dictate to the market—to increase prices not simply in spite of, but even because of, a contracting market—one of the new structural causes of this unprecedented situation? I think so.

That idea dates all the way back to the Depression itself. At that time, Gardiner Means argued that prices in concentrated, monopoly industries fell much less than those in the competitive sector. That theory has been vigorously debated ever since. Some scholars, like J. Fred Weston and Steven Lustgarten, think the opposite is true since World War II; others, like Alfred Kahn, hold that the "decisive evidence is not in." But I believe that Means has made a convincing case and that his analysis explains much of what happened in the early seventies. That is also the conclusion of a very thoughtful review of the argument by Willard Mueller and of a study by Michael Wachtel and Peter Adelsheim. I will not, of course, go into the scholarly details of the dispute here. I simply want to acknowledge that the position I present has been challenged and has, I think, survived that challenge.

Means had defined this trend in the thirties. Then in the fifties others became aware of the problem. Steel prices, it was noted during the 1954 recession, went up even though plant utilization dropped from 95 percent in 1953 to 71 percent in 1954. Charles Schultze, later to become President Carter's chief economic adviser, noted the same phenomenon between 1955 and 1957. In the sixties, steel prices did not rise so fast, in some measure because of John Kennedy's bitter fight with the industry on the issue and because of the Kennedy-Johnson guidelines. But when Richard Nixon came in and refused even to jawbone (up until the dramatic reversal of August 1971), the old pattern reasserted itself. It would be wrong, however, to give Nixon all of the blame since, if this analysis is right, his election more or less coincided with a structural downturn in the economy which led to stagflation.

The administered price theory does not, however, work very well in the 1969–70 recession when the price markup in the competitive sector was greater than among the oligopolies. In part, that was because of a trend in which all firms tended to behave like the giants; in part it was the result of fierce foreign competition in the monopoly sector. These anomalies are freely conceded by proponents of the administered price theory, like Michael Wachtel and Peter Adelsheim, who then go on to show that their hypothesis has very great power in explaining the stagflation of 1974–75. For instance, Means produced data to show that in 1973–74, fuel and chemicals both went up by 60 percent (which refracts developments in OPEC), concentrated industries other than fuel and chemicals by 30 percent and competitive industries by less than 10 percent.

Even more to the point, there are serious people—the Council of Economic Advisers as well as the socialist and trade unionist Charles Levinson—who persuasively argue that prices now go up *because* of a recession. Notice that this is a total reversal of the traditional assumption according to which high unemployment forces companies to lower their prices as they compete for sales on a contracting market. As their capacity utilization falls and unit labor prices climb, Levinson notes, corporations raise their prices in order to maintain their cash flow. In a comment which is a masterpiece of euphemism, the Council of Economic Advisers made the same point in 1978. Since the assertion clearly implies a critique of the Adam Smith idyll which is still holy writ in the United States, it had to be made with considerable diplomacy.

"Price reductions," the council said, "are not seen as a means of sustaining revenue and profits during periods of decline in the total market, since each firm perceives that its competitors will match any price cuts. . . . The responsiveness of supply to changing demands is also reduced by the importance of fixed costs in manufacturing industries: decisions to enter into new markets must be based on long term considerations rather than on more immediate changes in market conditions. *The cost of entry into many major industries by new firms is often great enough to allow some pricing discretion by those already there"* (emphasis added). The italicized sentence is, I think, one of the most tactful descriptions of monopoly policy one can imagine. It also provides a kind of mainstream and official approval to the central point in the administered price thesis. Huge companies, effectively insulated against competitive pressure by the very monopoly structure of their industry, target profit goals and fix prices to meet them. In a recession, when demand falls, they must charge more to meet their goals.

Even the seemingly contrary evidence—the recent tendency of the competitive sector to raise prices in bad times—may fit into this analysis. In a good many cases, seemingly independent companies are affiliates of conglomerates with access to the parent corporation's capital and consequently aspects of monopoly power even in the nonconcentrated sector. And second, there are industries where production is dispersed and distribution, which sets consumer prices, is not. Apparel is a case in point. In the fifties, prices in that industry behaved according to the standard scenario when steel was violating it—but in 1969–70 and 1973–74 they went up during recessions. The producers are small in size but the retail networks are not. The entire economy, then, may well be more concentrated than we imagine.

There is, however, a more serious objection to the view being presented here. It admits that corporate monopoly power is part of the problem and then puts the unions on an equal plane. So it was that Walter Heller wrote in 1979: "In the face of strongly organized producer groups—powerful unions, oligopolistic business and politically potent farmers—the economic answer [to whether price stability and economic freedom of choice can coexist] was a pessimistic one. With each group pushing for a larger slice of the economic pie, it seemed very doubtful that increasing productivity could satisfy those rising claims." But is it true that the workers and their wages are as important to this process as the corporations and their profits?

A fascinating account of "cost pass-along management" by Byung Yoo Hong, an economist at Columbia University, provides data to show that Heller is wrong on that count. In a careful and sophisticated mathematical analysis of the available figures, Hong demonstrates that in the stagflation era—in this case, the years since 1965 —wage increases declined relative to price increases as compared to the immediate postwar period of 1945–65. And within approximately the same time frame, there was a significant increase in the rate of profit as a percentage of stockholder equity. That, of course, is in keeping with the proposition advanced earlier that our current problems do not result from "demand pull," from wage increases bidding up prices.

But then even Alfred Kahn (in his scholarly days before he joined the Carter administration), who holds that the administered-price theory is not yet proved, insists that the notion of labor monopoly power does not hold. Given the fact that about 80 percent of the nonfarm labor force is not in unions, "it becomes very difficult . . . to attribute general economy-wide wage-price inflation to market power on labor's side."

Finally, an investment banker testifying before the Joint Economic Committee, Gary M. Wenglowski, Director of Economic Research for Goldman, Sachs, gave a striking demonstration of how business now operates in terms of the administered-price theory. He commented that ". . . if you lower the cost of capital to business by a tax reduction in capital gains, that tends to reduce the rate of increase in prices that would ultimately be necessary to raise rates of return." In short, exactly as Means says, management starts with a concept of a "justified profit" which it will maintain regardless of what happens on the supposedly sovereign market. If the taxpayers will subsidize that profit through tax expenditures, then the company will hold down prices; if not, the prices will be raised to meet the target. This, Mr. Wenglowski tells us, is not simply a hypothesis about the behavior of one economy; it is a working rule in the boardroom.

That fact points in an important policy direction: monitoring, and ultimately controlling, oligopoly prices and profits but *not* wages. There is no economic reason for wage controls under conditions of stagflation since wages have chased after, but not caused, high prices. There is, however, a clear case for price controls since there is abundant evidence to suggest that giant business dictates to, rather than obeys, the market. If this huge source of monopoly power is not checked by the workings of the economy—and it is not—then there must be conscious political intervention to get results which were once supposed to be produced by Adam Smith's invisible hand.

The evolution of corporate power, its increasing concentration and its unresponsiveness to the market are thus structural determinants of the crisis of stagflation. *So also are the specific conditions in four key sectors— food and fuel, housing and health—three of which are not concentrated.*[4]

___ **IV** _____

The idea that inflation was particularly marked in those four areas—which are, no so incidentally, critical necessities and major components in the budgets of most Americans—was first developed by Leslie Nulty in an analysis undertaken for the Exploratory Project for Economic Alternatives. Those four items, she found, accounted for more than 70 percent of the expenditures of the bottom four-fifths of American income recipients. More to the point, in the period, 1970–76, the prices of the four necessities increased 44 percent more than those of nonnecessities. For the average citizen, then, inflation is even more of a problem than the gross numbers of the consumer price index indicate. "If," Nulty wrote, "inflation had been concentrated on air fares, electric toothbrushes and yachts, or even spread evenly, it would not have put such a powerful squeeze on the budgets of most

Americans and might not have become the major issue it is today."

That theme was then taken up by many people—including the Coalition Organized Against the Inflation of Necessities (COIN)—and it was corroborated by a number of comments in the 1979 Report of the Council of Economic Advisers. Housing, the council said, is the largest single component of the consumer price index, accounting for one-third of the expenditures. It was, the council then wrongly commented, the area in which there was a classic "demand-pull" inflation in 1978, an error which will be dealt with shortly. Health care, it was noted, outpaced all other costs and constituted a "steadily escalating share of our national output." And food was also recognized as a major source of inflation even though the behavior of prices in that case is sometimes erratic (and there are even reductions!).

Nulty's argument, however, did not merely identify four problem areas. It stated that each of them was a problem precisely because of structural factors. Since she did not use that term in exactly the same way it is employed here, it is important to define it before proceeding to cases. Inflation of the necessities is not inherent in the overall structure of late capitalism itself. Indeed, since the causes are sectoral it is important to stress that macromeasures, like shifts in fiscal and monetary policy, have little effect on these substructures. In one case, housing, anti-inflationary macropolicy is itself a significant source of inflation. So what has to be examined are the peculiarities—and sometimes the very American peculiarities—of the ways in which these goods and services are produced and delivered.

Moreover—and this is obviously relevant to the discussion of the last section—Nulty found that wage costs were *not* the cause of high rates of inflation in *any* of these sectors. Again, the 1979 Economic Report supports this conclusion for the society as a whole, noting that despite tight labor markets in 1978, wage increases were moderate, particularly in the last three-quarters of the year. So we are, the data clearly show, dealing with an area where the "classic" demand-pull patterns cited by the council in another section of its report simply do not apply.

What then are the special structural factors at work producing inflation in these four areas of critical necessities?

In health, the answer has been obvious for a long, long time. The United States is the only advanced country in the world without a national health system, It therefore spends more of a percentage of its GNP on medical care than any other advanced country, capitalist or Communist. That expenditure—8.3 percent of GNP in 1975—represented almost a doubling of real outlays over a twenty-five-year-period. Yet in 1974, the United States was only fifteenth in the international rates of infant mortality; in 1973, it was nineteenth in terms of life expectancy. Clearly, one of the main reasons for the medical backwardness of the richest nation in human history is that it relies on fee-for-service care which is mainly paid for by third-party insurers.

The centrality of that fact is a commonplace in discussions of the problem—yet nothing is done about it. Thus, Senator Henry Bellmon of Oklahoma referred to it as an established truth in 1977 and yet the debate went on and on. One of the pernicious things about this system is that it tends to conceal the real price of health care. Nulty cites studies under the auspices of the Council on Wage and Price Stability—hardly a center of radical research—which show that people make medical decisions on the basis of net cost, i.e., the part directly paid for by the patient. They do not understand that they will be charged the full cost indirectly in the form of higher premiums.

Similarly, the absence of comprehensive public planning leads to a proliferation of extremely expensive medical technologies. And the third-party insurers are also unconcerned about cost or quality since both have only a tangential effect upon their business. Indeed, public subsidies for the health care of the poor often lead to unnecessary—and sometimes fatal—surgical operations. The answer to this problem is, and has been for some time, obvious: for the United States to develop a national health system. But proposals to that purpose by Senator Edward Kennedy of Massachusetts and Congressman Ronald Dellums of California have never even come to the point of serious debate on the floor of the Congress. And as this book is being written there is reason to fear that powerful forces from the medical profession and the insurance lobby will prevail in insisting upon regressive financing in any new legislation which will be adopted.

In the 1979 version of his comprehensive national health bill, Senator Kennedy clearly decided that he could not possibly succeed in passing legislation which would deny the private insurance industry the right to a federally guaranteed profit. He therefore included those companies in the new draft of his bill. So it was that the conservative forces in America, so proud of their commitment to penny-pinching, have apparently won in their battle to force Washington to pay billions for nonservices from the private sector. But then, the Carter administration regarded even Kennedy's proposal as too radical and contented itself with pushing for catastrophic care, i.e., socializing the high risks of the affluent and leaving the rest of the system in its normal, costly and chaotic condition.

Housing is a second case in point. It is, as chapter 6 shows, an area where construction is victimized by roller-coaster monetary policies and perverse public outlays which discriminate in favor of the upper middle and upper classes. In 1978, it was widely held that a new federal policy—allowing thrift institutions to issue certificates of deposit based on Treasury bills—would guarantee that there would be plenty of money available for mortgages. It was usually then noted in an aside that the money would, however, fetch very high rates of interest. Between 1971 and 1974, Nulty notes, the financing costs of a house went up by 147.9 percent (while labor costs went up much less).

The irony in the housing sector is that it is an antiinflationary policy which is inflationary. When Washing-

ton tightens up on money in order to restrain price increases, that increases the price of a house—and it is
doubtful whether it has much of an impact on giant corporations. So it was that in January 1979, even with the
new funds for mortgages in thrift institutions, there was a
sharp decline in the number of housing starts. That trend
was in process as this book was being written but, on the
basis of past experience and even with the new modifications in savings and loan banks, it is likely to continue.

Food is the third necessity which is subject to hyper-
inflation. Here, as Nulty points out, the problem is exacerbated because the price increases have been more
pronounced in staples, like flour and rice, than in the more
expensive items. It is, of course, clear that volatile, noneconomic factors are at work in this sphere, the vagaries
of the weather, first and foremost (and including the mysterious disappearance of anchovies off the South American coast in the seventies which deprive American
farmers of one of their important sources of livestock
feed). But here, again, the structure of the economy—and
the specific substructure of the farm system—have a profound impact upon such accidents.

There is, for instance, the American system of subsidizing nonproduction through payments to farmers—
rather than simply guaranteeing farm income and enjoy-
ing the benefits of maximum output as is done in some
other countries. That does not simply impose a direct subsidy cost—which goes disproportionately to agribusiness
and big market farmers. It also generates an artificial and
expensive scarcity which bids up consumer prices. "Price
increases for crops in 1978," a Data Resources analysis
said, "were initiated and sustained by federal agricultural
policies which withdrew land from production and established a restrictive long-term grain reserve." Moreover,
agricultural products are a critical component of American exports—we and the Canadians, I have suggested,
constitute the Organization of Wheat Exporting Countries, a cartel as effective, cohesive and profitable as
OPEC—and Washington works with the gigantic corporations which dominate the world food market. So it was

that in 1972 American taxpayers underwrote the profits of huge export firms—and the cost of bread in Moscow.

In addition, the American food system is characterized by layers of intermediaries between the farmer and consumer: processors, refrigeration, transporters, supermarkets and the like. Each one of these stages operates on a "markup" principle which in effect subjects the final buyer to a compound-interest charge. Furthermore, the entire system is extremely energy intensive: it is not unusual to fly frozen fish from the North Atlantic to restaurants perched on the ocean in South Carolina. The fabled productivity of the American farmer is quite real, but it is neither a miracle nor a result of some innate Yankee ingenuity. It is rather the consequence of an industrialized, wasteful, government-subsidized system oriented toward agribusiness rather than family farmers. I addition to all of the other objectional outputs (corporations in the fields presiding over the food system, etc.) it also produces inflation.

If this analysis sounds radical, it is not. In the late forties, when the liberal Democratic administration of Harry Truman was in power, it recognized almost all of these trends and proposed to do something about them through a proposal—the "Brannon Plan"—which was quite similar to successful policies in Canada, Sweden and other countries. The legislation was quite complex but its philosophy can be simply stated: to support the income of family farmers who would be encouraged to produce as much as they possibly could in order to bring prices down. In short, abundance was to be subsidized, not, as has been the case for an entire generation, scarcity and a corporate-dominated scarcity at that.

Finally, there is the energy crisis. I pointed out earlier in this chapter that the OPEC price hike was not simply a "onetime shock," although it certainly was a shock. It was a shock mediated by a generation of federal policies which followed corporate priorities and spent billions of dollars in order to purchase a shortage of domestic energy. Here, as in the case of agriculture, federally induced, and even mandated, waste is a very important component of the problem. And the policy is to be explained, not in terms of the irrationality of those who decided upon it and carried it out, but as an adaptation to the needs of the dominant corporation in the energy and agriculture sectors.

One way to begin to change this intolerable situation would be through the creation of a publicly owned gas and oil corporation which would rip away the veil of corporate secrecy which now makes the government dependent upon information supplied by the very multinationals it is supposed to control. Such a policy, as the next chapter will show, could also make a major contribution to the achievement of full employment. More broadly, there is obviously a sectoral solution for each of the other sectoral causes of stagflation: A national health system; federal planning for housing and land use (a theme which will surface again when we consider the urban crisis); a food system oriented toward family-sized farmers and consumers rather than to agribusiness and corporate intermediaries. Each one of those measures has been on the liberal agenda for at least a generation.

None of them has been adopted. In the area of the necessities we are in the presence of inflationary sectors which have established and structural resistance to any kind of serious reform. At least one of the reasons why the Carter administration engaged in symbolic attacks on inflation rather than dealing with its real sources is to be found here: an effective program would require measures which are, for American but not West European politics, radical and the Carter administration is moderately conservative. Like Herbert Hoover in the face of a seemingly inexplicable Depression, a Democratic heir of Franklin Roosevelt could neither comprehend nor master the problem of stagflation.

That problem, we have seen in this chapter, was not the result of government social spending or high wages for workers. It was built into the Keynesian strategy which favored the corporate infrastructure and only intervened to the extent necessary to get private business moving. When the economy turned a historic corner in the late sixties, that tactic, which had worked tolerably well on the upswing, suddenly exhibited basic structural flaws. That problem was in turn exacerbated by a political business cycle imposed upon the economy by Lyndon Johnson's war and Richard Nixon's reelection campaign. At the same time, administered pricing, which had been developing for a generation, spread from concentrated to nonconcentrated industries. And the specific structural characteristics of those sectors producing the basic necessities of consumer life helped make the resultant inflation all the more vicious in its impact upon the poor, the working people and even the middle class.

At every point in the process—though in complicated and uneven fashion—corporate structural power was a major determinant of the crisis. That is, at the very minimum—say, in the Truman administration's analysis of the agricultural crisis—a rather radical liberal truth. At the maximum, when the basic soundness of corporate domination of the economy is called into question, it is a radical truth, pure and simple. The failure of the men and women of established vision to perceive these things is thus not a function of their lack of intelligence but of the fact that the problem is so unprecedented that conventional eyes cannot see it. That systemic failure of understanding does not simply perpetuate inflation; it also fosters stagnation, the subject to which we now turn.[5]

_____ Notes _____

1. LBJ: CEA, Economic Report, 1969, p. 4. CEA, 1969: chart 8, p. 95. Samuelson: Quoted in Goldschmid et al., p. 299. Heller: _New Dimensions of Political Economy_, p. 106. Moynihan: _Maximum Feasible Misunderstanding_, p. 29. Short-term borrowing: CEA, 1979, table B-85, p. 282.

2. Keynes: _The General Theory_, pp. 14 and 303. Seligman: _Main Currents in Modern Economics_, p. 733. Keynes, 1940: _The Collected Writings_, vol. XXII, pp. 148–49. Inflation and Vietnam: CEA, 1979, p. 54. 1969–70 budgets: CEA, 1979, table B-69, p. 263; Schultze: _Setting National Priorities, the 1972 Budget_, p. 2. Prices: CEA, 1979, table

B-45, p. 239. On Nixon and 1960: Tufte, *Political Control of the Economy*, p. 17. Nixon in 1971: *A New Road for America*, pp. 267 ff. 1970 shift: Ibid., p. 250. Federal Reserve governor: Tufte, op. cit., p. 3. Okun: *The Great Stagflation Swamp*, p. 2. *Business Week:* "The Great Government Inflation Machine," May 22, 1978. CBO: *The Disappointing Recovery*, p. 9. *Business Week:* "Can Fiscal Restraint Win for Carter?" January 29, 1979. New Jersey Standard: Robert Engler, p. 135. Energy Future: p. 4.

3. Burns: *John Herling's Labor Letter*, December 27, 1978. Brown: "The White Horse of Victory," *The Wall Street Journal*, January 10, 1979. Vietnam expenditures: JEC, *Economic Stabilization Policies*, p. 197. Potential output: Perry, p. 98. House Budget Committee in JEC, *Economic Stabilization Policies*, p. 36. Corporate taxes: Harrington, "Full Employment," p. 25. CEA on private sector: 1979, p. 131. Blumenthal: AP dispatch, *Detroit News*, February 9, 1979. Credit: Mandel, p. 29; Heller, "Balanced Budget Fallacies," *The Wall Street Journal*, March 16, 1979. Weidenbaum: *The Costs of Government Regulation of Business*, pp. 5 and 13. Kelman: "Regulation That Works." Robert Eisner: "Sacrifices to Fight Inflation," *The New York Times*, August 11, 1979. CEA on pollution: 1979, p. 69. *London Economist* on productivity: "American Jobs," April 14, 1979. Aaron: *In Setting National Priorities: The 1980 Budget*, Pechman, ed., p. 140.

4. 1929 and 1933: Harrington, "Full Employment," table III, p. 18. Means on thirties: In Wachtel and Adelsheim, *The Inflationary Impact of Unemployment*, p. vi; Weston and Lustgarten in Goldschmid et al., pp. 312–13; Kahn in *The Roots of Inflation*, p. 263. Means: JEC, *The Federal Trade Commission and Inflation*, passim. Mueller in Goldschmid et al., pp. 286 ff.; Wachtel and Adelsheim, op. cit. supra, pp. 3 ff. Steel prices: Mueller, op. cit. supra, p. 286; Schultze, JEC Study Paper #1, p. 98; Wachtel and Adelsheim, op. cit. supra; table 1, p. 18. Means on 1973–74 in JEC, *The Federal Trade Commission and Inflation*, p. 8; Levinson, pp. 44–45. CEA, 1978: p. 144. Apparel prices: CEA, 1979, table B-51, p. 241. Heller: "The Realities of Inflation." Byung Yoo Hong: "Inflation Under Cost Pass-Along Management," pp. 63 and 66. Kahn: op. cit. supra, p. 246. Wenglowski: JEC, *Special Study on Economic Change*, pt. 3, p. 933.

5. Nulty: *Understanding the New Inflation*, passim. Necessities: Ibid., pp. 7–8. CEA, 1979: pp. 43, 84–85. CEA on wages: 1979, p. 66. Health care statistics: Sidel and Sidel, pp. 27 ff. Bellmon: *Congressional Record*, p. S10861. Net cost: Nulty, op. cit., pp. 42–43; Mortgages: CEA, 1979, p. 31. Food: Nulty, op. cit., p. 26. Farm subsidies: *Statistical Abstract*, 1975, table 1048, p. 620; Data Resources: Gough and Siegel, "Why Inflation Became Worse." U.S. agriculture: Harrington, *The Vast Majority*, chap. 6. Brannon Plan: Belden, pp. 70 ff.

3

The Dinosaur Returns

The National Bureau of Economic Research (NBER) is the nation's quasi-official keeper of the conventional wisdom about business cycles. At the bureau's Fiftieth Anniversary Colloquium in 1970, Paul Samuelson ebulliently informed the audience: "Now that the National Bureau is fifty years old, it has worked itself out of one of its first jobs, namely the business cycle. I don't know when the American Cancer Society was founded, but by similar reasoning, fifty years after the date some optimist could hope to cross cancer off his list." And a little later in the proceedings, Samuelson joked about how the experts would now have to redefine their subject matter if they wanted to operate in a recession-free world.

He analogized: ". . . if we think of a man who is an expert on dinosaurs—let's say in a university or in a museum—and he runs out of dinosaurs, well he can, of course, redefine a lizard to be a dinosaur and keep up his budget." Others at the colloquium, like Solomon Fabricant, had talked of the study of "growth cycles" rather than of recessions and expansions. In the bad times of a growth cycle, the rate of increase of production slowed down but there was no absolute decline. That, one could assume, was one of Samuelson's lizards in dinosaur's clothing.

In the first quarter of 1974, real gross national product, measured in constant dollars, began to go down and continued to do so until the first quarter of 1976. In that first quarter of 1976, GNP achieved a level slightly higher than in the last quarter of 1973, the first time that had happened in more than two years. In three years—1974 through 1976—it was conservatively estimated that the nation lost $435 billion in production computed in constant dollars. At the same time the federal government failed to collect more than $170 billion in revenues even though its expenses—including outlays for unemployment compensation—soared. And by 1976, the National Bureau itself began to recognize the new reality. The full employment consensus, its annual report said that year, was breaking down.

In short, the dinosaur had returned.

In the previous chapter, the analysis focused primarily on the inflationary component of stagflation. In this chapter, the emphasis will be upon the chronic unemployment which is part of the same phenomenon, that critical aspect of the problem which all but disappeared from public view in the late seventies. One of the reasons that the very topic vanished from the agenda was the mistaken belief that unemployment concerned only the unemployed, while inflation was a threat to everyone. It was unfortunate, almost everyone—but not everyone—would concede, that the jobless rate fluctuated around 6 percent after several years of "recovery." But that still meant that 94 percent of the labor force had its mind on prices and not unemployment.

That reasoning, the first section of this chapter will show, is false: unemployment menaces employed workers, women, minorities, people on pensions, as well as the Third World, the cause of peace and the protection of the environment. Indeed, the fact of the matter is that an America suffering from the jobless rates which have become commonplace and accepted in recent years will be unable to find a progressive solution to *any* of its problems. Therefore the attainment of full employment is a precondition of the social happiness of everyone in the country, not a special plea made only on behalf of those out of work.

One way of trying to evade that fact is to define, or rationalize, the intolerable levels of unemployment out of existence. The seventies, we have already seen, were particularly adept at solving problems by statistical sleight of hand. Samuelson had been afraid that analysts of the business cycle faced with obsolescence because their subject matter had disappeared would turn lizards into dinosaurs—growth cycles into recessions—in order to keep their jobs. Less than five years after this pronouncement, the tendency was in the opposite direction: dinosaurs were being solemnly defined as lizards. With millions of people out of work, there were reputable scholars who announced that we had in fact achieved full employment.

One critical theme in that statistical confidence game had to with women. If only, it was said, so many of them had not come into the labor market, then we would have neither high rates of unemployment nor of prices. Females, in this analysis, are a major cause of stagflation, a notion that has now been approved by the Council of Economic Advisers. This theory, and some of the statistical juggling which it facilitates, will be discussed in the second section of the chapter. Then, having dealt with some of the marvelously ingenious excuses which our plight has evoked, I will deal with the dinosaur as dinosaur: with the crucial role of the old-fashioned business cycle in any economy which was supposed to have mastered it a generation ago.

At this point, an extraordinarily revealing aspect of American life will become apparent. In 1978, the Congress passed the Humphrey-Hawkins Bill and the president signed it into law. That measure had originally been intended as a radical and progressive revision of the Employment Act of 1946, an act which stated that it was the public policy of the nation that every worker should have a job. Humphrey-Hawkins was supposed to turn that pious wish into a guaranteed right to a job. The first drafts of the law were, however, subjected to bitter criticism, from economists as well as from politicians. The economy, a liberal thinker like Charles Schultze said, was incapable of achieving traditional liberal goals.

Eventually a watered-down version of Humphrey-Hawkins did pass and it was that very mild measure which the president signed. But then, if one reads between the lines of the 1979 Report of the Council of Economic Advisers and similar analyses of the Congressional Budget Office, a shocking fact becomes visible: the administration does not really believe that it can meet the exceedingly moderate goals which the law mandates. It would be impolitic—not to mention illegal—for the government to say this openly, but it is clear that American society is now retreating from commitments which were at least formally acknowledged by every president since Harry Truman. The final section of this chapter will try to explain why this is so—and that has to do with the return of the dinosaur—and, more importantly, why it need not be so.[1]

_____ I _____

First of all, the chronic unemployment which is characteristic of stagflation is a menace to everyone in the society and not just the jobless.

It is, to begin with, an assault on the living standards of employed workers. Management, as the third section of this chapter will show, is quite frank on this count. One of the functions of a recession and its joblessness is to weaken the bargaining position of the unions and to restore discipline in the plant. And in fact that cruel strategy works. If, for instance, one compares rates of unemployment and the real wages of employed workers between

1953 and 1975, there is an obvious pattern. When the jobless rate goes up the buying power of workers goes down.

That is clearly bad from the point of view of the individual whose living standard declines. But it is also an evil from the point of view of the society as a whole. The 1970s, with its chronic and high rates of unemployment and its limping and lagging real wages, thereby made recovery from recession all the more difficult. After the 1974–75 recession, everyone noted that the recovery was much less positive than after other postwar downturns. One reason was the unprecedented (since 1945) severity of the crisis; another had to do with the impact of stagflation on wages. The economy was 5 percent below the normal trend in 1977, the Congressional Budget Office said, because of the "stagnation of real income in recent years . . ." There was, I would add, a vicious circle at work: unemployment held down real wages; stagnating real wages impeded recovery; a weak recovery prepared the way for pushing unemployment to an even higher plateau. In the process, men and women out on the street lost, of course. But so did everyone else, including business people.

This impact of unemployment on the entire society has another dimension which has been generalized by James O'Connor in *The Fiscal Crisis of the State*. Between 1974 and 1976, as we have seen, the federal government lost $170 billion in tax revenues at the same time that its outlays for the famous "built-in stabilizers" increased drastically. The result was the highest deficit in the history of the nation. That consequence, it should be carefully noted again, was *not* a function of prodigal spending by Washington. For one thing, it occurred under the presidency of Gerald Ford, the most conservative chief executive since Calvin Coolidge. For another, it was caused by stagflation rather than by social outlays, and came after the crisis, not before it.

In its 1977 midyear review of the economy, the Congressional Joint Economic Committee provided a dramatic illustration of my point. In fiscal 1976, the committee noted, the federal government lost $50 billion in tax revenue because of excessive joblessness. If one then added in the transfer payments for unemployment compensation, food stamps and other benefits which were caused by the very same phenomenon, that added $17.3 billion to the total direct cost of stagflation in that year. We paid, then, $67.3 billion for our miseries. "Since the actual deficit was about the same as this amount," the committee commented, "the budget would have been roughly in balance had the economy been at full employment."

More generally, the government under our mixed economy is assigned the task of socializing more and more of the operating costs of the corporate economy, like stagflations, railroads ruined by the private sector and the like. At the same time, those very responsibilities make it impossible for Washington to balance the budget or anything like it. So there is an inherent "fiscal crisis" in a system in which profits are private but more and more costs of those profits are social. This is then blamed, not upon its structural sources in a contradictory economy, but upon the excessive liberalism of the policy makers. The resultant demands for austerity then hurt everyone in the nation as social services are cut for the middle class and the working people as well as for the poor (but are cut, of course, most drastically for those least able to bear the burden).

So the real wages of employed workers, the resilience of the economy and the tax structure of the country are victims of unemployment along with the unemployed. So are people who are not even in the labor market.

The aging are an obvious case in point. There was a tremendous scare in the Social Security system during the seventies when it seemed that America was soon to run out of money needed to fulfill its legal obligations to people over sixty-five. Why? A Senate Committee answered clearly: ". . . the short-term deficit is caused by our extraordinary economic situation: substantial unemployment coupled with high inflation. The net impact is that Social Security is being strained at both ends. Benefit payments are rising because the cost-of-living adjustments are higher than initially projected. Yet income for the system is reduced because unemployment in 1975 reached its highest level in 34 years."

That short-run crisis could be handled. But in the long run—as the portion of the population over sixty-five moves from 18.6 percent in 1973 to a projected 28.3 percent in 2050—dealing with the problem will not be so simple. The American Social Security system is not funded, i.e., the monies of the present generation at work are not set aside for their future but are paid out to the present generation of retirees. As the new demographics of zero population growth take over—and one should always note that such projections are subject to considerable error—there will be a smaller work force which must provide, not only for its own needs but for those of its parents and grandparents as well. Under such circumstances, if the United States accepts high levels of joblessness as necessary and normal (which, the next section will show, is precisely what is now happening), then there could be a generational conflict in the not too distant future as the different age groups fight over scarce resources. Indeed, during the 1974–75 crisis of the Social Security system, President Ford proposed to "cap" the cost-of-living allowances at a level well below the actual rate of inflation. That is, he proposed to reduce the real living standard of the aging in order to deal with the problems of the economy.

There is another group which is composed of people who are not in the labor market and yet is profoundly affected by the ups and downs of stagflation: the poor. Most of them, as chapter 7 will detail, do not work because they are too young to do so. Yet when that fiscal crisis hits, they are the least able to defend themselves and their benefits, unlike those for Social Security, are not indexed. Even more to the point, the young, who constitute a major portion of the other America, are denied the opportunity of making contact with the society outside the slum or ghetto by means of a job. So the nation will be paying the social costs of the Depression levels of unemployment among, say, minority youth over the next generation in the coin of crime, prison expenditures, family breakdown, alcoholism, drug addiction and the like.

That obviously relates to the problem of racism, which will also be discussed in chapter 7. The joblessness of the seventies fell, of course, with discriminatory effect upon the black, the brown, the female and the young. Indeed, as we will see in a moment, women in particular were scapegoated as the principle cause of stagflation. Therefore, no matter how profoundly America purges its psyche of racist and sexist feelings and attitudes, racist and sexist outcomes will be institutionalized into the very structure of the economy under conditions of chronic unemployment.

But then, there are people who are not even citizens— or inhabitants—of America who suffer from our unemployment rates. On the one hand, multinational corporations range to the far corners of the globe in order to get cheap labor. Many of the radios in Ford automobiles in the United States are "imported" from a Ford subsidiary in Brazil. As *Business Week* generalized in 1978 about the multinationals, ". . . their basic aim is to maximize worldwide profits, without regard to sources of profits or national boundaries. U.S. multinational managers have no reason, therefore, for preferring to export American made products rather than producing the same goods in foreign plants."

That, obviously, favors the foreign worker in the sense of providing him or her with a job though, it should be noted immediately, an even more exploitative job than those held by Americans. But it also sets in motion a reaction within this country and particularly in industries, like steel, which are still nationally based and feel themselves menaced by alien competitors. Therefore as unemployment goes up, American workers often join "their" capitalists in demanding protectionist measures against impoverished countries which, it now turns out, are quite capable of turning out steel or even modern ships. So it is that the Third World, which has been victimized by four centuries of Western progress, suffers anew from the Western failures of stagflation.

The environment is affected too. In the late sixties and early seventies it began to dawn upon the American consciousness that the side effects of an irresponsible, profit-maximizing technology were often more massive than the intended benefits. And this country, which had been retrograde from the very beginning in terms of occupational safety, also began to adopt some measures to deal with the carnage which takes place on the job. Yet, as the last chapter documented, with the onset of stagflation the corporations mounted a major offensive around the theme that environmental and occupational protection were too costly. It can be safely predicted that, if the current levels of joblessness continue to be accepted as "normal," then there will be a new degradation of the quality of American life in these two areas.

World peace is also affected by unemployment. This point, as I stressed in the first chapter, must be carefully argued. The American labor market is not primarily dependent upon the military economy for jobs. Indeed, as a study by the International Association of Machinists (IAM) in 1979 documented, additional federal outlays for the military produce decreasing amounts of work in the private sector. Moreover, those expenditures are inflationary because they create income without putting goods and services on the market. So it would be a mistake to argue that the United States cannot achieve full employment on a peacetime basis short of a revolutionary transformation of the system. That "radical" proposition, of course, plays into conservative and hawkish hands given the fact that such a transformation is not exactly imminent. Still, understanding all of these things, the fact remains that certain groups of workers, and certain geographic areas, feel themselves—sometimes wrongly—to be dependent upon military expenditures.

If there were full employment planning and alternate jobs for those workers, it would be possible to persuade them to accept disarmament. But as long as there is chronic unemployment as part of stagflation, they are almost certain to be committed to expanding the military economy. And that becomes a serious—though not a decisive—impediment to the negotiation of nuclear and conventional disarmament. At the same time, the Carter budget for 1980 was precisely based on a guns *or* butter concept. Given the notions of fiscal frugality underlying that document—notions based, not so incidentally, on an obsolete and discredited "demand-pull" theory of inflation —it was therefore all but inevitable that the 3 percent increase in real spending for the Pentagon be balanced by cuts for Social Security, students and public-service jobs. Yet, as that Machinist study shows, the expenditure for the means of annihilation will be much less labor intensive than investments in social decency. The strategy, then, will make joblessness all the more tenacious.

One could go on but the point is plain. Unemployment is a problem for every American even when the jobless rate is "only" 6 percent. It affects the employed, the aging, the minorities, women, the environment, the Third World and the very possibility of world peace. This issue, then, is not a special interest of people looking for work; it is a decisive determinant and precondition of every single progressive policy in the land. This is one of the many reasons why the recent attempts to pretend that the problem does not even exist are so deeply disturbing.[2]

II

In 1977, with the unemployment rate at 7 percent, Herbert Stein wrote an audacious article in *The Wall Street Journal.* "To admit that we are now at full employment," he said, "requires that we exorcise some ideas we have had from infancy. Most important, it requires getting rid of the idea that 7 percent unemployment *cannot* be full employment."

It is one of the peculiarities of the American concept of

full employment that it is defined by an unemployment rate. That is based on the theory that there are a certain number of the unavoidably unemployed, e.g., individuals who are between jobs looking to better themselves. There are, to be sure, other ways of coming up with a definition —full employment, Sir William Beeridge, the architect of the British welfare state, used to say, occurred when there were more jobs than people looking for them—but America has rejected them.

The problem is, that "full employment unemployment rate" can be shifted upward. As recently as the Kennedy administration the official goal was 3 percent unemployment with a 4 percent rate as an interim target. Then the aim was defined as 4 percent unemployment, and then Stein, in that amazing revelation, decided that 7 percent —which meant almost seven million people out on the street—was full employment. Almost two years after that *Wall Street Journal* article, Stein was appearing as a witness before the National Commission on Employment and Unemployment Statistics. Sar Levitan, the commission's chairman, needled him: "Now that the Bureau of Labor Statistics reported that unemployment has declined to 6 percent, would you say that we are having super-full employment, or would you want to modify that statement?"

On the record, Levitan had Stein dead to rights. If 7 percent unemployment had been full employment, then 6 percent unemployment—again, almost six million people without jobs—would be seen as a dangerous, threatening situation, as a tight labor market. Stein was not daunted. Full employment is defined by a jobless rate that "you could not get below without an acceleration of inflation," he replied. "All right, so we are below 7 percent; we have the inflation accelerated. Now you can draw the conclusion you like from that." So one of the possible ways of dealing with the problem of stagflation was, here again, statistical: the unemployment component of the phenomenon could be made officially tolerable if it were defined as inevitable. After all, what rational person can rail against necessity?

This point should be carefully distinguished from attempts to make the unemployment figures more precise. Levitan himself had long argued that a "hardship index" should be constructed which would assign complex weights to various kinds of joblessness. An out-of-work student, he argued, should not be counted as equal to a primary breadwinner walking the streets. There were many controversial aspects to this proposal and they are being discussed by the National Commission at this writing. However, it should at least be noted that one version of his index put the "hardship" figure at a higher level than the official unemployment count. As usual, however, the conservatives only took note of the evidence of possible overcounts of the unemployed; they did not even notice the copious data on undercounting.

Such technical matters seem academic and irrelevant to the lives of people in the society. Yet, it was of great moment that in 1979 the president of the United States adopted a point of view which was almost, but not quite, as radically audacious—and callous—as Stein's. The economy, Mr. Carter said in his economic message, "is operating at close to its capacity . . ." But if that point had been reached when there was still 6 percent of the labor force unemployed, there were momentous consequences. The Council of Economic Advisers was specific about them. Since a "high employment economy"—that phrase was delicately substituted for "full employment" for obvious reasons—is compatible with 6 percent joblessness, that means that the government can no longer expand spending in order to put people back to work. The traditional fiscal and monetary tactics for fighting the problem are declared inoperative and one must now rely on special programs which will upgrade the skills of the unemployed and thus make it possible for them to be hired without increasing the risks of inflation.

The problem with that last solution is that it was once tried in the much more propitious labor market of the sixties with very ambiguous results. (Those will be examined in greater detail in chapter 8.) Therefore, even though there is no reason to doubt the sincerity of the president and his advisers, these statements have the extremely probable effect of consigning millions of Americans— mainly, it should be noted again, black, brown, female and young—to the scrap heap. During the euphoria of the sixties, The National Commission on Technology, Automation and Economic Progress had said that rapid increases in productivity and economic growth with 2.9 percent unemployment were quite possible. Now, a scant thirteen years later, one was being told by even more prestigious and powerful figures—including the president— that, in good times, the nation had to suffer 6 percent joblessness. Why did that momentous change take place?

Arthur Burns provided a typically dyspeptic analysis. In a 1978 speech, he said that ". . . as far as skilled or experienced labor is concerned, it may be fairly said that our economy is close to full employment. The unemployment that remains is largely structural in character, reflecting an archaic legislative approach to minimum wages, inadequate preparation of young people for jobs in industry, reluctance of some men and women to exchange generous governmental benefits for low-paying work and inability or reluctance of others to take available jobs for family or personal reasons." In short, the excessive humanity of the welfare state and the perversity of the jobless account for our situation.

Other analyses were much more subtle and less nasty. Perhaps the most popular thesis made women responsible for the new and high levels of "necessary" joblessness.

That idea was raised to the level of a theory by George Perry of the Brookings Institution in 1976. In the postwar period, there was a sharp and steady increase in female participation in the labor force. Between 1950 and 1975, the women's percentage of the total working population went from 30 percent to 40 percent; in 1990, projections see it rising to 43 percent. Women are concentrated in the low-paid, relatively marginal jobs, which is the chief explanation for the fact that their wage is about 60 percent of the male wage and why they suffer significantly higher rates of unemployment than men. Even more to the point, female joblessness has been rising relative to male.

The result of this shift, Perry's analysis held, is that there are now in effect two labor forces and two unemployment rates. The "prime" labor force is primarily male, skilled and in the major industrial and service sectors. The other labor force is much more heavily female, black, brown and young; it is relatively less skilled and absolutely less paid. Here is how the Council of Economic Advisers put the problem in 1979: "As the over-all unemployment rate declines, demand for skilled, prime age workers exceeds supply of these workers and puts upward pressure on their wages, even though unemployment among minorities, teenagers and women may remain uncomfortably high."

When this theory is put forward there is often an extremely reactionary implication: that women's unemployment is not as important as men's, that if only the females would go back to the kitchen and the children, then the American economy would function well. After all, in this theory women are the primary cause of stagflation. Their high unemployment (along with that of the minorities) puts pressure on policy makers to undertake expansive measures at the very time when the shortage of prime workers is setting off inflationary tendencies. If they would only retreat from the workplace, the current crisis would be solved.

Indeed, in Europe there are conservatives who are trying to develop a strategy based on just such an analysis. In West Germany, for instance, they have proposed to give women "upbringing money" so that they will go home and take care of small children. That subsidy is less than normal unemployment compensation and the Christian Democrats have refused to back the mother's right to return to her job. This is, after all, a tactic of trying to deal with unemployment by driving women out of the work force. But then Americans should not be shocked. One of the reasons why women's Social Security benefits were designed to depend on the husband's pension—and thus normally gave no credit for the amount contributed to the system by the wife—was a conscious desire to limit the number of workingwomen during the Great Depression.

Ironically, it is at least possible that the major premise of this reactionary attack upon women is without empirical foundation. In 1977 a Joint Economic Committee report suggested that changes in the composition of the labor force, particularly the influx of women and teenagers, accounted for only three-tenths of 1 percent in the unemployment rate. That left 90 percent of the increase in "necessary" joblessness to be explained. If the committee is right, even if the female proportion of the labor force reverted to 1956 levels, that would not begin to solve the basic problem.

But if the committee turned out to be wrong that would not justify the sexist implication of many of the current theories which essentially argue that our difficulties "only" stem from female unemployment, i.e., from the joblessness of secondary earners who are merely supplementing an income supplied by men. There is a long tradition that discounts women's work in this way. It has been, I believe, wrong throughout our history but I will confine myself to a narrower point here: Are women today working for incomes which are not basic to their families' standards of living? Do they labor for frills and "mad" money?

We know that the stimulus for the recent surge in female labor force participation came from World War II. In those years full employment was a precondition for military victory and it was taken seriously in a way that has never held since. The government spent around 50 percent of GNP, joblessness fell to 1 percent and patriotic appeals were made to get women into the factories. With the war's end, it was assumed that female workers would return to the feminine mystique. It didn't turn out that way. Too many of them had learned the advantages of independence, of earning their own way. There were the first beginnings of a feminist consciousness which was to culminate in one of the most important movements of the late sixties and the seventies.

Something else happened. In the post–World War II period, the United States entered the phase of "high mass consumption," a fact which was immediately celebrated by all of the official eulogists of the society. What is not often noticed is that this transformation could not have taken place were it not for the sharp increase in the percentage of workingwomen. The figures are clear. In 1974, white women accounted for one-quarter of the family income, black women for almost a third of theirs. In 1974, the "intermediate" budget for an urban family of four, according to the Bureau of Labor Statistics, was $14,333. In that year, the average white family made $17,983, the black family, $14,317. If the white woman's contribution to that total were taken away, then the family income would fall back below the intermediate level, to $13,500, and in the case of the black family the husband-only income would be $9672.

One would think that economists would be aware of the disastrous economic consequences of a sharp reduction in female labor force participation. But it is not surprising that the practitioners of this discipline have overlooked a revolution in social structure and morals. It is an occupational hazard of their profession to be naive, or insensitive, about sociology, psychology and the whole range of factors which do not fit easily into mathematical models. Take one example. In her testimony before the National Commission on Employment and Unemployment Statistics, Dr. Nancy Smith Barrett pointed out that "something like 40 percent of all children born in America today, including upper, lower, all income strata, will at some point be supported solely by their mothers." That is only one striking index of the change taking place in woman's position in the society. How, then, can one use, not only the jobless figures, but the social criteria, of the 1950s—of another age—in dealing with women in the 1980s?

This is one more example of the way in which the persistence of the unemployment component in stagflation impacts upon, not simply the labor force or the unemployed, but the quality of life of the entire society. In this case, that chronic joblessness becomes an incentive for a reactionary attack upon the social gains made by the female one-half of the population. In the name of hard economic "fact" there are demands for a march to the rear. But then that is happening throughout the society and is perhaps even more dramatically visible when one turns to the dinosaur that was supposed to have been slain but suddenly reappeared among us—to the business cycle.[3]

III

Since Karl Marx developed the first, comprehensive theory of the capitalist tendency toward periodic boom-and-bust there has been a library of books written on the subject. Schumpeter's *Business Cycles,* one of the best of those studies, was cited in the first chapter and at the fiftieth anniversary meeting of the National Bureau of Economic Research, the economist Victor Zarnowitz, presented a brief survey of the recent literature. And yet, for all of the insights and analyses since Marx, his theory remains the best single account of the phenomenon, one which can integrate almost everything of value which has been produced about it since. But this is clearly not the occasion for a book-length detour in that topic, particularly when I have written on it in some detail in *The Twilight of Capitalism.* So I will very briefly state, rather than argue, that Marxist framework and then proceed to relate it to the present.[4]

What is the nature of the dinosaur that continues to thrive in our very sophisticated economy?

I expand on the brief statement about structural imbalances in the last chapter. The system of production is basic. It is, for all of the changes brought about by the welfare state and the evolution of the corporation, still an unplanned, profit-maximizing system in which the critical decisions about investment are made by private owners or their surrogates and which therefore requires inequality as a precondition of its existence. That inequality provides the surplus which the private decision makers then invest according to their profit priorities. Because the system is unplanned, it tends to expand capacity in good times as if there were no tomorrow; because it requires maldistributed wealth to work, it periodically "overproduces," not in terms of human need, but within the framework of limited consumer demand which is a consequence of the organization of production. Keynesianism, the last chapter suggested, was an attempt to offset that systematic overproduction and underconsumption by means of a controlled inflation, leaving the structural tendencies toward crisis intact but ameliorating their effects. We have already seen some of the limitations of that strategy. Now its impact upon employment and unemployment will be explored.

For the fact of the matter is that in such a system unemployment is functional and desirable. In his 1978 speech to the American Enterprise Institute, Arthur Burns, it will be remembered, talked of the "unavoidable function" of recessions in lowering interest rates, enforcing efficiency and the like. Ten years earlier, Dr. Burns had speculated that perhaps recessions would no longer take place, "merely a reduced rate of growth . . ." But now he was back at the stern and true faith in which such periodic miseries are to be welcomed like a bad-tasting medicine or a necessary surgery. Why?

Prosperity is not an unalloyed good from a business point of view since it menaces profit margins. Combative workers bid up wages and become undisciplined; inefficient producers compete for scarce resources; the interest rate climbs; the good times curdle. Recession brings relief. Wages recede and discipline returns; the inefficient are driven out of business; the interest rate falls. This is not simply a theory about economic behavior. It is a deeply held conviction within the business community, one which people act upon. Here, for example, is a remarkable report by Leonard Silk, the economic columnist for *The New York Times*, in April of 1978, i.e., at a time when "recovery," as the seventies defines the term, was proceeding apace.

Silk wrote, "Wall Streeters, far from worrying that the Federal Reserve may be tightening the reins on the economy too much, are bitterly expressing the view that nothing would be so good for the market and the economy as a minor recession—stiff enough to reduce inflation and the trade deficit, although not so steep as to disrupt business plans for new investment or to wreck prospects for strongly rising profits in the next expansion." In December, *The Wall Street Journal* corroborated Silk's perception. "The economy is likely to slow down next year," Ralph Winter wrote, "and a recession may start by mid-year, say the economists. 'Good!' respond many corporate executives."

The businessmen, Winter continued, have "no illusions" that recession would cure inflation. That would take a "balanced Federal budget over a period of some years with only a modest deficit permitted during a recession." But they did think—without knowing how utterly Marxist their consciousness was—that a recession would help union leaders accept lower wages and would drive down interest rates. At no point did the strategists chronicled by Silk and Winter make any mention of the human cost of their tactic, much less of the rippling social consequences which were detailed earlier in this chapter.

In its 1980 budget, the Carter administration more or less adopted the same outlook. In a brave show of anti-inflation purposiveness, it held the projected deficit to $29 billion—even though there was not a single economist anywhere, in the administration or without, who would testify that such a gesture would have any significant impact upon the inflation rate. It would increase unemployment, however, as Mr. Carter himself admitted, and take away benefits from a number of people who had helped to vote the president into office. Indeed, the spectacle of the president of the United States and his advisers advocating a policy which they themselves suspect will not work is one more sign of the structural nature of the present crisis.

In 1978, Carter's Council of Economic Advisers considered whether "a reduction in demand sufficient to produce a modest and short-lived amount of economic slack would eliminate inflation quickly," i.e., whether the corporate program for a small recession would help banish stagflation. They concluded that wages and prices would respond very slowly to such a maneuver. It would take, the council said, six years of 6½ percent unemployment to cut inflation from 6 percent to 3 percent and that would cost $600 billion in lost output at 1977 prices. Moreover, this tactic would hold down investment which would mean that once inflation was reduced, there would be shortages (which, presumably, would be a new source of inflation). All of this was stated quite clearly and yet Mr. Carter embarked on something like the doomed strategy in 1979.

In that same 1978 Report, the council had made a shamefaced case for the Humphrey-Hawkins Bill, emphasizing its price stability, rather than its full employment, features. And it also noted very carefully that the proposed legislation gave the White House the right to change the full employment targets in the third Economic Report after passage of the law. This came as no surprise to anyone who knew about Washington politics: Charles Schultze, the council's chairman, had played a major role in making Humphrey-Hawkins much less ambitious than the original draft and had resisted accepting even the extremely modest goals of the text which was finally signed into law. So it was that in the 1979 Report, the council all but openly stated that it doubted that the government could fulfill the responsibilities which had been so solemnly imposed upon it only a few months before.

One hardly needs to read between the lines; the skepticism of the council is flagrant: "Achieving all of the goals, and particularly 4% unemployment and 3% inflation by 1983 would demand not only a performance by the American economy that is unprecedented in peacetime history, but also general programs that can deal effectively with some of our most intransigent problems, particularly inflation and structural unemployment." And a little later: "The likelihood of achieving rapid and sensational economic growth while inflation remains high is very small." Clearly, the council was preparing the way for a future White House announcement stating that it was impossible for the United States to have both full employment and price stability—and indeed questionable whether either goal could be fulfilled.

In short, Washington itself was admitting that the problem was structural and could not be solved by traditional Keynesian monetary and fiscal policies. But then Washington had no solution, which was why the Carter administration pursued a tack which its own theories showed to be unworkable. Why did such intelligent and serious people who had so much to gain politically from economic success behave in this fashion? Was it a failure of the intelligence? Or of the will? Neither, I would suggest. An innocuous sentence in the last report of the Ford Council of Economic Advisers gives an important clue to the real reason.

That council said in 1977: ". . . the full employment unemployment rate is generally understood to mean the lowest rate of unemployment attainable, *under the existing institutional structure*, that will not result in inflation" (emphasis added). Serious solutions to the problems of stagflation—and the achievement of full employment in particular—required measures that transcended the "existing institutional structure." But the manifest intelligence, expertise and will of the Carter administration operated under a profound constraint: to deal with the crisis of the seventies and eighties without changing any of the basic arrangements which date back to the thirties (or before). A Council of Economic Advisers composed of Solomon, Marx and Keynes could not square such a circle.

Public-service employment is a case in point, one which is relevant both to the analysis of the present and the changes which the future requires. There are countless studies showing that such a social investment generates more jobs than any form of federal spending (i.e., compared to tax cuts and public works). But, as the next chapter will show, public-service employment cannot, so long as one is committed to existing institutional structures, be allowed to challenge the corporate domination of the economy. So if any jobs are to be funded, they must be low-paid and temporary or else they would bid up wages in the most exploitative areas of the private sector. And permanent, well-paid public positions, providing the people with a useful good or service and financing themselves in the process, would be a violation of the nation's commitment to "free enterprise."

Ironically, the original Humphrey-Hawkins—which focused on full employment planning and envisioned the possibility of a major public component—would have been a much more effective tool against stagflation than the bill which actually passed. By compromising the measure in the name of realism, the experts, like Charles Schultze, made it most unrealistic. When, for instance, one considers an area of economic and social desolation like the South Bronx, it is abundantly clear that no amount of "trickle-down" benefits will persuade profit-maximizing corporations to locate there. Either there will be direct public investments for social purpose or the social pathology of that area will persist and worsen. (This whole issue is treated at greater length in Chapter 6.)

The achievement of full employment, then, requires a redefinition of the institutional limits of the public and private sectors in the United States. That transformation, which is radical for this country and a commonplace in most other capitalist societies, is a precondition of fulfilling the official goals of the nation. What is envisioned here is not, let me emphasize, the temporary, make-work, underpaid kind of a job which is usually created for this purpose. Neither am I thinking of one more nationalization of enterprises ruined by private business, like the shamefaced take-over of the Penn Central Railroad. Rather, I am saying that the public must run some profitable operations which can be used, among other things, as a major tool of full employment planning.

The Tennessee Valley Authority provides a good example of the possibilities—and dangers—of such an approach. To begin with, the TVA is not a department of the federal government. It is a corporation whose board is nominated by the president and subject to Senate approval which then operates as an independent entity. I stress this point since the very idea of social property conjures up in the American mind an image of centralized, bureaucratic ownership inevitably located in Washington. That is not the case with TVA (whose headquarters are in Tennessee); it certainly should not be the case in the program I am outlining. Indeed, one of the most important models for emulation is the rural electrification effort begun under Franklin Roosevelt which provided cheap federal money for the encouragement of local cooperatives.

To return to TVA. Per capita income in the valley—which includes parts of seven states—rose from 44 percent of the national average in 1933 to 79 percent in 1976. Indeed, TVA is now the largest utility in the country. But at the same time the authority has been suffused with corporate values. In the early fifties, it moved from hydroelectric power toward steam, and over the years it underwrote the strip mining of Appalachia. As *The New York Times* summarized this sad aspect of TVA in a 1978 editorial: "In recent years . . . TVA has continued to plan large increases in generating capacity even though critics stressed the need for conservation. It has committed itself heavily to huge centralized generating plants and been slow to explore alternatives. It has backed the Clinch River demonstration breeder reactor. . . . It has been chided by Federal energy officials for inadequate attention to rate reforms that might encourage more efficient use of electricity. And it has resisted efforts by the Environmental Protection Agency to cut air pollution with the result that TVA, a Federal agency, spews dirtier air than some other utilities."

Clearly, then, public property is no panacea. But just as clearly, it holds open the possibility of locating jobs in areas of need—a tactic which the private sector adjures.

As James Galbraith, a brilliant young economist, put it, "Private employers, many of whom are not practicing bigots, avoid the hard-core unemployed for business reasons. They are, or are thought to be, low-profit workers: ill trained, poorly educated, transient, sometimes hostile or obstreperous, often located in run-down, dangerous remote or (the inner cities) high wage and thoroughly unionized districts." One way of getting to those people and places—the only way I suspect—is to make direct, profitable social investments in a planned way. Hearings held by Senator Edward Kennedy in March 1978 demonstrated how this could be done in the case of solar power.

For all of the talk of a national energy plan, Senator Kennedy pointed out, no one in government had discussed the employment aspect of that commitment. Yet, evidence was presented to the committee he chaired that an investment in solar energy would generate three times the number of jobs produced by similar outlays for nuclear power (a form of energy which is, given the current state of technology, dangerous and objectionable on many other grounds in any case). The energy crisis, William Winpisinger, the president of the International Association of Machinists, testified, "gives us an unparalleled opportunity to develop a rational, fair, democratically controlled, national energy policy. . . . We can continue to develop all sources with private investment, but we can also develop energy sources with direct public investment."

Winpisinger's point is extremely important. The oil industry, which controls all forms of present and future energy, has made it clear that it will not make the investments into research and development necessary to create new, and alternate, sources of energy like solar power. There are a whole series of proposals—from Democrats like President Carter and Senator Henry Jackson as well as from Republicans like Gerald Ford—in which Washington will pay the cost of development and then turn the finished, and quite profitable, product over to the private sector. That is not simply objectionable on grounds of distributive justice; it also relates to both the kind of technology we will get and the employment impact it will have.

In 1978, *Business Week* examined the potential of solar power. The "energy establishment," it said—oil companies, utilities "and others associated with the centralized power system"—were keeping an eye on Washington's activity in this area. A General Electric vice-president was quite frank: ". . . the real key is that the government is willing to spend a lot." The Establishment, *Business Week* went on to say, was fearful that the federal effort might lead to a dispersed and small-scale technology which would escape corporate control. They were therefore ready to join in the undertaking as soon as it showed any signs of success and they would do so in order to shape the technology to their own taste, i.e., to make it centralized.

Similarly, the corporations would have no incentive to take social objectives, like full employment, into account if they won control of the federally financed project. But why, then, not follow Winpisinger's advice—and that of many of the other witnesses before the Kennedy committee? Why not public ownership, both as a means of creating a technology on a human scale (which could also be used in the Third World) and as a tool for full employment planning and area redevelopment?

Here is how the Congress's own Office of Technology Assessment put the potential of such an approach: "Onsite solar energy appears to be more labor-intensive than contemporary techniques for supplying energy; thus, in the short term, the introduction of solar energy devices might create jobs in trades now suffering from serious unemployment. In general, the new jobs will be distributed widely across the country and most workers would be able to find jobs near their homes. Work on solar equipment, for the most part, should necessitate only simple retraining programs, although there may be shortages both of engineers and architects . . ." On one count, however, this analysis is overly optimistic. If the private energy establishment gets ahold of the development of this technology, it is unlikely to have the beneficial consequences indicated.

In one exchange before the Kennedy committee, Senator George McGovern generalized this point. He did so in the form of a series of questions addressed to the secretary of labor. "Making reference to the efficiency of rail transport, you noted that you get more performance out of a mile of track than you do out of 9 miles of superhighways. What, in your judgment, would be the relative impact on the employment situation of investing that proposed $25 billion tax cut [President Carter's proposal at the time, later withdrawn] in an alternative way? For example, in public investment, say in rebuilding the rails and providing support for the construction of solar collectors across the country and the reprofiting of public buildings . . . ? Wouldn't we really get more jobs and more economic stimulus out of carefully selected public investment of that kind than we would get out of the tax cut?"

Ray Marshall, the secretary of labor, answered, "Yes; you do get more impact out of direct expenditures, if you are concerned mainly about employment, than you do out of tax cuts." But if that is publicly acknowledged to be the case by a cabinet member of the Carter administration, and if that same administration is simultaneously implying that it cannot meet the Humphrey-Hawkins job goals, why not build those railroads and that solar system in order to achieve full employment? A personal anecdote might help to answer that question.

In 1974, I addressed the Democratic Study Group of the House of Representatives, an association of liberal Democrats. In the course of my remarks, I attacked the hidden nationalization of all losing railroads in the Northeast and the continued private operation of all the profitable carriers. It should be, I said, public policy to develop a single, efficient, restored-rail system in the Northeast and Midwest, under direct public ownership, in which profitable operations would subsidize the unprofitable. It was, I argued, insane for the nation to pay only costs without gaining any control or any benefits. That, one Congressman said to me, is absolutely right and convincing —but it transcends the "ideological limits" of American society. Those ideological limits are as much a part of the system of established power as corporate lobbying. Indeed, because the limits are internalized and "freely" chosen, they are often more effective than other forms of political influence.

There is, the last chapter showed, a workable anti-inflation program aimed at the macro- and sectoral structures, like administered pricing and an antediluvian health system, which cause soaring prices. There is, this chapter demonstrates, a road to planned full employment. We do not adopt these rational solutions because major economic interests would lose in a more sane and just society. But we are also paralyzed by our own beliefs, by those superstitious "ideological limits."

In the 1970s, the American ideology became even more openly procorporate than ever before. Since that fact is going to be a major determinant of the 1980s, it is the subject of the next chapter. Unless this country is able to see through the corporate ideology, the dinosaur of recession and joblessness will remain with us as we stumble toward the twenty-first century.

___ Notes _____

1. Samuelson: National Bureau of Economic Research, *The Business Cycle Today*, pp. 167 and 175. Fabricant: Ibid., p. 135. GNP numbers: CEA, 1975 and 1976, table B-2. Losses in recession: Harrington, "Full Employment," p. 4. Annual Report, NBER, 1976, p. 1 ff.

2. Unemployment and wages: Harrington, "Full Employment," table 1, p. 3. CBO: *The Disappointing Recovery*, p. 5; O'Connor, passim. JEC: *Midyear Review of the Economy*, 1977, p. 39. U.S. Senate, Special Committee on Aging: Report, p. 66. Aging trends: Ibid., p. 67. *Business Week:* "The Reluctant Exporters," April 10, 1978. Machinists: Marion Anderson, "The Impact of Military Spending on the Machinists Union," IAM (AFL-CIO), January 1979.

3. Stein: "Full Employment at Last," *The Wall Street Journal,* Sep-

tember 14, 1977. National Commission: Vol. 1, p. 36. Levitan index: JEC, *The 1978 Economic Report of the President*, pt. 1, pp. 286–87. Carter and CEA: Economic Report, 1978, pp. 3 and 25. National Commission on Technology: p. 15. Burns: *John Herling's Labor Newsletter*, December 23, 1978. Perry: Owen and Schultze, eds., pp. 301 ff. Women percentage: Harrington, "Full Employment," p. 13. CEA, 1979: p. 119. European conservatives: Ratner, ed. JEC on women: *Midyear Review*, 1977, p. 12. Women's income: Harrington, op. cit., p. 14. Barrett: National Commission, vol. 1, p. 60. Nulty: Testimony for the International Association of Machinists, p. 8.

4. Zarnowitz: National Bureau of Economic Research, *The Business Cycle Today*, pp. 17 ff. Burns in 1968: Quoted in NBER, op. cit., p. 3. Silk: *The New York Times*, April 27, 1978. Winter: "Businessmen: Let Slowdown Come," *The Wall Street Journal*, December 18, 1978. CEA, 1978: pp. 149–50. On Humphrey-Hawkins: Ibid., p. 95. CEA, 1979: pp. 110–11. CEA, 1977: p. 48. *The New York Times* editorial: "Tapping the Potential of TVA," April 17, 1978. Galbraith: "Why We Have No Full Employment Policy," p. 30. JEC, Subcommittee on Energy, p. 28. Winpisinger: Ibid., p. 163. Jackson and Ford: Harrington, *The Twilight of Capitalism*, pp. 258–60. *Business Week:* "General Electric Hedges Its Solar Bets," October 9, 1978. Office of Technology Assessment: Subcommittee on Energy, op. cit., p. 277. McGovern and Marshall: Ibid., p. 151.

4

The Corporate Ideology: Triumph of Illusion

In the second half of the 1970s, the United States saw—or rather, welcomed—the triumph of illusion over reality.

Federal and state tax laws were changed in favor of the rich and against the interest of the people, often with the enthusiastic and militant consent of the people who thus helped discriminate against themselves. In analyzing how this happened, one does not merely gain some insight into events of the last decade. One also begins to understand the role of the corporate ideology in preserving the structures which prevent America from solving its problems. And that understanding is, of course, the precondition for action in the two decades which remain in the century.

What happened in the last five years is hardly new. In every social system illusion has always been a very real constituent of power. Indeed, it is normally more effective than the police or the army in controlling the people. No society can organize itself for long on the basis of simple repressive force. That guarantees constant opposition, counterviolence, revolt. So every society must produce an ideology which legitimates its inequities and thereby persuades those at the bottom to accept, and even revere, their own inferiority. Prior to the rise of capitalism, that ideology was usually religious: God, or the gods, wanted men and women to submit meekly to divinely inspired and sanctioned injustices. At the extreme, the untouchables of India accepted a status as permanent and hereditary outcasts because an ancestor was supposed to have broken holy law.

Religion could not play such a dominant role in the capitalist ideology. The system was created in opposition to a feudal order in which the Church sanctified the status quo and it appealed to individual conscience (Protestantism) or reason (the Enlightenment). So the system had to seek its justification in this world, not the next. It did so by stating and restating a basic theme in many, many guises: that the differences in income and wealth which it not only tolerated but created were functionally necessary for the expansion of production and therefore for the happiness of all.

In the seventies, many Americans—including millions who should and could be part of a progressive majority— were persuaded by a new statement of this hallowed theme. That does not, however, mean that wily plutocrats carefully worked out a myth and foisted it upon the people. Those who profited from this half-truth (and an ideology is always a half-truth since outright lies have a limited staying power) sincerely believed in the illusion they perpetrated. And this is so even though economic reality in this country is increasingly, and necessarily, at odds with the corporate description of it. Under these circumstances, the intellectual confusion and moral guilt of the corporate rich testify to their honest faith in their own myths.

For instance, since the New Deal the government has played a critical role in stimulating the prosperity of the private sector. Indeed, from Franklin Roosevelt through the Nixon-Ford administration, business flourished when their liberal Keynesian enemies were in the White House and did rather poorly when their conservative friends achieved power with corporate assistance. If the boardroom had been occupied by tough and cynical realists, the executives should have become liberals. With one understandable exception—the presidential campaign of 1964 when Barry Goldwater tried to move the Republican party back into the nineteenth century—they did not. They remained true to a free enterprise ideology which not only countered reality but, if put into practice, would have subverted the public basis of their private wealth.

This contradiction was resolved in a number of ways, from Goldwater's utopian attempt to repeal recent history to the liberal businessman's attempt to embrace it. Thus, there is no one corporate ideology but a whole series of variations on the basic theme which adapt it to the politics and preoccupations of a given period. So part of the work of this chapter will be to describe the historical genesis of the particular version of the capitalist myth which proved so effective in the second half of the seventies. Fads, it will be seen, are not confined to women's fashions or youthful rebellion; they hold sway in the minds of businessmen who pride themselves in being eminently practical and real-worldly.

But then the corporate leadership is also guilt-stricken and that has something to do with the intensity, the seeming doctrinal purity, of their ideology in the seventies. They somehow agree with Joseph Schumpeter's critique: " 'Capitalists' cease to believe in the standards and moral superiority of their class. They adopt, or connive at, many things which their predecessors would have considered not only injurious to their interests but dishonorable . . ." But if the conflict of welfare state fact and *laisser-faire* ideology gives rise to an uneasy business conscience, it is also the source of a paranoia. In one part of their mind, the corporate leaders believe that every intervention of the government into the economy is a despotic threat to their well-being even though forty years of experience prove the contrary.

Thus Walter E. Hoadley, the chief economist for the Bank of America, said in 1978: "The fear across America —and it's just beneath the surface—is that there will be a redistribution of income and wealth. The Carter administration has become a symbol of that fear." This fantasy exists despite the fact, documented in chapter 5, that there has been no redistribution whatever during the past generation—and despite the fact that the Carter administration made the winning of "business confidence" a prime goal. It is reminiscent of the massive opposition of the corporate rich to Franklin Roosevelt at a time when that president was saving the system from itself.

So if I argue that the corporate ideology has played a significant role in perpetuating the nation's crises in the recent past—and will continue to do so in the future unless it is demystified—that is not to suggest the existence of a seamless, all powerful and carefully crafted illusion. Business beliefs victimize businessmen as well as the rest of the society, though with less viciousness. They also exercise a spell over those social classes and groups whose objective interest is anticorporate and sometimes even consciously so. Those forces detest the unjust outcomes which the corporate ideology facilitates yet they unwittingly share so many of their opponent's prejudices that they are unable to mount a sustained and effective attack upon them.

So it is not really so surprising that Arthur B. Laffer, the economist who acted as theorist for an important strand in the corporate ideology of the late seventies, could say, ". . . I consider myself very much of a Jack Kennedy economist." For, as we will see in a moment, Kennedy-Johnson liberalism shared some critical premises with seventies conservatism. This was not because the architects of the New Frontier and the Great Society were deficient in abstract understanding. It was because they were part of a structured system which tended—tended, not was predetermined—to place fundamental ideological limits upon liberal reform. The basis of that tendency was outlined in the discussion of the New Deal in chapter 1. In what follows, it will be seen at work in the area of ideas and policy-making.

This account of the corporate ideology will begin with

that sixties liberalism. It will then move on to define the conservative seventies version of the functional justification of the status quo in some detail. And finally, there will be a brief outline of alternatives to this cherished, and destructive, American myth—in both theory and practice. For this is an area in which those two polar terms regularly go hand in hand.[1]

———— I ————

The sixties are, of course, remembered as a period— almost a golden age—of liberal reform. Keynesianism triumphed in economic policy under John Kennedy and laid the basis for Lyndon Johnson's Great Society programs; the civil rights movement under the leadership of Martin Luther King, Jr., struck down three-quarters of a century of Jim Crow in public accommodations and voting; the college campus was the stage for a dramatic revival of youthful social conscience; and an antiwar movement, which was sometimes called a "children's crusade," effectively unseated an incumbent president of the United States and forced a basic change in the nation's foreign policy.

All those events did take place and the sixties were certainly much more of a time of social change than either the fifties or the seventies. And yet, the memory plays tricks on the mind. Take an excellent analysis by Michael Kinsley of the procorporate tax nostrums of the late seventies. "The old view," Kinsley wrote, "labeled Keynesian, emphasized that a tax cut (or a Federal budget increase) stimulates aggregate demand by putting more spending in people's hands. The new conservative theory emphasizes that cutting tax rates can stimulate the supply of goods and services by increasing the after-tax return for productive activity. The difference in emphasis is crucial. The Keynesian theory encourages tax cuts aimed primarily at poorer people who are more likely to spend the money right away."

It is certainly true that there is a considerable difference between the conservative tax theories of the late seventies and John Kennedy's Keynesianism in the early sixties. And yet, Kinsley overstates the point by failing to recognize the degree to which Kennedy liberalism was also a variant of the corporate ideology, and therefore not quite so unambiguously dedicated to poorer people. The Kennedy tax cuts, for instance, provided investment tax credits and accelerated depreciation for business, setting off what the AFL-CIO called a capital goods boom which did much more for heavy industry than for the poor. That was "supply side" economics with a vengeance. And in terms of individual income taxes, the period 1964–73 (with a tax structure formed by Kennedy-Johnson policies) saw the bottom 16.1 percent of the people filing returns receiving 7.9 percent of the cuts, while the 4.7 percent in the upper middle class got 10.3 percent of the benefits and the 0.6 percent of the rich got .9 percent of the reductions.

Those figures are not an accident. In the first days of the Kennedy administration, some of the new president's advisers—John Kenneth Galbraith, Leon Keyserling, economists from the labor movement—were for stimulating the economy through direct spending on social projects. Others, in the Council of Economic Advisers, urged tax cuts which would be much more congenial to—and profitable for—the corporate rich. It was, of course, the latter group which prevailed. As Henry Aaron commented, ". . . Kennedy promoted only fragments of the liberal agenda and was curiously ineffective in securing acceptance even of those items he chose to embrace." Moreover, Aaron notes, Kennedy's famous statements on Keynesianism were contained within a framework which asserted the end of ideology and politics. Most of the nation's problems, the young president said, "are technical problems, are administrative problems."

In saying these things I am not asserting that proposition which sectarian radicals repeat over and over like a prayer: that there is "no difference" between liberal Democrats and conservative Republicans. Of course there is a perceptible and politically relevant difference between humane and mean-spirited readings of the dominant ideology. And yet—and this is the point to emphasize—the Kennedy-Johnson years did not challenge that ideology even if they gave a somewhat liberal interpretation of it. So, for example, Lyndon Johnson's Great Society talked of a "partnership" between business and government as the key to progress, a theme which evoked a positive response in the corporate sector.

I resurrect this history for a present purpose. The victory of a conservative version of the corporate ideology in the late seventies was partly the result of the fact that many of its liberal critics were disarmed. They could dispute the details of the right-wing proposals, but they could not make a principled challenge to them because they shared the basic principles. Positions taken during the seventies by Hubert Humphrey, Daniel Patrick Moynihan and Jimmy Carter are cases in point.

In a Senate speech in April of 1977, Humphrey gave a classic statement of the underlying premise of the nation's ruling illusion: "It is reported that business leaders continue to show a lack of confidence in the Nation's near term economic future. This, in turn, means that the commitment of financial resources necessary to create desperately needed new jobs through financing new plants and facilities is being made at a rate which is far from adequate." The conclusion to be drawn from this analysis? That the Democrats are truly probusiness, that they will see to it that the corporations are given the incentives to persuade them to open up new jobs.

A month later, Humphrey acted on his theory by engaging in a classic maneuver: demonstrating how essentially conservative his own Jobs Bill was. Federally financed job training and public works, he insisted, "are included in the bill as supplements to help meet private sector labor needs . . ." Allaying other fears, Humphrey went on to insist on the planned inferiority of the employments his proposal would create: "These positions would be temporary, confined to the lower levels of skill and pay, be subject to careful screenings to prevent cross over from private employers and could not be utilized for at least two years following enactment."

These statements are not a personal aberration on the part of the late liberal leader. Since official American liberalism accepts—uneasily, with contradictory instincts—the principles of an essentially conservative ideology, it seeks its leftist legitimacy on the Right. So there is a standard argument, which Humphrey was using, showing that liberal proposals are not only compatible with, but will shore up, the status quo. In part, that is obviously a political tactic in a society in which each major party tries to reach out to the broadest possible consensus. But it also has to do with the enormous power of the corporate myth and it eventually has a very practical effect. To prepare the way for the conservative arguments in favor of liberal programs, liberals make those programs more conservative.

Daniel Patrick Moynihan's enthusiastic support for right-wing Republican analysis is an example of this process, even if a somewhat ambiguous one. Moynihan talks of himself as a New Deal Democrat and had the support of the Meany wing of the labor movement in his campaign for the United States Senate. But he also worked for Richard Nixon, praised that president on leaving the White House, and has been associated with the neoconservative (ex-liberal and ex-socialist) intellectuals gathered around the journal, *Public Interest*. Still, on economic issues he pictures himself in the Roosevelt and Kennedy traditions and that is why I take his advocacy of the corporate ideology as an example of how liberals sometimes work very hard to defeat liberalism.

In a Senate speech favoring an increased investment tax credit in areas of high unemployment, Moynihan said, quite candidly, that he was proposing "an interest free loan to businesses" in such places. In coming to that conclusion, he accepted the proposition that America's economic troubles stem from a low rate of investment, as a portion of GNP, compared to European countries. This fact, he said, "has the quality of a revelation about it." It pointed inexorably to a lowering in the ratio of investment per worker and therefore to lower living standards. "The principal reason why this happens," Moynihan said in terms reminiscent of the Gerald Ford wing of the Republican party, "is that the economic return from investment has not been high enough; and in turn one of the reasons for that has to do with our tax structure and the curiously somnolent, grudging way in which capital equipment is allowed to be depreciated under our tax schedule."

The substance of Moynihan's theory will be dealt with in the next section (where it will be demonstrated that it has no substance). For now, what is to be stressed is that a senator who ran as the heir to Robert Kennedy adopted a position somewhat to the right of Richard Nixon. In some ways, the distance traveled by President Carter on a similar issue was not as great as Moynihan's, yet it had more serious consequences since it involved the chief executive of the nation.

In his acceptance speech after winning the Democratic nomination in 1976, Carter had talked of the tax system as a "disgrace to the human race." But then, almost as soon as he was elected, he placed a critical priority on "winning business confidence." Democratic presidents traditionally do that by adopting major segments of their Republican opponent's program (one of Kennedy's depreciation measures had been turned down by Eisenhower as too blatantly procorporate). So it was reported in April of 1977 that Bert Lance, then one of Carter's closest confidants and economic advisers, met with twenty-eight representatives of financial institutions, like Morgan Guaranty, Lehman Brothers and the Oppenheimer Fund. Two columnists said, "Lance's rhetoric was as impeccably orthodox as William Simon's, if not Andrew Mellon's. The Carter Administration sees the route to recovery led by investors not consumers."

Thus it was that *The New York Times* editorialized on the economic policy of the Carter administration: "If investments can be made more profitable by cutting taxes,

the Administration believes, business will be more inclined to invest. Some economists, particularly Republicans, have been saying that for years." In fairness to
Carter, it should be noted that he did not embrace the
entire conservative program. If he proposed an investment tax credit which would help the corporations more
than the Nixon-Ford policies, he also fought—unsuccess-
fully—the attempts to reduce capital gains taxes radically
and thus make the tax code even more of an antiegalitarian "disgrace to the human race." The point is not that
Carter or Humphrey, or even Moynihan, are philosophi-
cally identical with the Republican Right. It is simply to
stress that they share so many of the prejudices and premises of the corporate ideology that they could not, and
would not, effectively oppose it when it became militantly
conservative in the late seventies.

But before turning to the corporate lunge to the Right
in that period, this history must be made somewhat more
complex. In the sixties, when liberal rhetoric was in the
ascendant—and liberal practice much less so—the conservative myth tried to adapt itself to the new fashions.
For all of their class struggle rhetoric about Democratic
liberals (and business is the most ideological, the most
"Marxist," sector of American society), the executives
understood how much they shared in common with their
supposed enemies. So it was that, after the Goldwater de-
bacle of 1964, big business tried to act on the principle, if
you can't beat them, join them. That is why the failures of
the Great Society must be understood as the joint responsibility of both private and public enterprise.

It is like going back in a time machine to reread the
statements of corporate conscience in the sixties. *Fortune*
magazine was perhaps the most vociferous advocate of
the point of view. ". . . U.S. history is making a major turn
from the politics of issues to the politics of problems," Max
Ways wrote in *Fortune* in 1966 as he discovered "Creative
Federalism." "Tens of thousands of professional and managerial types, in and out of government, are shaping and
executing Great Society programs." And a year later, the

same author commented: "Industries cannot buy cleaner rivers or cleaner urban air for themselves. Government agencies are going to make these purchases but corporations are going to sell the equipment that launders the atmosphere." *The Wall Street Journal* joined in, editorializing that "business is turning into an important force for pushing embattled domestic programs through Congress." *The Journal* then quoted the secretary of Housing and Urban Development: ". . . the private profit motive and the national interest can merge at exactly the point of greatest urban need—and that is help for low-income families." In another comment, *The Journal* said that "private industry concern with slum rebuilding is the product of the Johnson Administration's encouragement and industry's self-interest."

There was even talk of the emergence of a "social industrial complex" in which business, bent on making money from doing good, would become a major ally of liberalism. And shortly after the 1964 Johnson landslide, Samuel Lubell asked, "Can the pro-business elements who voted for Johnson find a comfortable home in the Democratic coalition? The new emerging era of American politics is likely to be shaped by the struggle to answer that question."

The answer to that queston was no. Or rather, it would have been had the war in Vietnam not intervened to give an entirely different focus to American politics, breaking up that Democratic coalition among many other things. But had Lubell's question been dealt with in practice, it would have turned out that the corporations could not stay within the Democratic party. They—and Lyndon Johnson —vastly underestimated the government effort that would be required to rebuild the cities and vastly overestimated the quick profits that were to be made off a limited federal involvement. That experience is documented in chapter 6. So the quid pro quo in the social conscience version of the corporate ideology did not really exist. But that did not become completely apparent until after one of the most bizarre episodes of recent American history: the emergence of Richard Nixon in the guise of a Keynesian liberal which was chronicled in chapter 1.

The point is not to rehearse that particular history once again. Rather, it is to emphasize that a reactionary can use Keynesian liberal techniques for conservative purposes. More broadly, these events show how relatively narrow the American political alternatives have become. Behind the (quite sincere) clashes of the mass Left and the mass Right in the United States, there is a remarkable, if incomplete, consensus. Liberals acted in the sixties upon the theory that discriminating in favor of corporations is the way to get social legislation—and opportunistic, faddish executives were happy to ally themselves with a reformism which had such a profound respect for established interests. The seventies, then, do not represent such a radical discontinuity. The decade's distinctive ideology—a particularly blatant variation on the theme that the public subsidy of private profit is the way to the common good—differs in tone and emphasis from that of the sixties, of course. But there is a surprising continuity of principle between the reformist and the liberal decades. They share ideological premises which are part of the underlying structure of American society in this period—and a source of its underlying problems, as well.[2]

_____ **II** _____

Ideologically, the 1970s began on November 9, 1972. The central theme of the late sixties, the war in Vietnam, dominated American politics through Nixon's landslide election in 1972. On domestic issues, as has just been seen, Nixon spent the period leading up to that victory doing an impersonation of a Keynesian liberal. Then, at the very moment of his triumph, he sharply reversed himself: wage and price controls were to go, federal spending was to be cut back, money was to be tightened. Those were the policies which were put into effect in 1973 and, as we have seen, they made a mighty contribution to the stagflation which began in that year. On the day after the 1972 election, in an interview with Garnet Horner of the *Washington Star,* Nixon went on the ideological offensive.

The failure of the sixties, he said, were the result of "throwing money at problems." That had led to a moral crisis of the nation, "a breakdown in frankly what I would call the leadership class of the country." Now that permissiveness would be ended and the average American, who responds well if treated like a child, would be dealt with sternly. The central assumption of liberal and corporate thought in the sixties—that government in association with business would cure America's ills—was now obsolete. If the corporation had been granted parity with Washington in the Great Society formulas, now it was going to be posited as the supreme good. Public was bad; private was fine. The small print then added an important amendment to this sweeping proposition: the bad public sector should subsidize the fine private sector.

This theme was elaborated in a number of ways, all of them interrelated, by the New York Stock Exchange, then Treasury Secretary William Simon, Arthur Burns and many others. There was, they said, a capital shortage and it was at the root of declining American productivity vis-à-vis Europe and Japan. It had developed because federal policies impeded capital formation: high taxes penalized the innovators and investors by holding down profits; Washington's massive borrowings "crowded out" businessmen in the credit markets. The proper response then was to hold down—or rather, cut back—on social programs, restrain wages and increase the return to capital. This last point, these apologists conceded, might look like special pleading on behalf of the rich. But if one treated the wealthy in a kind and decent fashion, they said, that would increase investment, which would lead to new jobs, which would benefit the workers and the poor.

If the eighties and the nineties are to be an improvement upon the seventies, one requirement is to see through these half-truths and basic falsifications.

First, there is the theme of capital shortage. As the New York Stock Exchange put the notion in 1974, there is going to be a capital shortfall of $650 billion between 1974 and 1985. This will happen because Washington penalizes investment and therefore avoiding such a disaster requires a reversal of a number of federal policies. The investment tax credit should be raised, the Stock Exchange said; taxes on capital gains should be lowered; the "double taxation" of dividends (once in the form of a tax on corporate profits; second as a personal income tax on the dividends received) should be ended; depreciation should be calculated on the basis of replacement, rather than "historic" cost.

Each one of the Stock Exchange's proposals, it will be noted, requires a "tax expenditure" in favor of capital. That is, by cutting the levy on corporations and the rich, this program requires either higher taxes for everyone else or reduced federal spending or an increased federal deficit. In short, this policy represents a massive subsidy from the society to capital, one which is advanced, not by sending a check to the rich (which would be rather gross), but by absolving them and their companies from making payments to the government. The rationale for this largesse is a version of the basic principle of the corporate ideology: that business investment is the key to the well-being of the entire society.

In 1975, Treasury Secretary William Simon raised the ante on the New York Stock Exchange. He projected a shortfall of $2.5 *trillion* between 1974 and 1985, i.e., a figure almost four times higher than the Stock Exchange estimate. It turned out that he managed to reach this number by fundamentally flawed methodology. Simon defined his trends from a past reckoned in current dollars; he then computed his future in terms of inflated dollars (at a 5 percent rate of inflation). Martin Feldstein of Harvard—who is anything but a radical and even shares important attitudes with the corporate ideology of the seventies—pointed out that this procedure permitted Simon to exaggerate the problem by a factor of ten! This inexcusable sloppiness on the part of a man who was then the second-most-important economic policy maker in the land raises a far-reaching question (particularly since there will be further examples of such spectacular "over-sights" in a moment).

Did Mr. Simon consciously falsify his numbers? I doubt it, though the possibility cannot be excluded. The explanation lies deeper than a reference to self-serving, conscious manipulation of the evidence. Ideology blinds, or limits the vision of, completely sincere people. Simon, honestly, even righteously, convinced of the holiness of his conclusions, was victimized by his own narrow point of view. Similarly, seven out of eight projections of invest-ment needs in this debate, Solomon Fabricant found, as-sumed that there would be no recessions over a ten-year period! That is the kind of otherworldly thinking which regularly seizes scholars who claim to be extremely em-pirical and anti-ideological.

The existence of such honest, functionally impaired vision explains why there is such a wild divergence of estimates of the capital shortage or, more precisely, a de-bate over whether it even exists. Thus the 1978 Report of the Council of Economic Advisers flatly states that there is enough capital. What is needed, the council said, "is a sufficient margin of the expected return on capital over the cost of the capital." More dramatically, Eliot Janeway and Pierre Rinfret testified before a Senate Finance Sub-committee in 1977 that the capital markets were "glut-ted." Rinfret figured that the corporations had a cash flow which would sustain $40 billion more than the investment projected for the year.

In some industries, the problem of glut described by Janeway and Rinfret was quite obvious to see. As *Busi-ness Week* described the difficulties of the oil corpora-tions: "The prospects of big pools of incoming cash presents industry strategists with a compelling need to find outlets for that cash—either within energy or, if need be, outside of energy." Senator Kennedy was even more explicit: "Exxon, for instance, could tomorrow buy J. C. Penney, Du Pont, Goodyear and Anheuser-Busch using only its accumulated cash and liquid assets." Earlier in the seventies, as chapter 1 documented, the steel industry raised prices in order to get capital to expand capacity— even though it should have been clear that the real problem was one of phasing out plants.

There is, then, very good reason to doubt that a capital shortage of the type projected by the New York Stock Exchange and William Simon even exists. Moreover, there is another objection to their thesis which has to do with its basic methodology. Their whole procedure requires an implicit rejection of the very free enterprise faith which these ideologues so passionately profess. In their own conventional wisdom, *a capital shortage is impossible.* Socialist planners—or capitalist apologists justifying tax expenditures for the rich and the corporations—may draw up lists of what society "should" have. The followers of Adam Smith are forbidden, however, to engage in such speculations. Their doctrine teaches that only those uses of capital which can pay their own way are "needed."

In this context, business investment is never determined outside of the market. It is, rather, a function of how much people and institutions save and how badly business wants to borrow it. If companies are really straining at the leash for capital, they will—in theory— bid up its price to a level which will call forth the supply. This idyll does not, of course, actually work; but then almost none of the pure market schemes operates in the real world. The point is that the capitalist ideologues are using a socialist—or at least a planner's—method in making a reactionary argument. And that is not an accident, even though it should be embarrassment to the New York Stock Exchange, William Simon and the rest. For it is of the essence of the corporate ideology in this period to provide *laisser-faire* rationales for statism, in this case for billions of dollars in tax expenditure subsidies.

This process, in which the corporate sector is becoming more and more welfare dependent even as it incants chapter and verse from Adam Smith, is quite visible in a second theme of the late seventies ideology: that low profits are the reason why there is not enough investment. The conclusion of that theory is not that business should innovate and thereby increase the returns it receives. It is that the government should provide the private sector with risk capital by legislating an increase in profits. The statistical arguments in this case are extremely complex and I will merely summarize a few of them. The main point has to do with the welfare "chiseling" of big business.

Arthur Burns stated the basic proposition in 1973: ". . . investment in new capacity was discouraged by the relatively low profits of our domestic non-financial corporations between 1966 and 1971." Then, in 1974, William Nordhaus published a very influential article on "The Falling Share of Profits," and it inspired more theories that the government was responsible for this situation (a view that Nordhaus himself did not hold). By 1977, Senator Moynihan was stating these ideas, not simply as truth, but as "revelation."

One problem with this revelation is that it has no content. In 1976, Martin Feldstein and Lawrence Summers reexamined Nordhaus's data in the light of revisions in statistics which became available after he did his work. They concluded that there is no underlying tendency for a fall in the share of profits and argued that Nordhaus had wrongly generalized normal cyclical fluctuations into a long-range trend. The Council of Economic Advisers came to a similar conclusion in 1978, noting that the after-tax return on corporate equity in 1977 "approximately matched" the 1955–77 average. There is even an amusing aspect to the whole debate. Two IBM economists have suggested that much of the differences can be explained when it is understood that the corporate pessimists were using "tax profits" reported to the Internal Revenue Service, which naturally minimized returns in every way possible, while the optimists focused on the "book profits" which were sent to shareholders and the Federal Trade

Commission. In fact, even when one adjusts realistic profit estimates downward to take inflation into account, they do not show any great drop.

An article in *Business Week* designed to prove that profits were too low unwittingly corroborated the IBM economists' point. For some time, now, corporate ideologists have been complaining that their earnings are exaggerated because of high inventory profits (money made by simply holding on to materials over a period of time when prices are rising—which vanish when those inventories have to be replaced at even higher prices) and the fact that depreciation allowances don't really cover the cost of new machines. *Business Week* restated that lament. But then it noted that those illusory profits could be done away with with a few bookkeeping changes—only that would make the company less attractive to present or potential stockholders. Business, in short, fostered its own profit illusions for its own profitable purposes and then blamed the resultant problems on the government.

But then government actually responds generously to this problem which the corporations had in considerable measure created for themselves. Congressman Parren J. Mitchell noted in a minority comment to the Joint Economic Committee Midyear Review of the Economy in 1979 that Washington had created accelerated depreciation, additional first-year depreciation and special industry depreciation provisions, as well as other concessions, precisely to offset the "illusory"—or rather, self-deluding —profits. He concluded that ". . . we have made provisions for inflation's impact on business much more than the provisions we have made for inflation's impact on the people of the country."

Mitchell's dissent from the general line of that Joint Economic Committee report is significant in more than one way. The document marked the victory of "supply side"—that is, conservative, corporate-oriented—economics in what had been the congressional stronghold of Keynesian liberalism. It was one more sign of the disarray of the traditional reform ideology of the past half century. The victors could thus point to very real failures in the policies which derive from the New Deal and the Great Society, but they then came up with imaginary, non-workable and reactionary alternatives. Rather than proposing to go beyond that traditional liberalism first defined by Franklin Roosevelt, they sounded a resolute call to march back to Herbert Hoover. And to do so they had to adopt systematically careless interpretations of problems like the fabled decline in the rate of profit.

This is not to suggest that the American economy was doing well in the seventies. It clearly wasn't and that fact is central to this book. It isn't even to argue that profits were as high as they always had been. They were not, even if the decrease was in no way as catastrophic as the special pleaders made it to be. The crucial question is: Was the mediocre performance *caused* by low profits, which themselves were a result of high taxes and environmental regulation? Or was it the other way around? Weren't the profit problems caused by the limping economy, and not vice versa? I clearly think that the latter question suggests the case. As the Council of Economic Advisers said in the 1978 Report, ". . . stronger overall performance of the economy holds the promise of raising the return to capital." Achieving that, however, requires solving the structural problems of this period of American life, a task somewhat more difficult than that of lowering taxes on the rich.

It is the latter that the corporate ideology demanded. It wanted to legislate a higher profit rate rather than achieving it through economic expansion. To be sure, one always added that the largesse to the wealthy would trickle down through the entire economy and set off a boom which would benefit everyone. That, after all, is a key rationale of every version of our ruling myth. But what is striking is that the free enterprise purists of the late seventies wanted the government to raise their risk capital through tax subsidies. That is a sign of a mature—one might even say decadent—capitalism.

Moreover, this thrust becomes all the more questionable when one considers that capital was already the recipient of enormous subsidies even before the campaign for greater handouts began. A 1978 Joint Economic Committee study estimated that "preferential measures" reduce taxes on investment income by more than $30 billion a year. And the liberal economist Robert Eisner stated an even deeper truth: ". . . the combination of capital gains exclusions, tax depreciation in excess of economic depreciation, tax deduction of interest costs, and equipment tax credits, particularly in a climate of expected inflation of capital goods prices, offers a considerable distortion in the direction of more business investment than would be undertaken in a free market."

This trend, it should be noted, is not an American phenomenon; it is found to an even more marked degree throughout the rest of the advanced capitalist world. In 1979, the *London Economist* estimated that any reasonably smart businessman could get at least 20 percent of his capital from the government through various subsidies. Private capitalism today, the *Economist* ruefully conceded, "cannot even supply its own capital . . ." In forcing the society to come up with those funds, there is not simply a further maldistribution of wealth. In the competition between governments (state governments within this country; nations in the global context), public monies are used to beggar some areas and to enrich others, a fact which has devastating social consequences, as chapter 6 will show.

In any case, the data demonstrate that the great "capital shortage" of the 1970s was, in some considerable measure, a figment of the corporate ideology. The related argument over declining productivity is much more complex.[3]

III

America's troubles, it is said, are the consequences of low rates of investment which are the source of declining productivity. That, it will be remembered, was the thesis at the center of Daniel Patrick Moynihan's revelation about the necessity for giving business an "interest-free loan." And Moynihan's proposal is, in turn, only one variant of a basic nostrum: that legislating a high return on capital by tax subsidies will spur investment and productivity, make America competitive on the world market once again and thus benefit everyone. Once that panacea is disposed of, which is a fairly simple matter, it will be possible to get on with the serious work of confronting the very real problem which has provoked such spurious solutions.

To begin with, there is an extremely important confusion which has to be cleared up. People "invest" in the stock market and "invest" in houses, but that is not investment which has any impact upon productivity. It is, however, precisely the kind of investment which the various tax schemes would subsidize most handsomely. For this reason, billions of existing and proposed tax expenditures are irrelevant to their stated purpose of increasing productivity. As a Joint Committee study put it, "A salaried worker's 'investment' in common stock or real estate does not qualify as an investment to the economist because it does not comprise an initial purchase of a new asset." Peter Drucker makes much the same point: "The residential home . . . has a 'trade-in value' but not 'wealth producing capacity'; it is not 'capital.' "

Yet, in stagflation America—and throughout the capitalist world—there is a tendency to "invest" in ways which do not add at all to "wealth producing capacity." As Olaf Palme, the former socialist prime minister of Sweden commented in 1979, "Instead of investing in production, the big capitalists buy unproductive objects and this has led to a pervasive speculation in real estate and luxury goods." A *New York Times* report corroborated that generalization, noting that more and more Americans were "hedging" against inflation by buying gold, houses, stamps, rare violins and the like. One reason for the trend, *The Times* said, was that one could avoid taxes by making such "investments."

It is obvious that putting money into rare violins does

not increase American productivity. But neither do most of the transactions on the New York Stock Exchange. In 1976, for instance, about 7 percent of the money raised by corporations came from issuing stock (70 percent came from internal financing, 24 percent from debt). And in 1975, it has been estimated, less than 10 percent of the sales on the registered exchanges in the United States actually provided new funds for business. The rest of the deals simply involved the shuffling, and reshuffling, of old stock certificates. Indeed, in 1970 a partner in Solomon Brothers and Hutzler complained of companies coming into the stock market to raise cash. "Every time you add $1 billion to the volume through new stock issues," he said, "you take out $1 billion that could be used to push up stocks already on the market."

So it was that in 1977, corporate saving was $149.6 billion and personal savings were only $66.9 billion. Most of that money from households went into mortgages and other such "nonproductive" uses (in the sense defined by Peter Drucker). Pension funds, almost all of which are beyond the control of the beneficiaries, provided $62 billion in that year. The American economy is, in short, *not* an Adam Smithian world in which individual investors decide the fate of productivity and new technologies. The sources of its truly productive funds are increasingly collective and social—retained profits, pensions, insurance companies. And yet the corporate ideology has successfully persuaded the Congress to provide huge subsidies to wealthy people who have only a tangential impact upon the development of the economy.

The fact is, as a Brookings analysis put it, that "only a small fraction of aggregate capital gains results from successful risk taking," i.e., from the kind of behavior which supposedly justifies giving public money to the corporate rich. And yet, in 1978 a conservative tax-cutting proposal from the late William Steiger, a Wisconsin Republican, won impressive support though it was based on the fundamentally flawed premises which have just been analyzed.

Steiger's bill lowered the rate of capital gains taxation and made it easier for the rich to avoid paying levies on their unearned income. This tactic was supposed to set off an enormous stock market boom as people rushed to take advantage of the newly legislated profitability of investment. Some of the Steiger supporters said Wall Street would make a 20 percent advance, others predicted 40 percent. The higher stock prices were supposed to result in lower interest charges which would stimulate investment, increase productivity and bring in still more revenues from a soaring GNP. This law, the economists at Chase Econometrics said, would "unlock" vast amounts of investment capital. This extreme version of the corporate ideology was not successful in the Congress, but it did help pressure the legislators into decreeing even more largesse for the wealthy.

So it was that the Congress reduced the effective rate of taxation on capital gains in 1978 by one-third. That move, the Council of Economic Advisers commented in 1979, was a most inefficient way of promoting productivity. It did, however, work marvelously well in increasing the maldistribution of wealth. The lion's share of that multibillion-dollar handout went to people earning more than $50,000 a year and the most spectacular gainers were individuals with annual incomes of more than $200,000! According to the proponents of this enormous handout to the corporate rich, it would immediately set off a stock market boom. On August 11, 1978, Congressman Jack Kemp, of Buffalo, New York, one of the most fervent apostles of this ideology, even argued that the emergence of a majority in favor of the tax cut on the House Ways and Means Committee in April 1978 had already set Wall Street soaring.

Six months after the reduction in capital gains tax went into effect, *The New York Times* reported that its impact on the market had been "minimal." Standard and Poor's average of five hundred stocks had gone up by a mere half of one point during that period. *The Times* concluded: ". . . the only clear winners from the tax cut ap-

pear to be the people who are actively taking the gains."
The fact that his prediction did not come true did not
phase Kemp. He reintroduced the "Kemp-Roth Bill," a
proposal to reduce personal and corporate taxes by about
$100 billion over three years. "Across-the-board tax reduc-
tions," Kemp and Roth had argued in 1978, "will increase
the incentive to work, save and invest . . ." In the Kemp-
Roth scheme, taxpayers with incomes of more than
$50,000 a year—2.1 percent of the total—would get 23.5
percent of the dollar benefits of the reduction while those
with incomes of $15,000 or less—50.3 percent of the total
—would get only 17.2 percent.

In one area, venture capital for small firms, it even
seemed that the tax cut philosophy was working. In 1977,
investors put a mere $20 million in such undertakings; in
1979, as a result of federal tax expenditures to the wealthy
of about $5 billion, venture capital seemed likely to pro-
duce $300 million. And even in this supposedly Adam
Smithian enclave, the tendencies toward concentration
were at work. The money no longer comes from individuals, *The Wall Street Journal* reported. It is provided by
firms and consortia of firms. In short, a mountain of relief
for the most affluent people had produced a mouse of venture capital.

One of the most revealing arguments in favor of this
discriminatory measure was made by Alan Greenspan,
the chairman of the Council of Economic Advisers under
President Ford. He held that Kemp-Roth did not discriminate enough in favor of the rich. "The structure of Roth-
Kemp," Greenspan testified, "is in the right direction. But
I would go further. I would prefer more emphasis on corporate tax cuts and cuts in the upper and middle income
tax brackets." It would be terribly wrong, Greenspan said,
to favor the middle- and lower-income groups.

So the Congress of the United States, in a time of talk
about fiscal austerity, gave away billions to the rich in the
name of an otherworldly dogma which is only tangentially
related to the productivity which it was supposed to increase. However, one should not conclude that, just be-

cause the "realists" in Washington acted on crackpot theories, the problem which they raised is imaginary. It isn't, which is why I now leave the flights of ideological fancy and turn to the reality to which they are so tenuously linked.[4]

At first glance the facts are clear enough. Between 1948 and 1955 the private business economy's productivity went up 3.4 percent a year. Then, from 1955 to 1965, the rate of increase was 3.1 percent. However, that pace slowed to 2.3 percent between 1965 and 1973 and dropped to a mere 1 percent between 1973 and 1977. Because of this pattern, the United States lagged behind every other major capitalist power in the years 1960–77. Japanese manufacturing productivity went up by 8.8 percent, West Germany's by 5.5 percent and Britain, often cited as the sick economy of Europe, experienced a 3.4 percent gain while the United States improved by only 2.6 percent. As a result, the Joint Economic Committee calculated, household incomes in America in 1978 were $3700 less than they would have been if the 1948–68 productivity patterns had been maintained. And projecting the trend into the future, 1988 would see a loss of income of $8500 per household.

All of those numbers do indeed describe a tendency in the American economy. But the first thing to emphasize in understanding that reality is that the statistics give a very false impression of numerical precision. Here, as in so many other cases described in this book, flaws in the measuring apparatus are a refraction of structural changes in the economy and society which subvert not only the old wisdom but its very vocabulary. When such transformations occur, concepts as well as machinery become obsolete and one must become innovative about definitions as well as technology. Without getting too deeply into the thicket of issues related to productivity, it is important to communicate some sense of the problematic in those seemingly straightforward numbers.

The American economy, it is well known, is shifting from the production of goods to the provision of services, a fact which is sometimes celebrated in theories of the "postindustrial" society. But how does one measure productivity in various areas of the service sector? One can easily compute how many automobiles are produced per worker hour, but what is the unit of output for the Department of Health, Education and Welfare? In 1978, according to the Council of Economic Advisers, productivity declined by three-tenths of 1 percent in service industries, went up by a mere one-tenth of 1 percent in government, but rose by 2.2 percent in nondurable manufacture. One reason for at least some of these trends was noted in the last chapter: that environmental protection is computed as a cost but not as a benefit. Thus, the output of a modern plant which makes automobile engines less of a threat to health is not counted in the nation's productivity. Because of such statistical decisions, the commissioner of the Bureau of Labor Statistics (BLS) told the Joint Economic Committee, ". . . there is a downward bias in the productivity figures . . ."

Part of the problem is that common sense seems to side with the reactionaries. Isn't it obvious that a worker with more sophisticated technology produces more? Therefore, why not give the corporate rich a subsidy if they will spend it on making their employees more efficient? As we will see in a moment, the evidence strongly suggests that under current conditions the rich will simply use that subsidy to inflate the price of non-productive goods. But doesn't that still leave the proposition about machines and productivity intact? Not quite. A New York Stock Exchange study—which can hardly be charged with leftist bias—suggests that 55 percent of the decline in productivity between 1973 and 1977 comes from two factors that are not at all technological.

During those years, the boom-and-bust cycle (which was mainly a bust cycle) caused 32 percent of the drop in productivity defined by the Stock Exchange. In other words, the genuine full employment policies urged in Chapter 3 would not simply help workers, and particularly the minorities and women among them; it would have also enormously spurred productivity. And secondly, changes in labor mobility—above all, the fact that there is no longer productivity gain to be found in shifting people from farms to factories since less than 5 percent of the work force remains in the fields—accounted for 23 percent of the productivity loss. In both areas, what is required is radical structural change, not trickle down. But then, one should not blame the people for being bewildered about such matters when the experts themselves are in such disarray.

It would be very wrong to think that this confusion among the experts is simply an academic matter. American society is profoundly prejudiced toward the "real," the concrete, the specific. It is, therefore, an enormous advantage to business that they can cite precise dollar costs of, say, environmental regulations, while the environmentalists have yet to work up quantitative measures of the benefits they have won for the country. It is this situation which leads to the outcome described in chapter 2: federal subsidies for more degradation of both humanity and nature. And a similar process is at work in the debate over productivity.

It is also possible that, contrary to the conventional wisdom, one cannot explain the differences in world productivity figures on the basis of the low rate of investment in the United States. That, a Joint Economic Committee study suggested, may be a statistical artifact of the cheaper prices charged for capital goods in this country. Even more to the point, it may be that we have basically misunderstood the significance of the shift from goods production to services. "Post-industrial society," the French economist Jacques Attali has suggested, "will probably be hyperindustrial."

An American expert, Irving Leveson, expands on this last notion. Productivity in the service sector is—and this directly contradicts the implications of the Council of Economic Advisers' analysis—increasing rapidly because of industrialization. Leveson describes "the shift to department stores and the shift to supermarkets; the growth of fast food restaurants and the recent rapid growth of self-service gasoline stations . . ." Even as I write, the check-out process in the supermarket is being automated with the use of scanners, a technology which was available twenty years ago but which is only now coming into its own.

There is no reason to multiply instances of the difficulty in talking with any precision about productivity. That point is made. It is now time to turn to the structural changes which give rise to the conceptual confusion.

First and foremost, productivity is profoundly affected by the return of the dinosaur known as the business cycle. In the reams of print that have been used to discuss the problem, one will find abundant reference to the deleterious impact of federal regulation, to the unfortunate role of women and all of the other scapegoats, but the idea that the malfunctioning of the system itself is the critical fact is hardly ever mentioned. After all, such an analysis points in the direction of structural change rather than toward legislated handouts for the corporate rich. That all but guarantees that it will not be discussed in polite American company.

There are exceptions to this rule. One was made by one of the Carter administration's chief—and rather out-spoken—economists, Barry Bosworth, the director of the Council on Wage and Price Stability until 1979. After the traditional seventies attack on federal regulations, Bosworth told a Senate committee: "I think the second major factor [causing the decline of productivity] is the fact that this economy has been on a roller coaster for the past decade. Whenever we have a boom, everybody switches and worries about inflation; and then we go into a recession and everybody gets upset about the unemployment rate. With that type of up-and-down behavior of the economy, no businessman can make an intelligent decision on what future output requirements will be. . . . The fundamental reason we are not getting more investments today [1978] is that nobody believes the expansion will continue." Bosworth compared this situation unfavorably to the sixties "where we had slow but sustained increase in economic activity. Then, people could make much better projections of what their investment needs were going to be."

In 1979, Peter K. Clark, a Stanford economist, presented a carefully documented paper at a Brookings conference. He asked, What are the causes of investment? He then took five models of business investment and compared their various predictions about the seventies with the actual train of events. He concluded, first, that "business fixed investment in the aggregate is only a little lower than might have been expected from its historical relationship to output and cost." So much for the shrill cries of William Simon and his similars. Secondly, and more important for this context, Clark found that investment responded primarily to good times—a point which one might have thought was obvious but which has often been carefully forgotten in the current discussions—and that the various tax incentives aimed at subsidizing the cost of capital for the businessman, and the interest rate manipulation are "not very helpful" in explaining real world trends.

That is the heart of the matter. For if, as Bosworth says [and I agree], the basic problem is the inherent instability of the economy in the seventies moving into the eighties, then all of the various solutions being urged are not simply irrelevant but also harmful. The corporate rich and their institutions will gratefully accept reduced capital gains taxes and put the money into rare violins, not factories; they will win the right to despoil the environment, but they will not consequently increase productivity. They will act in this manner, not because they are psychologically perverse or antisocial, but because investment in productivity is not justified in terms of that most primitive of capitalist criteria, making money. If, then, the full employment program outlined in the last chapter were actually put into practice—if the cycle of boom-and-bust were really tamed through structural transformations— that would not merely help the workers. It would do more to motivate business to invest than all of the wasteful handouts we have recently legislated. The productivity problem, like every other issue before the society today, is systemic in character.

Indeed, there are other structural factors at work in addition to the business cycle. Some of the high productivity gains in American society came from shifting people from agriculture to industry. But now that less than 5 percent of the labor force is in the fields—now that farming itself is an industrial activity—that source of progress is closed off. Then there is education. It has been computed that, between 1929 and 1969, changes in the quantity and quality of labor—a rising population with more education —were responsible for three times more growth in measured output than the inputs of capital. But if, as chapter 8 will argue, there are, under present structural constraints, declining yields from education, then another source of our past achievements is disappearing.

I return to a basic theme. Somewhere toward the end of the sixties, the United States seemed to turn a corner as an era ended. That huge, structural fact, which can be countered only by policies which are at least as structural as it is, caused the decline in productivity insofar as it exists in reality and not just as a statistical artifact. So a solution to this crisis requires planned full employment under unprecedented circumstances. But where, it might be fairly asked, is one going to get the monies necessary for such a change? I would answer: by the democratic socialization of at least part of the process of capital formation in the United States.[5]

IV

World War II, we know, demonstrated that federal military expenditures could vastly expand the nation's industrial plant while ending mass unemployment. The space program of the sixties showed how Washington's commitment to research and development could have an impact, not simply upon the exploration of the moon, but on the entire economy. And if America created the energy alternatives suggested in the last chapter, or dealt with the deteriorating cities of the Northeast and Midwest along lines which will be proposed in chapter 6, that could have a similar effect. The critical point of investment policy, then, is to organize the economy consciously so that there are productive uses for both public and private funds.

That, we know, does not mean that planned full employment would then allow all the rest of our institutions to go on as before. As has just been seen, the corporate ideology, with its theory that private investors are the main source of funds for new jobs and economic growth, does not correspond to reality, even though it effectively rationalizes privileges for the rich. Retained profits within corporations, and institutional investors, are where the monies mainly come from. It is thus high time that American government policy is based on such existing trends rather than on a Horatio Alger myth. And they hold out the very real possibility—which did not exist under *laisser-faire,* entrepreneurial capitalism—of democratizing investment. For one merely proposes to socialize the control of monies which are already social in origin.

First, there are pension funds, one of the most important institutional sources of capital. They are theoretically —but only theoretically—owned by millions of American workers.

In an interesting, if fanciful, book, *The Unseen Revolution,* Peter Drucker laid out some of the basic statistics. Writing in 1976, Drucker argued that private employees already own 25 percent of that sector's equity capital, while the self-employed, public employees and teachers account for another 10 percent. By 1985, Drucker estimated, the pension funds would own 50 percent—and perhaps 60 percent—of corporate stock and 40 percent of debt capital. He calls this reality "socialism" on the grounds that "the 'worker' and the 'capitalist' are one and the same person . . ." But then, even though the admission destroys the subtitle of the book ("How Pension Fund Socialism

Came to America"), Drucker is forced to concede that "nothing has happened to either work or worker. The relations at work between worker, work group, task and boss have not been affected at all."

Moreover, under the law the employee with a "vested interest" in a pension fund "cannot draw out the money until [retirement], borrow against it or, as a rule, assign or sell it." In short, this "ownership" is without any of the prerogatives which go to capital—and is not ownership in any real sense at all. This is important to emphasize, since some conservatives want to capitalize the value of the pension funds and then count it as the "wealth" of the potential beneficiaries. Using such a device, they then prove that there is "a continuing redistribution of income and wealth" in America. How the corporate rich would feel if similar limitations were placed on their money is easy to imagine. They would denounce it as Red Revolution.

Drucker's fantasy, the *London Economist* rightly noted, is based on ". . . a quarter truth. Ownership is no substitute for control and in the case of the pension funds, control is firmly in the hands of managers and trustees. Their potential power has more in common with the corporate, than with the socialist, state." Indeed, the *Economist* described this trend as heading toward a "private corporate state." It told, for instance, of how the major fund managers in Britain had deliberately engineered a dramatic decline in the stock market in order to change public policy in 1974. And it continued, "Chastened, the government drastically reduced industry's tax bill." Private investors—those heroes of recent American legislation—will, the *Economist* said, never again be the source of investment monies. And so far, the "owners" of all that wealth have had no control of it.

But what if this theoretical "socialism" became more real, i.e., what if the worker "owners" actually began exercising rights of ownership? Drucker favors putting workers' representatives on the pension fund boards as a way of making it "possible for management to regain legitimacy," i.e., as a reform which would shore up, rather than transform, the basic relations of hierarchy and subordination. George Cabot Lodge, of the Harvard Business School, came to a similar, but much more liberally motivated, conclusion in *The New American Ideology.* The democratic Left should adopt such an idea, both as a means of providing more investment funds *and* as a part of a commitment to change the very nature of work and authority in America. That is the exact opposite of Drucker's interpretation flow and goes well beyond Lodge.

Indeed such a development would help solve one of the very real problems of capital formation today. Investment now comes mainly from pension funds, insurance companies and retained profits. That pattern, economists in both the Left and Right have recognized, can lead to a bias against innovation. As Jacques Attali has pointed out, when retained profits are crucial, the most established, often least future-oriented, companies are at an advantage. And Drucker complains that "the capital market decisions are efffectively shifting from the 'entrepreneurs' to the 'trustees,' from the people who are supposed to invest in the future to the people who have to follow the 'prudent man rule' [mandated under American law] which means, in effect, investing in past performance."

If, however, pension funds were free from the compulsory conservatism of corporate prudence—and it is interesting that a probusiness thinker like Drucker recognizes the problem—they might, under genuinely democratic control, be a source of needed monies for new areas of socially relevant innovation. This does not mean that the pensions should take up only the risky investments while the private sector would be allowed to "cream" off guaranteed profits. It does, however, mean that pension funds under the actual control of their beneficiaries and working within the framework of a national economic plan could be somewhat more imaginative, and infinitely more socially responsible, than private money managers are today. In Sweden the public pension fund reserve—Allmana Pension Fonderna—is allowed, with the approval of

Parliament, to make risk capital investments. Indeed, Martin Feldstein of Harvard, a mainstream academic moderate, cited the Swedish case approvingly in testimony before a Senate subcommittee on economic growth.

So a basic reorganization—democratization—of pension funds would be one element in a new investment policy. A social approach to profits is another.

A number of actual experiments in this direction have been, or still are being, undertaken. In Peru under the "military socialism" of the seventies, a portion of the profits was distributed to the workers in the form of stock; in Denmark, a percentage of the wages is used as the base. In the Netherlands, a system of capital growth sharing is being debated. A payment, based on "excess profits" (defined as the excess over a yield of basket of government securities plus 2 percent for risk-taking), is made in the form of certificates distributed to individuals which are marketable, and of allocations to a fund run by the trade unions and the government. And in Sweden, the Meidner Plan, first urged by the unions and then adopted, in modified form, by the Socialist party, provides for a corporate tax to be paid in stock to a worker-controlled mutual fund.

I have obviously only made the briefest sketch of these developments, yet they give a clear sense of direction. In the United States today, workers are asked to forgo consumption so that there can be more investment; business even tries, sometimes successfully, to get them to support tax preferences for the rich on these grounds. That, however, is clearly wrong since it gives the corporate wealthy public subsidies which increase the inequality of the society. But if workers were actually to participate in the management of, as well as in the benefits from, investment, there could be a positive incentive for them to defer their present consumption in the name of a better future.

This point becomes clearer when one compares a democratizing of the investment process with a similar, but quite contrary, proposal, that of profit sharing. This is the idea that the employees of a company should share in the "ownership" of the enterprise for which they work by investing their own pension monies in it. In the United States it has taken the form of the Employee Stock Ownership Plan (ESOP) urged by Louis Kelso and enthusiastically supported by Senator Russell Long, the chairman of the Senate Finance Committee. A corporate analyst like Drucker is opposed to this approach on solid grounds. If it worked, it would mean that the employees at the most profitable companies would gain enormously compared to those who belonged to pension funds invested in low-profit, or even losing, operations. An analogous problem can be seen in Yugoslavia, where publicly owned, worker-controlled enterprises sometimes exhibit an anti-social, but collective, egotism, refusing, for instance, to put their surplus funds into risky, underdeveloped parts of the country.

Second, the socialist trade unionist Charles Levinson has rightly emphasized that profit sharing takes place *after* capital formation. Under those circumstances, the workers could well come to be hostile to investment, preferring to take corporate growth in the form of distributed income rather than to see the managers and private owners use it for expansion. So what is being proposed here is not simply a share in the profits but a share in the investment-decision process in which the workers as a collectivity (through unions or directly elected boards voting the stock assigned to the employees) would participate in making the basic choices about the future.

In addition to providing new possibilities for capital formation, such an approach might well make it possible to fight inflation more effectively. Under present conditions, talk of "equal" sacrifice by labor and management is so much nonsense because those two parties are in structurally unequal positions.

Wage and price controls have suffered from a similar flaw. It is relatively easy to hold down the wages of great masses of workers since they are quite specific and stored on computer tape. But prices and executive compensation are problematic. A nominal price can remain stable while quality or quantity is decreased, which is an effective price increase. Executives can be given various options, with future but not present value, which will make them more wealthy yet not show up as current income. So it was that one of the chief wage and price controllers for Richard Nixon said that he and his associates had determined to "zap" labor and had managed to do exactly that.

But if workers were to share in investment decisions and benefits, it would become possible to cope with many of these problems. That fact, plus the egalitarian tax program described in chapter 5, would move in the direction of eliminating the structural inequalities of the system. If, under such circumstances, it were important to defer consumption, either to fight inflation or to provide for capital formation, there would be a realistic basis for seeking the cooperation of working people.

A democratic and social allocation of credit is another reform which moves in a similar direction.

The federal government is, of course, already massively involved in the allocation of credit, more often than not to the detriment of the average citizen. The Federal Reserve manipulates the money supply with the explicit and conscious desire of controlling the supply of credit: "easy" money to spur a boom (or elect a Richard Nixon); "tight" money to fight inflation (and set off a recession as a side effect). The problem is that gigantic corporations, with enormous retained profits and the ability to make, rather than take, prices, are the least affected by such policies. People paying off a home or holding their money in savings accounts—working people, the middle class—are hard hit. So it was that federal policies in this area were responsible for wild fluctuations in the housing market of the seventies: from a 1970 low to a 1972 high to a new low in 1974, housing starts rose by 125 percent and fell by 65 percent.

More broadly, a recent study indicates that federal credit rationing and tax expenditures in this area—worth "well over $18 billion a year"—redistributes money from the poor to the well off. In some cases, this is done quite directly, e.g., in the establishment of interest rate ceilings under Regulation Q of the Federal Reserve. So the issue is not whether the federal government will allocate credit, but whether it will continue to do so in the current, antisocial, antiegalitarian fashion.

There are a number of ways in which credit could be democratically and socially allocated. At the simplest level, banks could be required (as a precondition for participation in a federal system which is of enormous benefit) to lend a portion of their monies to specified purposes, like housing for "ordinary" people, in a given area. The geographic restriction would be extremely important in combating "redlining," the procedure whereby banks raise money in a neighborhood or a city and then ship it to high-profit uses somewhere else while ignoring the decay where they themselves are located. The New York City banks, the Securities and Exchange Commission revealed in 1979, did that on a massive scale when they profiteered in municipal paper (with the connivance of a Republican administration in Albany) until the crisis hit, concealing their own suspicions about the worth of those bonds, and then quietly abandoning the city when default seemed imminent.

Second, where major banks are about to collapse, there is no point in a federal bailout which returns them to private hands. If Washington has to intervene, it makes sense for it to take over the bank and make it a public corporation, with employees and consumers on the board of directors. Third, the individual state can establish banks and make them the chosen repository for various state funds. And the states, as Sam Brown demonstrated during his tenure as treasurer of Colorado, can also use their deposits to influence the social policies of banks, i.e., by refusing to place money in institutions which do not meet certain criteria with regard to minority and women's lending.

Such specific measures, and the proposals with regard to pensions and the democratization of investment, are illustrative and hardly exhaust what can be done. Rather, they define a beginning. Beyond that, they all have a common purpose: to demystify the corporate ideology in practice as well as in theory. It is hard to reconsider an illusion which has the status of a commonsense truth, but that is what is necessary. Why should a small group of individuals, and their hired representatives, have the right to make the major economic decisions? Why should the government be forced to adapt its policies to the wishes of this elite? Because the millionaires "abstain" from consumption? That is preposterous on the face of it. Because they incur a "risk"? But most of the monies for expansion are now clearly social in character, coming from retained profits or institutional investors like pension funds.

So there is a productivity crisis but it is not the one which is debated in this country and it is totally unaffected by the "solutions" which have been offered to it. Planned full employment, achieved in part by the democratic socialization of investment, would be a profound source of productivity growth. Tax subsidies to the speculation of the corporate rich is not. Moreover, the process of solving the macroeconomic problem in this way would help transform the microquality of life for individuals. For the means would be an expansion of freedom by means of democratizing production from the shop floor to the boardroom. And they would also include the social redistribution of a wealth which is already social in fact. That theme points to the next chapter, which will survey the social and economic consequences of the maldistribution of wealth in America. That is another one of the basic constituents of the institutional complex which must be radically changed if this nation is to deal with the challenges of the eighties and the nineties.[6]

___ Notes ___

1. Untouchables: Moore, pp. 55 ff. Schumpeter: *Business Cycles,* vol. II, p. 699. Hoadley: Michael C. Jensen, "National Economic Summary," *The New York Times,* January 18, 1978. Laffer: Michael C. Jensen, "The Principles of a Tax Cut Guru," *The New York Times,* June 17, 1978.

2. Kinsley: "Alms for the Rich." Tax cuts: Harrington, *The Twilight of Capitalism*, p. 233. Aaron: *Politics and the Professors*, p. 2; p. 167, n. 1. Humphrey: *Congressional Record*, April 5, 1977, p. S5570; *Congressional Record*, May 20, 1977, p. S8243. Moynihan: *Congressional Record*, April 29, 1977, p. S6731. Lance: Roland Evans and Robert Novak, "Lance Versus Wall Street," *New York Post*, April 4, 1977. *The New York Times* editorial: October 30, 1977. Max Ways: "Creative Federalism" and "The Road to 1977." *The Wall Street Journal:* April 19, 1967; November 14, 1966. Lubell: *The Future of American Politics*, p. 6.

3. Garnett Horner interview: *Washington Star*, November 9, 1972. New York Stock Exchange: *The Capital Needs and Savings Potential of the U.S. Economy*, passim. Simon error: *Capital for Productivity and Jobs*, Shapiro and White, eds., p. 146. Fabricant: Ibid., p. 33. CEA, 1978: p. 113. Janeway and Rinfret: *Congressional Record*, June 9, 1977, p. S11129. *Business Week:* "The New Diversification Oil Game," April 14, 1978. Burns: Shapiro and White, eds., p. 3. Nordhaus: "The Falling Share of Profit," pp. 169–208. Feldstein and Summers: "Is the Rate of Profit Falling?" pp. 211 ff. IBM economists: Leonard Silk, "The Issue of Profitability," *The New York Times*, December 16, 1977. *Business Week:* "The Profit Illusion," March 19, 1979. Mitchell: JEC, *Midyear Review*, 1979, p. 46. CEA, 1978: p. 69. JEC: *U.S. Long Term Economic Growth Prospects*, p. 64. Eisner: JEC, *The Role of Federal Tax Policy in Stimulating Capital Formation and Economic Growth*, p. 149. London *Economist:* "Enterprise and the State," February 24, 1979.

4. JEC: *U.S. Long Term Economic Growth Prospects*, p. 50n. Drucker: *The Unseen Revolution*, p. 76. Palme: in Lowenthal, ed., p. 42. *The New York Times:* Jerry Flynt, "The Inflation Wary Invest in Objects, Not Dollars," February 3, 1979. Stock: Shapiro and White, eds., table 2, p. 11; Magdoff and Sweezy, table 6, p. 107. Solomon Brothers partner: Richard Martin, "New Offerings," *The Wall Street Journal*, June 20, 1970. Sources of funds: Federal Reserve Bulletin, February 1979, XX A-45 and A-46; *Survey of Current Business*, July 1978, table 5.2. Brookings: Pechman, ed., *Setting National Priorities: The 1980 Budget*, p. 149. Steiger: Michael Kinsley, "Alms for the Rich." Capital gains: CEA, 1979, pp. 94 and 131; *Congressional Quarterly Weekly Report*, February 24, 1979, pp. 341 ff. *The New York Times:* Karen W. Arenson, "Minimal Effect . . . ," April 30, 1979. Kemp and Roth: Senate Finance Committee, Hearings on Individual and Business Tax Reductions, July 14, 1978, p. 51. Benefits: Statement of Andrew J. Biemiller, AFL-CIO (mimeo) before Senate Finance Committee, July 14, 1978. Venture capital: William M. Buckley and Lindley B. Richert, *The Wall Street Journal*, June 15, 1979. Greenspan: Senate Finance Committee, pp. 172–73.

5. Productivity: CEA, 1979, table 15, p. 68. JEC: *Notes*, vol. V, no. 7, March 2, 1979. 1978 productivity: CEA, 1979, table 16, p. 71. BLS com-

missioner: JEC, *Employment and Unemployment*, Hearings, p. 2199. New York Stock Exchange: JEC, Hearings, *The 1979 Economic Report*, pt. 1, p. 156. World productivity: JEC, *U.S. Long Term Economic Growth Prospects*, pp. 51 and 20. Attali: *La Nouvelle Economie Française*, p. 134. Leveson: JEC, *Special Study on Economic Change*, pt. 3, p. 766. Bosworth: JEC, 1978: *Midyear Review of the Economy*, pt. 3, p. 584. Peter K. Clark: "Investment in the 1970s." Education: *Data on the Distribution of Wealth in the United States*, table I, p. 19.

    6. Drucker: *The Unseen Revolution*, pp. 11, 34, 47, 133. Pension fund "wealth": *Data on the Distribution of Wealth*, p. 169. *London Economist*: "A Private Corporate State," April 11, 1978. Drucker on boards: Op. cit., p. 92. Attali: Op. cit., p. 80. Drucker on investment decisions: Op. cit., p. 71. Swedes: Branco Horvat in *Solutions Socialistes*, Kolm, ed., pp. 171–72. Feldstein: JEC, *The Role of Federal Tax Policy*, p. 175. Peru and Denmark: Horvat, op. cit., pp. 170–71. Netherlands: "Vad Lives," *London Economist*, March 11, 1978. Drucker on profit sharing: op. cit., p. 37. Levinson: *Capital, Inflation and the Multinationals*, p. 301. Housing: Shapiro and White, eds., pp. 88–89.

5

The Dirty
Little Secret

Fairy tales, Sigmund Freud taught the world long ago, are
not merely an innocent source of childish delight. They
are also the veiled expression of very adult emotions of
love and violence and, above all, of the "dirty little secret"
of sex. Since Freud, people have been talking openly, end-
lessly and tediously about their sex lives. But there is another scandal which is still so shameful that it must be
dressed up in its own fairy tale. It is the maldistribution of
income and wealth in the capitalist democracies.

In this contemporary, and quite functional, fairy tale,
everyone in the nation is paid in proportion to his or her
economic contribution. The rich and the poor alike are
thus subject to the law which rewards individuals according to their marginal productivity. Moreover, the talented
and enterprising poor can become rich, the impecunious
rich can become poor. Idyllically, this system of allocating
wealth according to merit also just happens to lead to the
most efficient use of scarce resources. And in case the real
world perversely deviates from this fantasy, the government is assigned the Robin Hood role of taxing those at
the top in order to ensure the welfare of those at the bottom.

In fact this fairy tale is a fairy tale. American (Western) society is characterized by institutionalized and perennial inequities of income and wealth. On rare occasions, individuals do found great fortunes but these few exceptions are best explained by the roll of the economic dice than by virtue and/or enterprise. The much more general rule is that one's place in the social hierarchy is determined by the accident of birth: rich fathers have rich sons. Surprisingly, it was a conservative economist who made one of the pithiest statements of this situation some time ago. Frank Knight wrote, "The ownership of personal or material productive capacity is based upon a complex mixture of inheritance, luck and effort, *probably in that order of importance*" (emphasis added).

Worst of all, the government does not play the role of Robin Hood but that of the Sheriff of Nottingham. It supports and even exacerbates the maldistribution of income and wealth.

It is, on the very face of it, outrageous that a democratic government should discriminate in favor of the rich and against everyone else. But that is only one of the evils involved in this case. As we have seen, the business cycle is an inherent mechanism in the capitalist economy. Periodically, an unplanned productive system "overproduces" in terms of the effective demand in a maldistributed system of wealth which is itself the result and the precondition of the system of production. The Keynesian solution, as chapter 2 documented, was to close this gap by means of a controlled and gentle inflation, a policy which, for reasons already given, was one source of the stagflation of the seventies. But to the degree that wealth and income are more fairly distributed, then the very structural source of all these ills is eradicated.

That is not to suggest, as well-intentioned radicals often have, that one can overcome the tendency toward boom and boost by simply making the tax laws more fair. For if, as this chapter will show, America's current maldistribution is not functional in the way in which the apologists for it imagine, it is still an integral part of a system in which private corporations dominate the investment process. Thus the analysis and proposals made in this chapter must be taken in conjunction with the last chapter's program for the socialization of at least some of the investment decisions in the United States. For the system of distribution can only be basically changed if the system of production is transformed too.

But if that qualification is understood, it can then be said that the redistribution of income and wealth would not simply make America more just. It would also help us to overcome the stagflation and chronic unemployment which we now face. And ironically, it would create the conditions in which one of the nation's favorite delusions might even become a reality. In theory, sovereign consumers dictate what obedient corporations will produce and therefore the exchange between them takes place, in Charles Schultze's phrase, on the basis of a "unanimous consent agreement." But Schultze himself admits, "If the income distribution is grossly unfair, the concept of voluntary decision and unanimous consent is a charade . . ." Only the naive will ask if Schultze, who made this comment in a book celebrating the glories of those unanimous consent agreements, inquired as to whether the distribution of income and wealth was "grossly unfair." To probe that point would have been to discover that the book's central thesis was a "charade." Still Schultze did concede that inequality frustrates the market system.

If, however, America could become a significantly more egalitarian society, then the market could actually function as it is supposed to—as a transmission belt for voluntary choices rather than as a stuffed ballot box dominated by the rich. At that point, the "consumer sovereignty" which is now a rationalization of producer domination might actually begin to exist.

Even more importantly, the redistribution of income and wealth would remove one of the structural imperfections of the democratic system in America. As it now stands, the concentrated power of corporate wealth forces democratically elected governments, whether liberal or conservative (or, in Europe, socialist) to adapt to the priorities of a tiny elite even when the latter's program has been decisively rejected by the voters. A combination of democratized investment and redistributed wealth would remove that institutionalized tendency toward the corporate control of political life.

In the late seventies, the countertrend to that possibility—increased and open corporate involvement in politics —became particularly pronounced. Corporate political action committees (PACs) boomed. A Conference Board study noted that frustration "has been largely replaced by an activist stance on the part of the business community. Defensive postures have been giving way to aggressive stategies." Between 1976 and 1978, the corporate PACs almost doubled in number (from 450 to 821) and they have only begun to tap their potential. Common Cause commented that "those PAC's could become the dominant force in Congressional campaign financing." In the bad old days of the robber barons, millionaires bought and paid for members of Congress in the classic manner of personal corruption. Now that tactic, like so much else in the society, is collectivized by giant and impersonal corporations. Thus, the political impact of economic maldistribution becomes both more crass and much more sophisticated.

In a simple world, the very existence of the systemic unfairness of the American mode of distribution would call to life a political movement demanding egalitarian transformations. That, alas, is a leftist fairy tale. Most Americans accept the official apology for the system or, even if they suspect that the established fantasy is a lie, hope that they, or their children, can participate in it on advantageous terms. So it is not enough to demonstrate the facts. One must politicalize them as well. The facts, as we will see, are easily come by; the politics are not.[1]

_____ I _____

Both income and wealth are maldistributed in the United States, but the allocation of wealth is by far more unfair than that of income.* The reason for this contrast becomes clear from the most cursory reflection. Income is taxed in America and wealth is not (except at death, when great fortunes are treated with great deference). The rich, therefore, prefer to maintain their wealth in stocks, bonds, real estate and trusts. Indeed, they have an incentive to *minimize* their income.

This fact provides the basis for a significant obfuscation. Earned income accounts for four-fifths of the national income in advanced societies; profits and interest are a mere two percent to three percent of the total. So, it is often said, redistributive policies would not have any great effect because they would only divvy up a very small pie. If, say, 80 percent of the people got an equal share of the profit and interest, 2 percent, that wouldn't make a great difference. That ignores two aspects of the essential. First, most profits are retained and reinvested in the company and therefore increase the wealth, but not the income, of the stockholders. Second, as Serge-Christophe Kolm has pointed out, the stratospheric salaries which the top executives decree for themselves—for example, more than $900,000 a year for the General Motors chairman—are really a share in the profits in the form of income. Does anyone seriously think that a single individual's "marginal productivity"—the contribution he or she uniquely makes to the last unit of total output—is really worth almost a million dollars? Is the GM chairman 140 times more "productive" than a worker receiving the minimum wage?

For the purpose of this chapter, however, it is not executive compensation but wealth which is the focus. That is the form which the superiority of the rich takes and which guarantees their dominion from generation to generation. In 1969, the top wealth holders (Americans with gross assets of more than $60,000) owned $1.224 *trillion.*

* The numbers clearly show that income and wealth are *unevenly* portioned. I make the judgment that this is a *mal*distribution on the basis of the social consequences of the unevenness which I have just listed and which I will further document in the rest of this chapter.

In late seventies dollars that would come to around $2 trillion. That is hardly a trivial sum. If it were simply redistributed to everyone—which I do not advocate—it would increase the holdings of every American by about $9000. We are talking, then, about huge accumulations of money.

Before making a first statement of how this enormous wealth is concentrated, a general comment about the statistics is needed. In citing various sources, I will skip back and forth between different years. Ordinarily that would be an invalid procedure since most economic realities change over time in relationship to the ups and downs of the business cycle. However, the *relative* shares of wealth in America do not follow the rhythms which torment ordinary mortals. Over the entire postwar period, as we will see, those shares are relatively constant. This is a classic illustration of a "structure"—a persistent and enduring social pattern—as that term was defined in chapter 1. Since we can thus use statistics from different years we are better able to cope with a very real problem: that riches are truly a dirty little secret in the sense that the government, which deluges us with income data, is notably reticent when it comes to talking about concentrated wealth.

Indeed, in 1975 a Senate committee revealed that the United States government was unable to find out who owned the nation. Stocks are often held by "nominees"— banks, trust funds and the like—which do not actually own them. This puts, the committee said, a "veil" over the true nature of that wealth. It also allows for a host of evils including the "use of inside information and unjust enrichment." But the Senate was unable to penetrate the veil and reported that fact with some irritation. Given this dearth of information, it is important to stress that statistics from 1962 are likely to be an accurate indicator of relative shares in 1979 or 1980. We have to use every bit of information if we are to unveil the dirty little secret.

The following are first approximations of the distribution of income and wealth in the United States:

Family Income Shares

	1947	1972
Lowest Fifth	5.1%	5.4%
Second Fifth	11.8	11.9
Third Fifth	16.7	17.5
Fourth Fifth	23.1	23.8
Highest Fifth	43.3	41.4
Top 5 Percent	17.5	15.9
Median Income (1972 $)	$5,665	$11,116

SOURCE: U.S. Bureau of the Census in Thurow, p. 5.

Percent of the Net Worth of All Individuals Owned by the Richest 0.5%

1933	25.2%
1938	28.0
1945	20.9
1949	19.3
1953	22.7
1954	22.5
1956	25.0

SOURCE: James D. Smith and Stephen Franklin, "The Concentration of Personal Wealth, 1922–1969," p. 163.

Smith and Franklin, who are the source of the figures on the net worth owned by the richest half of a percent of the population, note that the fluctuations in the post–World War II period are largely the result of the way the data are gathered and reported and do not reflect real world changes. It is thus fair to say, as a rough but meaningful approximation, that "the distribution of wealth (1) became significantly more equal in the 1930s and early 1940s, two periods of massive intervention in the marketplace, and (2) has remained essentially unchanged since 1945."

What form does this enduring maldistribution of wealth take? In 1972, the richest 0.5 percent owned 49.3 percent of the corporate stocks; the top 1 percent held 56.5 percent of that total. Smith and Franklin comment: "One can say that the top 1% of the population literally controls all corporate assets in the United States via that half of the value of corporate shares." The top 1 percent owned 60 percent of the nation's bonds, 52.7 percent of its debt instruments and 89.9 percent of its trusts. However, the top 1 percent held a mere 15.1 percent of the country's real estate, which refracts the dispersal of home ownership in the United States—but not the fact that the average "owner" pays his or her rent to a bank which holds the mortgage.

That last point emphasizes a critical difference between the rich and almost everyone else. The bottom quarter of the society has no wealth at all—or, more accurately, has negative wealth since many of its members are net debtors. The next 55.9 percent of the people have 23.8 percent of the wealth. Adding those two groups together, the cumulative figure shows that 81.3 percent of Americans hold 23.8 percent of the wealth. In short, four-fifths of the people own somewhat less than the top 0.5 percent. Moreover, the wealth of the "ordinary" (nonrich) citizen takes the form of homes (which are, as has just been noted, heavily mortgaged), automobiles (purchased on credit) and other consumers' durables, like washing machines and television sets. In other words, most of the "wealth" of four-fifths of the population does not itself generate income or wealth.

It is otherwise in the upper reaches of the economy. The wealth of the rich is capable of parthenogenesis, of virgin birth; it produces more wealth all by itself. But if that is the case, aren't the rich even more subject to the vicissitudes of the business cycle than other people? In the case of a major collapse of the system, like the Great Depression, yes. Robert Lampman attributes a significant drop in the net worth of the top 0.5 percent—it went from 32.4 percent in 1929 to 25.2 percent in 1933—to the stock market crash. But the Depression was a catastrophe of unparalleled dimensions and it even engendered somewhat egalitarian government policies during the thirties and the war years. In the seventies, however, there is evidence that the rich manage to escape the consequences of the ups and downs of a stagflationary economy. In making a conservative argument that inflation had raised capital gains taxes and stockholders thus deserved special treatment, Martin Feldstein discovered that this problem only existed for those with incomes of $100,000 a year or less. The rich have found their own ways of "indexing" their wealth and protecting themselves against inflation.

So the rich have money that makes money in almost every season. Moreover, they are able to pass that enormous advantage down, from generation to generation. A significant figure was cited earlier: that the top 1 percent have roughly 90 percent of the trusts. That incredible concentration provides, Professor James D. Smith has noted, "a particularly beneficial way for the rich to transfer wealth from one generation to the other." This point will be examined in greater detail later on. For now, let it stand as a preliminary statement on how the rich pass on their wealth.

All that has just been said about the maldistribution of wealth, some argue, is biased, one-sided and overstated. The analysis, they would charge, has failed to take into account two factors which make the system much more egalitarian than the conventional statistics suggest. "Social Security wealth" has not been counted; neither has the cash value of the in-kind transfers received by the poor. These criticisms are, I will show, demonstrably wrong, yet they must be taken quite seriously since they come from liberals as well as conservatives.

"Social Security wealth," Martin Feldstein writes, "is the present actuarial value of social security benefits for which a worker and his dependent spouse become eligible at age 65." Using this criterion, Feldstein estimates that the share of the top 1 percent in the national wealth falls from 28 percent to 19 percent. This hardly turns America into a classless society; it does—if true—clearly moderate the country's inequality and invalidates at least some of the charges made in this chapter. Is Feldstein right? I think not, on two major grounds. His concept is flawed; but then, even if one accepts that concept, he makes an omission which invalidates his point. This seemingly technical issue is worth a moment or two since even a liberal like Henry Aaron accepts Feldstein's view, and the resultant confusion makes it impossible to give the redistribution of income and wealth the central place which it should have on the agenda of the movement for social change in the United States.

First, the very concept of "Social Security wealth" is most questionable. A. B. Atkinson, a thoughtful British specialist in this area, has plausibly argued that the value of wealth includes the freedom and possibility of maneuver which it confers upon an individual; the control over decisions which it brings; and the right to convey that wealth to whomever one wants. But Social Security "wealth" has none of these qualities. It cannot be cashed in, borrowed on or conveyed prior to retirement. One could thus be forced to go on welfare even if one had a considerable "wealth" in Feldstein's sense. Second, there is no power of control which derives from this "wealth." As owners of the nation's stocks and bonds, the real rich get disproportionate economic and political power: Presidents are forced to adapt to their priorities. They, or their agents, decide on how much will be invested, where, when and at what price the resulting products or services will be sold. This point applies with similar force to that claim of Drucker's that employee "ownership" of pension funds makes the workers the socialist rulers of America. In a political and economic sense this "ownership" has about as much to do with control as the "ownership" of the means of production by Russian workers under Stalin, i.e., it is purely passive, does not change the "owner's" social or economic position one whit and should be regarded as a fiction rather than as a fact.

Moreover, both Social Security and pension fund "wealth" are anything but secure. With the passage of the Retirement Income Security for Employees Act in the seventies, the most outrageous possibilities have been foreclosed. In 1963, when Studebaker folded, 4500 workers lost 85 percent of retirement rights which theoretically had been "vested." That cannot happen again, yet private plans only cover a minority of workers (44 percent), and their provisions fluctuate wildly with the best paid employees getting the most provisions for their retirement. Social Security "wealth" is even more insecure. The American system is not funded and the actual amount which is to be received is determined by political decisions which are by no means predictable. In the very mild and controllable crisis of Social Security caused by the recession-inflation of 1873–74—joblessness reduced the monies being paid into Social Security while higher prices automatically pushed up the indexed benefits—President Ford proposed a 5 percent cap on the cost-of-living escalator. That would have meant a reduction in the real income of the aging. If Feldstein insists upon his definition of Social Security "wealth," then he must face the fact that this is the only form of riches which a conservative Republican casually proposed to expropriate. On all of these grounds, I think it wrong to allege that present Social Security claims upon the future should be capitalized as "wealth."

But put these conceptual objections aside and consider a more narrow criticism of Feldstein's notion. The value of trust funds is excluded from the estate tax returns which provide the basis for most of our estimates of wealth in America, Feldstein's included. Yet, as we have seen, this is precisely a form of wealth which is designed to ensure that inequalities are perpetuated. The top 1 percent hold 90 percent of the trusts. So, John A. Brittain has rightly suggested, if one adds in Social Security "wealth," which improves the relative position of the nonrich, the trust funds should be counted, too, which improves the standing of the very, very rich. Those two operations, Brittain reports, then roughly cancel one another out. Those at the top remain securely in possession of a quarter of the nation's real—without quotation marks—wealth.

There is yet another argument, however, from those who say that America is not as unequal as the data seem to indicate. They say that when one computes the cash value of the in-kind goods and services received by the poor—like food stamps and Medicaid—that also makes us less unequal. That point will be dealt with in depth in the chapter on poverty and race where it will be seen as a central device in a show of statistical legerdemain which abolishes the poverty of millions of people in theory while leaving it alive—but ignored, neutralized, rationalized— in practice. For now, there is just one striking figure which adequately serves the purposes of the present analysis. In-kind transfers in the United States, like almost every government program, actually benefit the upper class much more than the poor, i.e., they are antiegalitarian. In 1970, households with an average income of $35,755 received $1915 in in-kind transfers; those with incomes between $1000 and $1999 got $756. Indeed, in that year those transfers mounted, with one unimportant exception, as income class rose; at every point, the better off received more than the worse off. The main reason for this startling statistic is that the upper classes got much greater education subsidies than anyone else. If, then, one is going to include "in-kind" cash values in the income accounts, that should be done with the benefits going to the rich as well as for those directed to the poor. When that is done, this category exacerbates, rather than moderates, the maldistribution of income and wealth.

Finally, there should be at least a reference to a comprehensive study of a country which is somewhat similar to America. Since we know so little about our own dirty little secret, we may be able to infer some knowledge about it from foreign data. This the British have provided us in the Report of the Royal Commission on the Distribution of Income and Wealth published in 1975. Income in the United Kingdom is about as maldistributed as in the United States; wealth is more unfairly allocated.

That contrast is revealing in and of itself. British capitalism developed slowly over a very long period of time and thus the mechanism of inheritance has had much greater opportunity to do its antiegalitarian work in that land than in *nouveau riche* America. But Britain also illustrates a contrary point. In part due to the redistributive policies of the British Labour party, the share of the top 1 percent fell by a third during the decade of the forties. That share then remained stable during the Tory fifties, and it began to decline again in the sixties when Labour came to power. It is possible, then, for conscious policy to impact on the structures of inequality.

But even if the recent trends in Britain are more egalitarian than in the United States, there is still an enormous inequality in that country. In 1973 (the last year which the commission studied) the top 20 percent of the population held 86.4 percent of the personal wealth; the bottom 80 percent thus had a mere 13.6 percent. In this country, as we have seen, the top 18.7 percent has 76.2 percent of the wealth, the other 81.3 percent has 23.8 percent. This suggests that these maldistributions, roughly similar despite quite different histories, are built into the structure of the capitalist system itself, and therefore require basic transformations if there is to be significant change.

In sum, wealth in the United States is distributed in a most plutocratic fashion, and the nation with the most egalitarian of myths—America, it has been rightly said, had "the socialist version of capitalism"—is almost as aristocratic in its social structure as a Britain with its hereditary concentration of riches. Let us turn now to those who do not dispute the fact but argue it away. These inequalities, it is said, are functional and even beneficial for the poor since they induce the rich to greater effort and thus increase the whole pie even if the relative size of the slices do not vary. In that image, everyone, even the worst off, profits from our inegalitarian arrangements and only the moralist or the ideologue could possibly object.[2]

II

The argument in favor of functional inequality is even found in an excellent book, John Rawls's *A Theory of Justice*, which consciously favors more equality. Inequality is permissible, Rawls says, "if lowering it would make the working class even more worse off." So an egalitarian like Rawls defers to the national myth. The distinguished—liberal—economist Arthur Okun is even more straightforward. "The contrasts among American families in living standards and in material wealth," Okun writes, "reflect a system of rewards and penalties that is intended to encourage effort and channel it into socially productive activity. To the extent that the system succeeds it generates an efficient economy. But that pursuit of efficiency necessarily creates inequalities. And hence society faces a tradeoff between equality and efficiency."

Both Rawls and Okun have a progressive version of the trickle-down theory and have even been attacked in the *Public Interest* as cryptoegalitarians. That article, by Marc Plattner, stated the philosophic basis of conservatism in this area: ". . . the bedrock moral premise of a liberal society is that those who devote themselves to 'honest industry' are entitled to reap—in the form of private property—the economic rewards that it brings. By contrast, the redistributionist view . . .[holds] that individuals do not deserve the economic rewards that are the fruit of their own talents and efforts and that the goods produced by their 'honest industry' are instead the 'common asset' of society as a whole . . ."

All that Plattner overlooks is the development of corporate collectivism. The capitalist economy is no longer (if it ever was) a free market of competing entrepreneurs.

No one's talents and efforts would yield any gains were it not for the pervasive intervention of the government in the name of the common good. That intervention, this book demonstrates, is financed by regressive taxes which fall most heavily upon the vulnerable people in the society; its benefits are disproportionately distributed to the richest citizens. Whatever worth John Locke's original labor theory of value might have had—that the effort of isolated individuals establishes their moral and political right to the full product of their toil—has been subverted by this corporate collectivization of the entire economy.

But then, the empirical basis of the corporate ideology is no more substantial than its tattered moral claims. To the champions of that view, the privileges of wealth are a positive boon to society, causing people to work harder. Here is a typical statement of this theme from the *The Wall Street Journal*: "People who are becoming millionaires are a cardinal motive force of a competent economy. They are the risk takers, the often competitive workers, the avid seekers of new technology and managerial innovation, the performers who set the highest standards of achievement and excellence."

Note, first of all, that this defense of inequality justifies it in terms of the superior performance which it incites. But, then, that is an argument for confiscatory inheritance taxes, which I am sure is not what the *Journal* intended. The transmission of great fortunes from generation unto generation provides a disincentive to the children of the rich; they need not take any risk, avidly seek anything or innovate. They are born at the top and if they prudently and passively invest their income—or better yet, trust that chore to a broker and become jet-setters —they will stay at the top. They are like those landlords of whom David Ricardo said that they grow rich in their sleep.

Recent empirical studies have demonstrated that inherited wealth of this counterefficient type plays an enormous role in the American system of maldistribution. John Brittain's Brookings study shows that 34 percent of the people with assets of more than $500,000 received a "substantial" portion of their fortune from inheritance; another 24 percent had some of their holdings handed down to them. And A. B. Atkinson has shown that the abstemious saver in Britain cannot ever approach riches within a lifetime. The same logic would apply in the United States. Someone with upper-middle-class income —in the top 2 percent, let us say—cannot, at ordinary rates of return, save his or her way into the charmed circle of the truly rich, where unearned income accounts for more of the annual take than earned income (in the mid-seventies, people with $200,000 a year and up fell into that category). The Horatio Alger myth, which is the appropriate fairy-tale description of the dirty little secret in this case, simply does not function in America.

But haven't there been some notable cases of large fortunes being made within a single lifetime? Xerox and the Polaroid camera are recent examples that come to mind. Two very different types of people—inventors and those who capitalize on inventions—are involved. Yet even though the actual creators perform a real economic function and are, in every dimension, superior to those who merely speculate on genius, both types share a critical quality: they are lucky. It is this factor, more than any Horatio Alger devotion, which explains why they make huge sums of money.

Most inventors who make a major—and enriching—breakthrough do it only one time. Even a man like Edwin Land, who seems to be an obvious exception to the rule, confirms it. Though he came up with many ideas after designing the Polaroid camera, none of his subsequent inspirations added materially to his wealth. Entrepreneurial and inventive bursts which lead to fame and fortune seem to occur infrequently and then only once in a single lifetime. Moreover, as Lester Thurow has suggested, the failures are probably quite similar to the successes and are distinguished from them primarily by luck. (In his provocative study, *Inequality*, Christopher Jencks argued that the factor of luck was critical at *all* levels of income.)

However, there is no point in pushing this argument to an extreme. The individual who actually makes a significant innovative contribution should be handsomely rewarded for his or her trouble. During the French electoral campaign of 1978—when the demagogic temptations of a populist egalitarianism must have been great—one of the chief socialist theorists, Jacques Attali, argued precisely that genius should receive such compensation. He then added the essential: that the rewards be enjoyed during a lifetime and not be handed down intact from generation to generation. In short, that tiny minority of the truly and effectively creative would receive tribute from the economy, just as *The Wall Street Journal* advocates. But that group should not be confused with the majority of the wealth holders today, who do not belong to it at all.

This last point applies with particular force to those who capitalize on genius, e.g., the people who simply bought Polaroid or Xerox shares very early. It is the proud boast of Wall Street that stock prices quickly and accurately reflect all known information about their value. If there is a stock which is dramatically undervalued by virtue of a lack of data on its real worth, then a fortune can be made. But that is, in terms of Wall Street's own definition, a lucky break rather than a socially useful innovation. The brokers do not beat the averages on the stock exchange and the possessors of great fortunes become like everyone else once they have made their once-in-a-lifetime score. Moreover, as the last chapter documented in detail, the stock market has a minimal role in generating funds for new investment and Wall Street functions most of the time as a casino for the middle class and the rich—but a casino which enjoys government subsidies. Las Vegas does not have a Horatio Alger myth to give it respectability.

Lester Thurow has developed a complex theory to explain how killings are made in this gambling system. Its details are too intricate to be recorded here but it should be at least noted that Thurow shows convincingly that the accumulation of great wealth is the result of a "random walk," rather than of hard work. Still, there is one last rationalization for the inequality of American society. The existence of these huge differentials, it is said, are necessary to motivate the best efforts of the talented. True enough, only a very few reach the summit of the pyramid, but its very existence keeps people working very hard throughout the society and particularly in the middle managerial reaches.

Short of a completely transformed society in which people work out of joy or service, *some* income differentials are necessary in order to get people to work hard. But does that generality mean that 0.5 percent of the society must be permitted to own more than do four-fifths of the people? Would the board chairman of General Motors stop striving if his $900,000 plus salary were reduced? John Maynard Keynes was a very successful money manager, a liberal antisocialist who had contempt for egalitarianism. Yet in his *General Theory,* he rightly remarked—just after he had proposed ending bonuses to the "functionless investor"—that executives "are certainly so fond of their craft that their labor can be obtained much cheaper than at present."

Keynes was speaking out of personal knowledge and intuition. Since he made his remark, there have been empirical studies which have confirmed it. In an exhaustive review of the literature, George F. Break showed that research suggests that there is a complex pattern of motivation at work and that higher taxes for the rich, or more income for the poor, would not necessarily reduce work effort among the executives. Lester Thurow and Robert Lucas reported to the Joint Economic Committee in 1972 that studies demonstrate that higher marginal tax rates actually make people work harder. But perhaps the most fascinating finding is the one reported by Charles E. Lindblom. It has to do with income conceived as a "score."

The scholarly literature, Lindblom says, shows that ". . . high income people are more motivated by the 'scores' they make—their pre-tax income—than by the disposable income they receive." That is, it is a psychological sense of being the top paid, rather than the actual money level of the top pay, which is important to corporate managers. The "key to the executive washroom" theme, which is so central to popular novels and films about the business class, is thus a serious insight. And it follows that the existing American disparities in income and wealth are not functionally necessary in order to motivate the middle and upper managers. The rewards could be reduced without any notable decline in efficiency. As Okun summarizes the evidence from all sources, there are "virtually no significant effects of the present tax system on the amount of work effort of the affluent."

So the enormous disparities of income and wealth—and above all, of enduring inherited wealth—are not justified by their contributions to economic efficiency. In the United States, the ratio between the income of the richest and poorest quintiles is 8 to 1; in Japan, which has significantly higher rates of productivity in many areas, the ratio is 5 to 1. It is, therefore, not economic necessity but belief in a fairy tale which justifies the maldistribution of riches in America.[3]

III

R. H. Tawney, the great British socialist, once said bitterly of his homeland's attitude toward equality, ". . . in England the instinctive feeling is one, not of sympathy, but of apprehension and repulsion, as though economic equality were a matter upon which it were not good taste to touch." In short, the victims of the dirty little secret don't want to think about it any more than the rich do.

In 1974, Alice Rivlin, then at the Brookings Institution, later head of the Congressional Budget Office, discovered that Tawney's insight applied to the United States. She told the American Economic Association: "Parents are not trying to narrow income differentials among the next generation; on the contrary, they think

larger differences between the income of the well educated and the poorly educated are just fine so long as their
own kids make it into one of the top groups." Alas, my own
sense of American society corroborates Rivlin's point.
This nation is psychologically individualistic, more so
than any other advanced country, for many historic and
cultural reasons. The outrageous differentials in income
and wealth documented here are the stuff of hopeful day-
dreams, not the object of angry resentment.

An anecdote might reinforce the academic generalizations. In the 1972 presidential election, a friend of mine
who is an official of the Garment Workers Union had supported Hubert Humphrey in the primaries, but then ral-
lied to George McGovern when he became the nominee.
He was campaigning actively for McGovern among his
union members, many of whom are black or brown and
female, most of whom receive relatively low wages from
an industry hard hit by runaway shops. I told my friend
that he must have had an easy time of it drumming up
support for McGovern since the latter's proposal to put a
high tax on inheritances of over $500,000 must have ap-
pealed to low-paid workers. I was wrong, he told me.
Those underpaid women, none of whom would ever see
$500,000 (or $50,000, or even $5000) were outraged that
the government would confiscate the money they would
hand down to their children *if* they made a million dollars.
One could explain patiently that the odds were a billion to
one against their ever getting a million dollars, but they
made up their minds on a critical issue with that extreme
improbability as their guiding principle.

But then this phenomenon is not confined to the
United States, though it is more of a factor there than
anywhere else. When the Swedish socialists acted on their
"solidaristic" labor policy in the sixties and seventies, they
sought to use wage bargaining as well as tax policy in
order to reduce the differentials in Swedish society. The
better-paid blue-collar workers, who would thus be asked
to put at least some of their bargaining power in the service of those less well off, did not object. But the white-

collar functionaries did. In a sense this is a sad confirmation of the point made in the previous section: that it is the relative position in the social structure which is very important, particularly in the managerial ranks.

In America, the only advanced industrial society without a major socialist current in the working class, this antiegalitarianism can be found at all levels of the society. How can it be dealt with?

In the chapter on education there will be several references to Fred Hirsch's seminal book, *Social Limits to Growth*. It will be shown how job competition in the United States incites young people to make "defensive" investments in higher education which do not translate into higher productivity for the society or even into significantly higher incomes for the students but which do protect them against downward social mobility. In short, the individualistic desire to get ahead results in a tremendous expenditure of money and energy simply to stay in place. The bitter knowledge of that fact is obviously spreading throughout the United States and it is one of the reasons why the seventies have seen a decline in the percentage of the youthful generation which is going to college.

Hirsch made an extremely important generalization about this situation: ". . . where individual preferences can be satisfied in sum only or most efficiently through collective action, privately directed behavior may lose its inherent advantage over collectively oriented behavior *even as a means to satisfying individual preferences themselves*, however self-interested. It follows that the best result may be attained by steering or guiding certain motives of individual behavior into social rather than individual orientations, though still on the basis of privately directed preferences. This requires not a change in human nature, 'merely' a change in human convention or instinct or attitude of the same order as the shifts in social conventions or moral standards that have gone along with major changes in economic conditions in the past."

Let me translate Hirsch's British generalization into American particulars. If, as chapter 8 suggests, the number of good, "middle-class" jobs will not satisfy the college educated during the next two decades, if, as some of the projections predict, there is actually going to be a "historic reversal" of the patterns of upward social mobility, then it is quite possible that the attitudinal shift which Hirsch describes could come about in the United States. That, obviously, would not happen automatically. It would require a political movement which would unveil the dirty little secret and show that our mythology has become perverse precisely for those who most earnestly believe in it. And this, in turn, would provide the basis for a politics which, interpreting the actual and bitter experience of the people, could channel our individualism into more social forms in an age when, as Hirsch's paradox shows, collective action is the only way to satisfy many individualistic desires.

But the individualistic psyche is not the only barrier to a redistribution of income and wealth. The American economic system is, too.

A system is defined, among other ways, by the fact that a change in any one element affects all the others. The most obvious illustration is the human body which reacts in dozens of ways to a tiny cut in a finger. As a result, there are "objective" limits on what can be done within a given system. In Chile, as Serge-Christophe Kolm has shown, restraining profits and increasing the real buying power of the masses, policies intentionally and rightly pursued by the Allende regime, had the unintentional consequence of feeding an inflation which became a major factor in the final overthrow of the regime. There are such limits in the United States, too.

Profits—or, more precisely, retained profits—are, as the last chapter documented, the major single source of new investment funds in the United States. Those profits are, in this system—but only in this system—appropriated by private corporations and invested according to their priorities. However, as long as this structure is in place there are "objective" limits to the amount of wealth and income redistribution which can take place. And even if one began the work of transforming the structures which impose these restraints upon the society—if, for instance, pension funds and retained profits were subject to the democratic control of beneficiaries, workers and the public, and investment were, to this degree, "socialized"— that cannot be done overnight. Therefore even the most optimistic assessment of the possibilities of reform must recognize that there are constraints which will exist throughout the foreseeable future.

Moreover, there are another set of limits, which are less precise since they are subjective and psychological, but quite real. In Britain, Charles Lindblom has noted, the Labour party's laws have hardly revolutionized the society. The British upper class is very much intact even if the workers have won some very important, though moderate, concessions to basic human decency. Yet British business responds as if it had been subject to the most radical, and egalitarian, transformations. And even though this is not the fact that the rich and the managers think it is, their thinking it has real consequences. They begin to act in a surly, noncooperative and socially subversive fashion even though their essential power has not been challenged. The limits of redistributive reform, then, do not merely derive from the objective limits imposed by a system which requires a certain level of private profit in order to function. They are also a function of the illusions of the corporate rich.

Late capitalism, Lindblom rightly argues, is based on a coalition of government and business. (It is corporate collectivism rather than free enterprise.) But then Lindblom asks about the capacity of such a society to deal with many social problems: "Is it possible to reconcile the minimum privileges required by business with a withdrawal of business privileges, including privileges of veto, that might help solve these problems?" Only, I would answer, under very specific—and unusual—conditions. One must look toward one of those periods, like the Great Depression in the thirties, when the guardians of the established inequality are in such disarray that they can be taken, so to speak, by surprise. Only then can one begin to deal with that tenaciously kept dirty little secret.

This does not mean that the redistribution of income and wealth is an either–or matter, that the status quo must persist until there is basic change. There is a long and patient work of demystification which must be carried on well in advance of one of those historic turning points. And there are significant approximations of the ideal which can be won in the here and now. The ideal itself, however, should be clear by now: the elimination of great disparities in income; the abolition of hereditary concentrations of wealth. I will deal with some principles and proposals which are relevant to immediate (ten- to twenty-year) action as well as to the longer run in which real structural transformations take place.

There should be a redistribution of income.

"Redistribution" is a word which should be taken quite literally. It would be a mistake simply to raise the incomes of the huge majority at the bottom of the pyramid since that would have the inflationary consequences which plagued Allende's Chile. Therefore policy should be redistributive in a double sense of the term. First, to lower the incomes of the very rich, whether they are earned or unearned; second, to transfer the monies thus gained to those at the middle and bottom of the society either in the form of lower taxes and higher individual incomes or in the form of increased social consumption. I stress that second way of increasing the incomes of the people for a reason. The tax cuts of the Kennedy-Johnson years all assumed that government should increase the effective demand of the people for the current mix of goods and services produced by the private sector. I am saying that there is a very good case for increasing planned social consumption, e.g., of health, rather than allowing the profit maximizers of the corporate sector to determine how the transferred funds will be spent.

This redistributive program, it should be carefully emphasized, would benefit the majority of Americans and not just the poor. Actually, tax policy has been *relatively* kind to the poor in recent years—which is cold comfort, given the other aspects of their lives—and the burden of a proportional Internal Revenue code has fallen most heavily upon working people and the middle class. What is proposed here, then, would not be charity for the worse off but equity for the overwhelming majority of taxpayers who are penalized by the shirkers at the very top of the income scale.

The focal point of this redistributive effort would be the tax law. The federal system is not truly progressive, but merely proportional. On the basis of realistic assumptions about the incidence of taxation, an authoritative study concludes the posttax income in the United States is only 0.25 percent more equal than pretax income, i.e., the impact is all but negligible. State taxes are straightforwardly regressive and one study, by Brooklyn, New York, Congressman Stephen Solarz, shows that under those levies families with $5000 a year pay more of a percentage of their income than those with $25,000 a year. That problem could be dealt with, as Solarz proposes, by giving federal deductions *only* for progressive state and local income taxes.

But the center of the problem is found in the federal tax system. The tax expenditure is a basic mechanism for maintaining the privileges of the rich in that code. It defines certain forms of income and certain kinds of expenditure as privileged and provides huge deductions for them. In the 1980 budget, as we have seen, almost $20 *billion* were forgiven on capital gains. The rationale for that enormous giveaway, as the last chapter showed, is spurious. Yet even more innocent-looking deductions are profoundly biased in favor of the wealthy. The exemptions for medical bills and insurance premiums provide $1.5 billion of benefits (out of a total of $11 billion) for the tiny elite with $50,000 a year and up. The same group gets 20 percent of the private pension fund benefits and almost all of the $1 billion in subsidies for business entertainment. The tax expenditures for homeowners are regressively proportioned, i.e., nothing for renters and the greatest relief for people with the largest houses and biggest incomes.

Clearly, then, a redistributive tax program would in fact be a more fair program. It would not confiscate income but simply require that the rich pay their fair share. A very interesting study from the Brookings Institution suggests what it would mean if the government tried to tax all income without making any of the myriad exceptions in the present code. There are numerous technicalities which need not be discussed here, but the results of one simulation are clear enough; as compared to the 1976 rates, the government's revenues would increase by 43.5 percent. This would take away some exemptions which favor the poor—under "comprehensive" taxation, as this approach is called, Social Security benefits would be taxed as well as capital gains—but it would materially increase the progressivity of the tax code. Moreover, a number of the advantages which the poor (and the working people and middle class) would lose by such a simplification would be made up by other programs. For example, when the country finally adopts a system of national health, we can do away with *all* deductions for medical care.

This, I have noted, is essentially a liberal program which merely finally honors the principle of ability to pay which we have theoretically—but only theoretically—observed all along. But it is almost radical in its political implications since any move in this direction evokes the most passionate and irrational opposition. For a generation now American politicians have been talking about moving more or less in this direction, yet every attempt at tax reform seems to end up with more loopholes for the rich.

Yet even though a fair tax system is extremely difficult to achieve, it is an absolute necessity, for all of the reasons given in this chapter. And the goal can be defined rather simply and in a way which should appeal to most Americans even if the implementation is problematic. Americans should be taxed on the basis of their "economic" income—"the money value of the net accretion to one's economic power between two points in time." All of the scandalous special privileges for unearned income should be abolished. A person who sells a share of General Motors stock should pay at a 100 percent rate just like the worker who makes a General Motors car now does (and always has). And second, once taxes are computed on the basis of real income, they should be clearly and obviously progressive. This would mean, third, that a truly just Internal Revenue Code would considerably *increase* the levies on the top 1 percent, and the added revenues could then be used either for useful social consumption for the other 99 percent or else to reduce their taxes.

At this point, however, a new complication arises. For even if this basic reform of the system were achieved, the analysis of this chapter suggests that a critical problem would still remain. The maldistribution of income would have been challenged, but the maldistribution of wealth —which is an even greater social evil—would persist.

The most significant single change in the system would address these hereditary concentrations of riches which create an economic aristocracy in theoretically democratic America. As it now stands, the inheritance tax is a feeble, ineffective attempt to cope with that outrage. There are estimates which show that roughly half of the property passed on in the United States involves "skipping" a generation to avoid the levies on inheritance. (Even as I write in 1979, Conservatives in Congress are unplugging a loophole in this area which was plugged a few years ago.) Then gifts can be used to transfer wealth and, within the generous limits of the code, avoid taxes altogether. Trusts can have the same effect, and there are dozens of other ways to engage in tax "avoidance" (which is perfectly legal, in contrast to tax "evasion"). The case for action is clear enough even in the light of our existing principles which are honored in the breach. And though many Americans may dream of one day being in a position to play the complicated tax games of the very rich, the wrongs described here mainly benefit the top 1 percent of the society. For the social psychological reasons which I have already noted, organizing a political majority of the 99 percent who stand to gain from fair inheritance taxation is not as simple as it might at first seem. Still, there is a very real objective possibility of doing precisely that.

Here again, there is no point in going into detail. That will be the work of experts once the formation of that political majority is under way. But two principles might at least be noted. First, the inheritance tax should be computed on the basis of the heir's wealth and income, i.e., it should be made easy to pass on, say, $50,000 to an heir who has no net worth and impossible to pass the same $50,000 to someone who is already wealthy. And second, some thought should be given to eliminating concentrations of wealth over several generations. That is, the amount of money which a father can pass on to a son should be considerably greater than the amount of that initial inheritance which the son could hand down to the grandson of the man who struck it rich.

The argument for acting in this matter derives from classic capitalist principles. The knowledge that a man or woman can pass a significant (but not antisocial) inheritance on to their offspring would be an incentive to work harder, to innovate, to act, in short, according to *The Wall Street Journal*'s mythic code of conduct. The offspring, as I already commented, would be given a disincentive since they could simply enjoy the fruits of their parents' labor. That could be dealt with by limiting the amount which they would receive but, in any case, their disincentive would be compensated for by their parents' incentives. When, however, one gets to the third and fourth generation of the transfer of wealth, there is no economic argument in favor of large inheritances and the political and moral arguments against them are utterly compelling. The drafters of legislation in this area might keep these facts in mind.

Here, then, is a preeminent example of a structural reform. The concentration of wealth in the United States is a persistent, enduring pattern, making—to paraphrase Orwell—some of our people much more equal than others.

The rationales which hide this dirty little secret are all fairy tales even when they masquerade as serious economic theories. Worst of all, this concentration of wealth does not simply have to do with money; it is basic to the maldistribution of power as well. This tiny, and often hereditary, elite is, precisely because of its ownership of the productive assets of the nation, able to veto the decision of a majority of the people. The policies urged here thus are critical to democracy itself. And they challenge the calculus which, as the next chapter will show, devastated cities in the name of private, antisocial gain.[4]

Notes

1. Knight: Quoted in *Inheritance and the Inequality of Material Wealth*, John A. Brittain, p. 1. Schultze: *The Public Use of Private Interest*, p. 17. PACs: *John Herling's Labor Letter*, June 2, 1979.

2. Income, profits and interest: Kolm, *La Transition Socialiste*, p. 116; CEA, 1979, table B-19, p. 204. Wealth: Smith and Franklin, "The Concentration of Personal Wealth in America," pp. 143–44; U.S., Senate, Committee on Government Operations, November 1975, pp. 6–7. Smith and Franklin on trend: Op. cit. supra, p. 162. Smith and Franklin on corporate ownership: in *Data on the Distribution of Wealth in the United States*, table I, p. 175; p. 9. Wealth percentages: Thurow, *On Generating Inequality*, p. 14. Lampman: Quoted, Smith and Franklin, op. cit. supra, p. 163. Feldstein: "Inflation and Capital Formation." Smith on trusts: *Data on the Distribution of Wealth*, p. 9. Feldstein: In Shapiro and White, eds., p. 187; Feldstein, "Social Security and the Distribution of Wealth," pp. 800–7. Aaron: *Politics and the Professors*, p. 40. Atkinson: *Unequal Shares*, pp. 27 ff. Studebaker: Furniss and Tilton, pp. 173–74. Brittain: Op. cit. supra, pp. 5–6. In-kind transfer funds: In Juster, ed., table 3, p. 12. Royal Commission: *Shares*, vol. I, p. 30, 1973; vol. I, table 45, p. 102.

3. Rawls: *A Theory of Justice*, p. 78. Okun: *Equality and Efficiency*, p. 1. Plattner: "The Welfare State versus the Redistributive State, *passim*. *The Wall Street Journal:* Editorial, August 16, 1978. Brittain: op. cit. supra, table 1–2, p. 18. Atkinson: Op. cit. supra, p. 53. Unearned income: Hacker, "Who Rules America?" Land: Thurow, *On Generating Inequality*, pp. 153 and 246, n. 22. Attali: *La Nouvelle Economie Française*, p. 177. Stock market: Thurow, op. cit. supra, chap. 6. Keynes: *The*

General Theory, p. 377. Break: In Blinder et al., eds., pp. 180 ff. Thurow and Lucas: *The American Distribution of Income*, p. 4. Lindlbom: *Politics and Markets*, p. 46. Okun: Op. cit. supra, p. 97. Japan: Thurow and Lucas, op. cit. supra, p. 4.

    4. Tawney: *Equality*, p. 17. Rivlin: "Income Distribution, Can Economists Help?" p. 9. Hirsch: *Social Limits to Growth*, p. 146. Chile: Kolm, *Solutions Socialistes*. Lindblom: Op. cit. supra, pp. 199 and 348. Tax progressivity: Pechman and Okner, p. 64. Tax expenditures: *Congressional Quarterly Weekly Report*, February 24, 1979, pp. 341 ff; Pechman, ed., *Comprehensive Income Taxation*, passim and appendix. Inheritance taxes: Tait, pp. 91 and 106 ff.

6

The United States of Appalachia

Fantasize a neo-Stalinist regime in an advanced Western country. It moves millions of its reliable supporters to new and desirable locations. Others, who do not fit into the plan, are left in the ruins of half-deserted cities. Still others, who stand in the way of technological advance in some underdeveloped regions, are transported to those decaying cities. This is not done by means of totalitarian force, like Stalin's collectivization of the Russian peasantry or the Cambodian Communist policy of driving entire populations into the countryside. This is Stalinism with a human mask and it only uses as much repression as is absolutely necessary.

If that were to happen, there would be angry, justifiable protest from American liberals as well as conservatives since such callous manipulation would deeply offend the nation's sense of human rights. Those hypothetical Stalinists would then reply that it is unfortunately true that eggs must be broken to make an omelet. They would regret the suffering which their plan had imposed upon some people, but they would point out that the undertaking had increased the efficiency of the economy and thus prepared the way for the eventual happiness of the majority. And the partisans of human rights in the United States would reply, echoing Kant's magnificent dictum, that you cannot treat people as means to an end; or, as our own history puts it, that the individual has certain inalienable rights.

Something like that outlandish Stalinist scenario took place within the United States during the post World War II period.

It was, to be sure, done so discreetly and democratically that many of the victims did not even know they had been victimized. And yet, millions of the better off—including some skilled workers as well as middle- and upper-middle-class people—were moved from the cities of the Northeast and the industrial Middle West. Other millions, disproportionately black, brown and young, were left behind, and millions more, displaced by mechanization from the fields of the South and from Puerto Rico, came to join them.

If what actually happened in this country in these years had been done according to a plan, the cruel bureaucrats who designed the gutting of vast areas of New York City and Cleveland and St. Louis would have been excoriated by every decent man and woman in the land. But it was not done by a plan and that is the beginning of rationalizing away the tragedy. It was, one is told, the work of the objective and impersonal Market. Or it was the unavoidable consequence of the development of Technology. Or it was the result of a biological rhythm which rules society as well as individuals: those older cities Matured. There is no person, no Who, responsible for what has been done; it is a What which is guilty, and that makes all of us innocent.

It is the theme of this chapter that the American political and economic system—and the individuals who dominate it—must be held accountable for laying waste to urban areas as effectively as a bombing raid. The results were not inevitable; they were chosen. To be sure, the market and technology and the very passage of time had something to do with what happened. But that process could have been shaped and controlled, its human costs could have been avoided and the entire society, and not merely the actual victims, would have been the beneficiary. Here, once again, the underlying reasons for our failure are structural. The nation blindly obeyed the dictates of corporate priorities, which constituted the basis of an unconscious plan.

In saying this, I do not propose to substitute a leftist theory of the inexorabilities of the system for those complacent rationales about the necessities of the market, or technology or the social-economic aging process. Our urban problems are indeed systemic—but the system itself is a human creation which can be consciously changed. Ironically, Americans who passionately reject what they think of (usually wrongly) as Marxist "determinism" are themselves often simplistic determinists. So it is one task of this chapter to remind the nation of the possibilities of freedom.

That will be done, first of all, by critically examining the determinist rationales for our urban disaster. Then, there will be an analysis which shows how political choices, made by a partnership of the corporations and the government, led to ruin of great cities in the seventies. And finally, the proposals—both good and bad—for dealing with our plight will be examined. We, unlike any Stalinist society one can imagine, have the democratic possibility of reversing our antisocial plan nonviolently. To do that, however, we have to recognize that it exists, and that is where I begin.

_____ I _____

When New York City teetered on the brink of bankruptcy in 1975, one of the most popular journalistic and political explanations for the catastrophe was that the nation's largest city was being punished for its profligate social decency. The journalist, Ken Auletta, later put that thesis, "New York City is the left's Vietnam. The traditional weapons—more money, more programs, more taxes, more borrowing—didn't work here; just as more troops, more bombs, more interdiction, more pacification programs didn't work there. And as that miserable war should have instructed military adventurists on the limits of American power, New York's fiscal war, unavoidably, teaches the limits of government intervention."

But then Auletta provides the evidence to subvert his own theory. Citing Robert Caro's *Power Broker,* he notes that Robert Moses's investment of $1.2 billion in 1955 for the construction of a second deck on the George Washington Bridge used money which would have been sufficient to modernize the entire New York City subway system and the Long Island Railroad. (Caro specifies that these improvements, all of which would have reduced the city's poisonous dependence on the private car, would have included two new subway lines and another tunnel under the East River!) That certainly demonstrates that government intervention on behalf of antisocial priorities is as perverse as military intervention on behalf of a corrupt dictatorship in Vietnam. But it also suggests that had those funds been spent on mass transit, then outcomes would have been utterly different—which is precisely the point of section II of this chapter.

Second, Auletta chronicles the political games which were played with the New York City budget and he is often right on target. He then goes on to praise Newark's mayor, Ken Gibson, for having refused to engage in the shoddy and spendthrift practices employed across the river in New York. And yet, Auletta fails to note the truly striking fact: that despite its balanced budget and greater prudence, Newark is in at least as deep trouble as New York. If that is the case, then the fiscal legerdemain of the politicians may have contributed to, or exacerbated New York's decline, but it did not cause it.

Most scholars who have dealt with the subject do not, however, see individuals and their policy errors as the source of decay in New York. They base themselves on the dominant tradition in the urban theory of the past generation: that cities' fates are determined by an impersonal, almost Darwinian, process of evolution. And they all rightly take the enormous exodus of good jobs and the immigration of people with desperate needs as the starting point of an analysis which comes to the wrong conclusions.

Between 1971 and 1977, New York City lost 624,900 jobs. During the depths of the recession, in 1974–75, 244,100 positions vanished; during the recovery of 1976–77, 153,300 disappeared. In considerable measure this was because the recession hit New York more viciously than, say, the Texas cities and the recovery was less of a boon. In 1968, when joblessness in the United States was 3.6 percent, New York was below the national average at 3.1 percent and was even slightly better off than Houston. But in 1976, when the national rate fell to 7.7 percent, New York City stayed at 11.2 percent (St. Louis, with 12.8 percent, and Detroit, with 13.1, were worse off). Industries which had become the backbone of the municipal economy were decimated.

New York's fate was dramatic but not exceptional. Between 1964 and 1975, per capita income in the Northeast, Middle Atlantic and East North Central declined relative to the rest of the nation. In the twenty-year period 1950–70, Chicago lost 140,000 households in the top 40 percent of the income structure and gained 150,000 in the bottom 40 percent. Cleveland, the urbanologist George Sternlieb commented, was "going out of business" in 1978. In all of these areas the pattern was the same: the exodus of middle-class and working-class taxpayers, the in-migration of poor people, usually black and/or Hispanic. In New England, for instance, the years between 1940 and 1970 saw 900,000 whites leave and 1.6 million blacks arrive.

So the fiscal crisis of New York and other cities was not primarily a result of spendthrift liberalism. It was caused by a flight of jobs and taxpayers which radically contracted the financial base of urban areas at precisely the same moment that there was a gigantic wave of new arrivals, unprepared for urban life and coming at a time of declining employment. The newcomers went on relief in large numbers, not because they were lazy or cheats, but because there was no work for them. Under such circumstances, the cities did not have to be prodigal in order to risk bankruptcy. Simple humanity was enough to precipitate a crisis.

As a result, urban war zones appeared in the great cities. The most famous was, of course, the South Bronx area of New York City. Once an entry point for working-class Jews, by the seventies it had become primarily black and Hispanic. The unemployment and welfare rates were around a third of the population. The tenements decayed, not because there was a rent control law, but because the people were so poor they could not even pay rents well under the legal ceiling. Buildings were abandoned and became the haunt of criminals and junkies. Fires broke out in confirmation of Tolstoy's insight that a city will burn itself down if no one cares for it. So municipal government, which inherited the ruins, tore down the old tenements simply to minimize the hazards. Thus in the midst of the largest city in the United States there was, and is, a vast man-made lunarscape, two hundred acres of rubble and desolation ringed by still more buildings waiting to be destroyed.

The major cost of this enormous failure was borne, of course, by the poor people who had to live in, or around, the collapsing neighborhoods. There were, NBC television reported in 1977, gangs of teenagers—and even preteenagers—who would commit murder for a small price. And although the poverty-stricken and the minorities were, as usual, the main victims of their own desperate violence, these hatreds and frustrations could not be kept locked up in ghettos. In New York, for instance, mugging and vandalism plagued the subways and the parks and effectively expropriated vast areas of the city from the middle class.

In 1969, the National Commission on the Causes and Prevention of Violence, made what might have seemed to be an apocalyptic prediction. "Lacking effective public action," the commission said, America would soon see deserted central cities at night, high-rise buildings which were "fortified cells," security features on taxis and cars, armed guards on public transit and at all public facilities. Every one of those prophecies has now come true in New York, and not only in New York. Indeed, one could make an ironic analogy. In the 1960 presidential primary in West Virginia, John F. Kennedy was appalled by the poverty he saw. So his administration, and Lyndon Johnson's, devoted a considerable amount of attention to the Appalachian problem. In large measure those efforts failed. Appalachia began to improve, not because of government programs, but because so many people were uprooted and then the energy crisis made coal a valuable resource once again.

The point is not to review what happened in Appalachia. It is to say that the Appalachian pattern—a decaying public infrastructure and a declining job market driving people out and making the place even less attractive and therefore allowing for more decay and job flight—has now extended to vast areas of the Northeast and Middle West. The classic heartland of American capitalism is now, almost all of it, caught in that self-reinforcing, downward spiral that was thought only a decade ago to be the problem of hill folks.[1]

II

There are serious people who say that these developments were not only necessary but that they are also good.

I have singled out three strands in the theory of the happy inevitability of America's urban disaster: the role of the market, of technology and of the social-economic aging process. Clearly, the three are interrelated, i.e., the market is seen as transmitting a demand which is determined by technological change or by aging. However, each of them is slightly different in the emphasis it gives in rationalizing the destruction of our cities.

Scholars tell us that it is the market, the impersonal, efficient market which decreed the South Bronx and all the other ruins and we are better off in the long run because of it. Thus George Sternlieb and James A. Hughes write, "The abandonment which now characterizes many central cities is, in substantial part, a function of the loss of demand as well as of deterioration in the physical amenities." Industry had become overspecialized, the workers had become highly unionized, many poor people were a problem, automation and rationalization allowed the corporations to move to new areas. So the older heartland "begins to falter with surging growth elsewhere."

In a similar mood, a Rand Corporation study concludes, "Over the years, rising costs, high crime, traffic congestion, increasing tax burdens and deteriorating services and facilities have made central cities progressively less attractive than the suburbs as places to live, work and conduct business." Moreover, "Without external intervention to improve the long-term economic outlook for the cities, there is little prospect for an end to the process of urban decline." And still another analysis, this one designed to help Northeastern policy makers, stresses the substitution of capital for labor, the decentralization of the economy, the shift of manufacture to the suburbs.

The old cities, you see, simply became too costly to afford and their ruin is common sense. As the Joint Economic Committee of the Congress stated this free enterprise fatalism in 1977, "To a large extent, the interregional migration of population and employment opportunities is occurring in response to real economic forces affecting the cost and efficiency of production *and has contributed to over all efficiency and productivity in the private sector and should not be discouraged*" (emphasis added). So the nation as a whole, the Joint Economic Committee tells us, gained; the inevitabilities inherent in "economic forces" are still working out benevolently, just as Adam Smith said, albeit with some side effects for millions of human beings.

This is, to use C. Wright Mills's marvelous phrase, "crackpot realism" with a vengeance. The principal objection to this line of thought—that it systematically ignores the degree to which the "economic forces" are the creatures of political choice—will be treated at length in the next section of this chapter. For now, a few comments on basic methodology are in order.

The market analysis of the urban crisis obscures both the real costs and the social and economic consequences of the process it describes. Not so incidentally, this flaw is in the interest of the rich and powerful and to the detriment of the most vulnerable people in the nation. In this theory, it is tacitly assumed that one must, in the name of "rationalization" and "efficiency," let the market forces do their work even if the result is havoc for millions and for entire communities. It is, of course, true that leveling neighborhoods in New York, Detroit, Cleveland and St. Louis is one way of getting rid of old plants and then investing in new areas is a way of increasing production. But it is not at all true that this is the only, or the best, way to modernize an economy. Who pays the adjustment costs in this scenario? Not the corporations which profit from the changes. They are allowed to walk out on their employees and their former city without so much as waving good-bye. Those who finance this "rationalization" by being subjected to the irrationalities of municipal decay are the ones who are left behind.

One can easily imagine alternatives to this cruel procedure. The corporations, as we will see, could be required to pay the real costs of their move as a precondition of obtaining the profits from it. The society itself could be required to equalize the burdens and fully compensate those who are injured by "progress." Such policies would, however, require that business pay its fair share, which is something it avoids in the name of a better bottom line. And therefore the market theory of the urban crisis, with its mythology of impersonal forces which must be obeyed in the name of efficiency, provides a marvelous rationale for social irresponsibility.

But then even the claimed benefits of this callousness are questionable. Intolerable costs, like the ruin of great cities, are paid for ambiguous outcomes. The Joint Economic Committee confidently asserts that these vast industrial and human migrations contribute to "over all efficiency and productivity." By what measure? Certainly, as we have just seen, not by the criteria of people in the South Bronx. The social costs of rationalization are imposed upon them. But even the more conventional measures of benefits are not reassuring. The growth of industry in the Southwest, for instance, has required huge energy investments in private autos, roads, air conditioning and the like; and it has created problems like smog, sprawl and, much more difficult to quantify, the alienation of rootless communities. These developments are one —and only one—factor in an economy which wastes energy more than any other in the Western world.

In a rare moment of candor in 1968, the Council of Economic Advisers at least posed this problem, even if it immediately ran away from it. The council asked whether "the separate decisions of millions of individuals and business firms, responding to the pull of economic opportunity and the push from their absence, tend to produce an 'optimum' distribution of population and economic activity . . ." The council concluded that there was not enough information to answer its question. It conceded that government policies might "influence the attractiveness" of various locations and even that conscious planning of such policies might "move us closer to an 'optimum'—assuming we knew what that was."

I find this agnosticism unconscionable. From the point of view of the Northeast and the Midwest it is painfully obvious that what has happened is not an "optimum," and even the growth areas might come to regret their success. Government policies did indeed "influence the attractiveness" of various locations and made a major contribution to the destruction of great cities. And those policies could have been shaped, as we will see, to yield social results. But that will not be done as long as the nation remains under the spell of the market theories of our municipal disasters, that marvelous alibi which tells the society that no one is responsible for evident catastrophes.

This critique permits some generalization about the function of markets. As we saw in the last chapter, markets are a marvelous and decentralized device for communicating individual desires if, but only if, the individuals are more or less equal. It they are not, then markets will frustrate the desires of those with less and overrepresent the desires of those with more.

The market theorists of urban collapse forget that fact. The best of them parenthetically concede that the market is rigged to transmit the desires of big corporations, and then forget the parenthesis; the worst do not even bother with the qualification. So it must be made clear that the "impersonal" market only operated in the way it did with regard to cities because the victims were systematically incapable of affecting the outcome, which was dictated by the power and wealth of those who benefited most.

Second, markets are by their very nature incapable of dealing with structural problems which require the posing of new alternatives. A market always presupposes a given distribution of power and it then operates to reinforce that given, often in a quite efficient manner. But if basic new options need to be introduced—if political policies must intervene on behalf of the Northeast and Midwest because their position has been drastically eroded—the market is useless to respond. It is an essentially repetitious—and therefore conservative—mechanism. It will continue to transmit the old priorities and block the new solutions. And that is what happened in the urban crisis of the seventies.

But then the market, as I have noted, is only one of the determinist excuses for the social tragedy of the American city. Technology is another, obviously related, impersonal force which can be invoked to absolve people for any responsibility for their own actions. So, for example, that

1968 Report of the Council of Economic Advisers interpreted the shift from the old industrial heartland in terms of technical advances in transportation, the construction of interstate highways, long-distance pipelines and the extension of coordinated electric power grids. These innovations, the council said, reduced the advantages of the older manufacturing sites and opened up the way to a migration of jobs.

Indeed, it was this line of reasoning which led some scholars from Harvard and MIT to conclude in the midsixties that there was no urban crisis. In *The Metropolitan Enigma: Inquiries into the Nature and Dimensions of America's "Urban Crisis,"* edited by James Q. Wilson, it was no accident that "Urban Crisis" was put in quotation marks. What was happening, these analysts said, was simply that new technology required single-story, spread-out plants and that developments in communications made it possible for offices to be much more dispersed than before. What these thinkers missed (and I pointed it out at the time, in *Toward a Democratic Left*) was only the essential: that those technological changes, and above all the new modes of transportation, could only have taken place because of huge federal investments, a point which will be expanded on in a moment.

The third rationale for complacency in the presence of so much urban disintegration appeals to a truth known to every man and woman in the world: that human beings age and die. From Plato to this moment, organic metaphors, which hold that a similar process takes place in political and social institutions, have had an enormous hold upon the Western imagination. In this perspective, the fate of the cities of the Northeast and Midwest is just one more confirmation of the inherent mortality of all human undertakings. It is thus natural that a city should begin to die, and no one should be surprised at the phenomenon. This proposition is not, of course, normally stated in its biological form. A 1978 survey by the *London Economist* gives a most sophisticated version of the basic image.

The *Economist* was enthusiastic about what was happening to New York City. "Small is more beautiful," read the title of the survey. Then the analysis: ". . . nothing can prevent New York from becoming a smaller city. America's population is now relatively static. The continent is vast and free, its citizens notoriously footloose. The national outflow of people from the overcrowded, overtaxed, cold, old area cannot be halted; indeed, for the United States as a whole, it is a rejuvenating and healthy migration." The South Bronx, the *Economist* said, "is the *natural* and *inevitable* consequence of a shrinking city. The destruction, poverty and helplessness that cluster around the burnt-out wrecks is abhorrent. That something should be done to stop it is the immediate reaction. That something should be done to speed it up is much nearer the mark" (emphasis added).

And yet, it takes only a moment's reflection to see that the biological metaphor used by the *Economist* is faulty. Cities are not necessarily subject to the same rhythms of birth and decay as humans. London, where the *Economist*'s editors live, is many hundreds of years older than New York and in much better condition. France has faced the problem of a relatively stable population for years and Paris has grown larger. Indeed, the French government has adopted a system of tax incentives and disincentives to encourage urban growth in areas outside of Paris. Cities, clearly, can have new lives; people cannot. The *Economist* prefers to forget this patent truth and to deal with sweeping, implacable necessities.

So we are told that the human agony of the South Bronx is natural and inevitable and ultimately rejuvenating. The North is cold and old; the emigration is a good thing. And that, of course, is the underlying thesis of all of these rationales: that nothing can be done and indeed that inaction is the best of all policies because it will allow the market, or technology, or inevitable processes to accomplish their benevolent work. The blacks and the brown and the young who are trapped in these cities are the victims of an inexorable progress, much as Stalin's kulaks were. There is no totalitarian force in this case, however, which is precisely what makes it so difficult to grasp. If the nation believes these catastrophes are good for it, then they cease to be catastrophes.

Why is this fatalism so widely accepted? There are many reasons, some historical, some cultural, but one which is particularly poignant has to do with the recent history of the United States. In 1966, the Report of the Council of Economic Advisers accurately and succinctly outlined the causes of the urban disintegration which was to come. It said:"Almost without exception, the central core cities, which are the heart of the metropolitan area, have experienced a gradual process of physical and economic deterioration. Partly as a result of people's desire for more space and home ownership, and made possible by the development of the automobile, central cities have been losing middle- and upper-income families to the suburbs. This movement is accelerated when cities become caught in a vicious spiral of spreading slums, rising crime and worsening congestion. . . . This process created an almost impossible financial situation for many cities."

In short, America knew what was coming. And yet we did nothing—or rather, as the next section will show, we adopted policies which made the trends ever more pernicious. And since we were so utterly impotent, since there was neither political will nor social imagination to cope with these miseries, theories which told us they were, and are, inevitable became quite popular. They saved us from both conscience and consciousness.[2]

III

In fact, the government—primarily, but not exclusively, the federal government—played a major role in creating the urban crisis. In some cases, its contribution to our social problems was direct and willful; in most cases, it was indirect and thoughtless, but coherent and systematic (that last paradox will be explained as we proceed). Given the critical role of federal policy in the ruin of great cities, we can leave behind the theology of economic predestination and turn to politics, to choices—to the possibility that things could be much better than they have been.

At the outset, it is important to avoid a futile misunderstanding, one that has already been briefly noted. It is obviously true that the federal government was not solely responsible for what has happened to the metropolis in the Northeast and Midwest during the past several decades. Of course, there were market, technological and aging factors at work. Social processes are always organic and complex, a reciprocal interaction of the economic, political and cultural. However, that is not to be agnostic about Washington's role. It was an indispensable—and reversible—influence at every point. Sometimes federal power was clearly the dominant force; at other times it merely reinforced trends which it found already in existence; but at all times it was a necessary precondition for the urban crisis.

So there is no point in haggling over the precise allocation of responsibility. A Rand Corporation study says that federal policy "played a fairly small role" in these developments, while "technological change and population movements played the decisive parts." A Department of Transportation analysis talks of actions in Washington that "heightened and accelerated" some of these problems. Whatever the exact modality, it is clear that Washington could have acted against the trends which, to some degree or other, it sponsored. And that becomes a crucial judgment when one remembers that most of the fatalist theories we are examining do not even mention the federal role at all.

The candor of the *London Economist* is, however, preferable to the reluctant admissions of the Rand study. "Demographic, social and economic developments," the *Economist* wrote in 1978, "have, of course, spurred the exodus from the nation's older cities. But the movement was clearly accelerated by government policies—the favourable tax treatment offered home mortgages, huge expenditures on motorways, investment tax credits that stimulated industrial decentralization." The *Economist*'s list of policies is far from complete, yet its conclusion is compelling.

The *Economist* mentioned the federal commitment to highways as a major factor promoting the exodus from the older cities; the Rand analysis admitted that this was an area where governmental influence played a role. And George Sternlieb and James A. Hughes, who were among the determinists described in the last section, say that the most significant shift of the postwar period was "the transportation revolution which generated an increasing reliance on air and truck transportation, gradually supplanting the dependency on the nation's rail system." At the beginning of 1978, *The Wall Street Journal* estimated that the completion of that subsidized road system on a minimal basis would bring the total investment to $80 billion and actually fulfilling the plan would cost $104 billion. So, it would seem, this is an open-and-shut case in support of my hypothesis. The government paid for roads which paved the way for the Northeastern–Middlewestern exodus.

The issue is more complex than that. How were the decisions made to channel billions of indirect subsidies to one mode of transportation with the "side effect" of undermining a good part of the advantages enjoyed by the older industrial centers? That outcome required hundreds of political units—the White House, various congressional committees as well as the Congress itself, regulatory agencies, state and local governments—to make thousands of choices which had the result of worsening the urban crisis. In what follows, a few facts and interpretations should give some insight into a development which could easily be treated at book length. That analysis will, in turn, establish a pattern which can also be found in the other cases in which Washington helped fund, and even plan, the attack on the older cities.

The numbers are plain and familiar. In 1940, the railroads had 63.2 percent of intercity freight traffic measured in transportation miles. In 1970 their share had dropped to 39.8 percent. During the same period the motor vehicle share more than doubled, going from 9.5 percent to 21.3 percent. (Oil pipelines made a similar gain, from 9.1 percent to 22.3 percent, but that is not relevant to the argument of this chapter since it did not impinge that much on the fate of the cities.) Ironically, the very same federal government whose subsidies to highways did so much to destroy the railroads had historically been the great patron of that mode. Between 1823, when Ohio got money from Washington for a "wagon road," and 1972 there were some $450 billion in transportation subsidies which, until after World War I, went mainly and massively to the rail system.

But in the last fifty years, and most decisively in the post–World War II period, the trains lost out in the competition for the subsidy dollar. In 1974, for instance, the secretary of transportation estimated that the handouts to the rails were a half of those to roads and a quarter of the federal investment in aviation. And, as will be seen in a moment, the monies for the trains in 1974 went to socializing the costs of their failure, not to expanding the mode itself. So the highway program—begun under Dwight Eisenhower—had turned out to be one of the most radical social programs in American history: it undercut the cities of the Northeast and Midwest, whose destinies were linked to the rails, and opened up the way for the expansion of the Southwest. It also helped change family life, sexual mores and contributed to the restless alienation of the whole society, but those effects lie beyond the scope of this chapter.

An economic myth helped to rationalize these policies. The highways, it was said, were paid for by "user" taxes and there were therefore no subsidies of any kind. Yet in 1969, the Federal Highway Administration figured that the taxes paid by heavy trucks—which impose a brutal physical burden on the roads—were $219 million short of the costs which they imposed. And in 1978, it was discovered that the system was deteriorating 50 percent faster than the repair crews could fix it up. This was in considerable measure because a 1974 law authorized a 10 percent increase in the truck-load limit. This led one critic to say that the interstate highways could be "the Penn Central of the next generation." These costs, it will be noted, are conventionally calculated. I have not even referred to the social costs—pollution and environmental degradation as well as urban destruction—which are clearly a part of the story.

These billions of subsidies to roads helped to wreck the rail system. In March 1975 the president of the Norfolk and Western Railway—a money-maker—told the Interstate Commerce Commission, "Admittedly, there is no way for all of the bankrupt lines in the Northeast to be restructured and operated viably as private enterprise." The issue, the corporate executive said, was not whether there would be some nationalization by the "area within which it can be contained." So it was that *The Wall Street Journal,* the bastion of dogmatic free market economics, came out for public ownership of the railroad structures and rights-of-way in the Northeast. And Senator Edward Kennedy, the most effective liberal member of the upper chamber in the 1970s, said in 1977 that studies by all of the federal agencies "indicate that the railroad industry as a whole is unable to meet from private resources, the capital requirements of maintenance, rehabilitation and modernization."

The government, Kennedy continued, had to take over right-of-way maintenance. And, he concluded, the point of the subsidies would be to permit the private sector to prosper and create jobs. This traditionalist rhetoric sounded somewhat strange coming from Kennedy but it has the virtue of focusing on a particularly vicious irony. It is a general principle of American governmental economic policy to socialize only losses and to keep profits private. Thus, after Washington's subsidies helped to destroy the railroads, the ruined system is purchased at an inflated price by the government. The public enterprise then loses money, since that was a precondition of its becoming a public enterprise in the first place. And this allows private-sector enthusiasts to cite one more "proof" of the superiority of corporate undertakings as compared to governmental operations.

But why did Washington behave in this way? The answer is fundamentally, but not simply, structural in character, i.e., it has to do with the institutional organization of the American economy. There is, however, no question that railroad management, one of the stodgiest and least innovative sectors of the nation's corporate leadership, made a personal contribution to its own downfall. The United States Railway Association, set up by Congress to propose a new system plan for the Midwest and Northeast, said of Penn Central that it had used "overly imaginative accounting procedures to bolster reported income." Less delicately put, that accused the company of having lied to the public. And in 1972 the Securities and Exchange Commission told how Penn Central officers used "insider information" to unload their stock in the company before it fell apart in 1970.

So human beings had their part to play in the ruin of the railroads and the related crisis of the cities. And the subsidy decisions were reached in a maze of government offices. We do not know—and probably never will know—the detailed history of the lobbying which produced such problems for American society. What is clear is that the decisions were made by competing corporate groups fighting over subsidy dollars. The railroaders were clearly no match for the truckers, the airlines and the pipeline owners. One might be tempted to interpret the victory of the latter as the triumph of more advanced technology over the retrograde railroads—only in Japan and Europe, where other political decisions were made about trains, that technology was, and is, extremely modern.

But how, then, claim that the transportation decisions which did so much to subvert the older cities were "structural" in character? Isn't the process just described one of old-fashioned political infighting? Part of the answer has already been presented in the summary statement in chapter 1. In a society where corporations are in control of the major investment decisions, government will, in almost every situation, defer to the priorities of the elite minority which thus commands the essential levers of economic power in a modern economy. In the case at hand, it was not structurally determined that the railroad management would be as inept as it was. Moreover, factors not immediately related to the domestic economy were at work: Eisenhower justified the initial highway program in the name of national defense and Cold War politics.

But what is unmistakably structural in these transportation decisions was that they were made according to corporate priorities and without regard to social cost, most dramatically, the social cost of the destruction of cities and the immiseration of millions of people in them.

This thoughtlessness is coherent in the sense that it systematically excludes the human and social from its calculations. Such ignorance, as Gunnar Myrdal has observed, is never random. From the corporate point of view it is functional; it is cruelly dysfunctional from the vantage point of men and women living in a deteriorating environment.

This structural character of the nation's transportation decisions can be seen in an area which is usually presented as the domain of "free will," par excellence. It is often argued that the American people are "in love" with cars and that the huge highway investments are nothing more sinister than politicians responding to the demands of their constituents. There is a half-truth and a huge falsehood in that thesis. Given the alternatives, which are in considerable measure shaped by government action, people will "freely" choose what seems to be best in the possible world. If they are offered inferior public transport or private cars, they will voluntarily opt for the latter if they can. In a sense, their choice is predetermined by what is available, and what is available is a political construct, not an economic or technological "fact."

This process then becomes self-reinforcing. As Fred

Hirsch put it, ". . . as public transportation deteriorates, we are given an extra incentive to use our own private mode of transport which in turn results in further deterioration of public vis-à-vis private transportation." So government policy sets in motion a self-fulfilling prophecy: that the American is somehow ethnically obsessed by the automobile and that Washington must build highways to satisfy this vehicular libido. Only that "American" psychology has clearly been molded by the narrow range of choices offered the people. It is the product of a politically engendered necessity, not of individual freedom. During the severe gasoline shortages in some areas in 1979, people flooded back to whatever mass transit was available. That was not a psychic transformation; it was a response to a new reality.

The investment in highways, then, is an obvious, if complex, example of how government policies indirectly, but systematically, undermined the economic position of once great cities. Tax policy is another case in point though it is not as simple as some believe.

In June of 1977, Daniel Patrick Moynihan of New York made a major speech in the Senate. At first glance, Moynihan's analysis would seem to be identical with the one presented now. Talking of New York he said, ". . . our decline has come about as the largely unintended, but nonetheless direct and palpable, consequence of the policies of the Federal government." Using recent figures, Moynihan then argued that New York State paid $10.6 billion more to Washington in federal taxes than it received in federal expenditures. And with some shrewdness, he commented that state and local taxes in New York were high because of the need to cope with problems caused by this federal drain.

Part of Moynihan's case is quite compelling. The cities of the Northeast and Midwest did not suffer simply from the indirect and complex results of federal policies. They were, in particular under Richard Nixon, directly, purposely and callously victimized. Nixon's "New Federalism"—the system of turning money back to the states and localities to use as they see fit rather than to earmark it for federally mandated programs—had the effect of penalizing the big cities. Between 1968 and 1975, the share of the federal dollar going to those metropolitan areas declined by 20 percent. In 1968, 62.2 percent of federal grants for cities went to those with more than 500,000 population; in 1975, 44.3 percent. And cities with less than 100,000 inhabitants increased their percentage during the same period, from 20.3 percent to 32.8 percent.

And during those Nixon years the federal programs that did remain intact were, in Robert Wood's marvelous phrase, administered by the "true disbelievers." It is no accident that funds were cut and programs sabotaged in big cities with Democratic electorates (including a concentration of blacks, who had voted more solidly against Nixon than any other constituent of the traditional Democratic coalition). That was done out of political malice and it does not require a sophisticated analysis to recognize that fact.

But even though Moynihan does grasp at least some of these trends—as a member of the Nixon administration from 1969 to 1971 he can hardly be expected to emphasize the role of his onetime leader in creating the catastrophes he now rails against—he oversimplifies and understates them in a way that bears very significantly on positive action. It is because of this last fact that I want to examine his analysis carefully. (I am not even going into other objectionable parts of Moynihan's speech, like the attack on environmentalism or the assertion that Washington has a "doctrinaire dedication" to free trade.)

To begin with, the very concept of comparing federal tax contributions with federal expenditures tends to be somewhat gross. As *Business Week* pointed out in 1977, Washington has been spending more money in the Northeast and Middle West in recent years. The problem is that the stepped-up expenditures represent stopgap and disaster aid which do nothing to change the structural disadvantages of the area, while the investments in, say, the Rocky Mountain states are in capital projects with permanent federal payrolls. That, however, would not be a decisive critique of Moynihan if the rest of his analysis were sound. It isn't, and the failure to make careful discriminations which was just described is a symptomatic flaw.

Moynihan sees only the consequences of direct federal expenditures. He does not see the "side effects" of programs which cannot be measured in dollar inputs. He also does not focus on tax expenditures, i.e., that multibillion-dollar hidden budget in which the government gives money to people and corporations by relieving them of the obligation of paying taxes they would have otherwise owed. Thus, *Business Week* was quite right to say "Carter's 1978 tax proposals on the investment tax credit actually do far more damage to the fundamental economic viability of the city than all the special tax credits, grants, loans proposed by the Urban and Regional Policy Group can undo." That proposal extends the tax credit to structure as well as machinery, i.e., it provides another incentive (worth more than $2 billion in foregone revenues in 1978) for companies to move. It is not an expenditure in Moynihan's calculus. Yet it will affect the fate of the Northeast more than the direct and palpable outlays.

Given this analysis, Moynihan can, in effect, seek salvation in the revival of a very old politics rather than through the creation of new coalitions with innovative programs. For if the problem is simply the result of the government taking too much from the Northeast and giving too little in return, then some horse trading in the Congress, some improved formulas for federal expenditures, and the decline of the area will be stopped. Only the crisis is much, much more profound than that and Moynihan's insight into the federal role in it is much too limited.

Moreover, Moynihan's analysis leads to more and more sectional rivalries, which cannot deal with the urban crisis, rather than to national solutions. Yet the fact is, as the Rand study noted, "The Northeast and Middle West still lead the nation in employment opportunities and median household income and have smaller percentages of their population below the poverty line than other regions." That point was regularly ignored in the seventies because of a fashionable journalistic distinction between the Snow Belt and the Sun Belt, in which the former was seen as poor and the latter affluent. In reality, 62 percent of the ghetto population of the United States is in the Sun Belt, and there were more families with an inadequate income, as defined by the Bureau of Labor Statistics, in the South than in the North.

So, sectionalism is a cause of the crisis, not its solution. A former public relations officer for a corporation stresses that the "business climate is a very important factor in determining the selection of states and communities in which to locate new plants." And the corporate respondents to a survey of the Academy for Contemporary Problems told how the "spirit of partnership" between government and business in the South was a factor in determining their plant location decisions. So it is that there have been fierce competitions between communities to see which one could offer the most inducements to capital.

This process, it should be noted, is international too. In 1978, the provinces of Ottawa and Quebec in Canada were competing with the state of Ohio for a General Motors plant, and in 1979, France, Austria and Portugal were matching subsidies to see which country would lure Ford to set up a new operation. To hide the reality—in which business sees how much tax money it can get for "risk" capital—it is often said that it is the greedy workers who price themselves out of the labor market. However, the Academy for Contemporary Problems discovered that it was not the wages which created the differential between North and South within the United States—wages per $100 of profit were about the same—but the total labor cost, including unemployment and workmen's compensation. That gives rise to a particularly antisocial competition: states and municipalities vie with one another in meanness.

But when all is said and done, the Academy concluded, there is "no net gain to the national economy and, not too infrequently, net near-term losses to the gaining as well as losing communities because of foregone benefits and added cost." The reality, then, is much more complex than Moynihan suggests and the solutions must therefore be much more radical than his. Yet, for all the complications, the devastating impact of tax policy upon the older cities is unmistakable. Direct federal expenditures, particularly in the Nixon-Ford years, discriminated against the urban centers directly, both in the sum spent and in the way in which it was invested. The rotting cities got disaster relief; the other regions, productive government investment. Tax expenditures, particularly those which cheapened new investment, gave corporations an incentive to move out of decaying regions rather than to refurbish their plant there. And state and local governments engaged in a battle without victors in which the older cities were the most severely vanquished.

A similar analysis could be made of at least three other areas of federal policy but there is no point in going into any detail since the patterns parallel those in transportation and taxes. Federal agricultural policy was, and is, oriented toward agribusiness and has provided subsidies for eliminating agricultural labor by mechanization, a process which also made small farmers noncompetitive and eventually drove them out of business. All of this had the result of uprooting a huge rural population which had been systematically undereducated and of driving millions into the big cities precisely when they were no longer centers of new opportunities. Puerto Rican development policy had a similar outcome.

Second, the very possibility of suburbia is a federal creation. As a 1973 congressional study noted, the most "significant achievements" of Washington in the housing area had to do with building a subsidized system of finance and mortgage support. It is literally true that the exodus from the big cities would have been impossible without this development. It is also true that the distribution of population and production in the United States was consequently a result of planners' choices—though no one spoke of the plan—rather than of impersonal forces.

Third, energy policy is the most complicated case in point. As chapter 2 summarized, federal import quotas and tax subsidies, as well as a supply which was rigged by oil state governments in cooperation with Washington, poured billions of tax dollars into the creation of a wasteful energy economy which was most prodigal, at the public expense, precisely in the areas of new growth. The freeway culture of the Southwest was one spin-off from this system in which the government followed the priorities of oil corporations to the detriment of the public good. In the summer of 1978, the costliness of this exercise in urban antiplanning became apparent. Smog alerts in the Los Angeles area were so numerous that business lost $200 million. Corporation executives even speculated that the problem might reach a "third-stage alert," which would involve $100 million a day in lost wages alone.

When these brief summaries of agricultural, housing and energy policy are added to the more extensive documentation about taxes and transportation, the proposition with which this section began is confirmed. The destruction of great American cities was not the result of economic "forces" acting autonomously and independent of the human will. Rather, those forces operated in, and were significantly shaped by, an environment created by political decisions which were systematically and coherently thoughtless as far as social cost and consequence were concerned. And since that is the case, since we are dealing with choices and not necessities, it is possible to propose a much better way of designing and building America.[3]

IV

America desperately needs pro-urban legislation already proposed and supported by a large, but not yet, effective, coalition. That part of a positive program is not

radical, but an extension and deepening of liberal principles to which the country already gives lip service. But
then there must also be significant structural innovation:
an urban and land-use plan as an integral part of national
economic planning.

Before detailing these generalities, some extremely
important caveats are in order. Only when these have
been stated will it be possible to turn to both the liberal
and radical measures which are required if the nation is
to reverse the catastrophic patterns of municipal destruction in the postwar period.

To begin with, the point is not to restore, or romanti-
cize, the cities that have been destroyed. What is past is
past, and even if it took place in outrageous fashion there
is no going back. Even more to the point, the neighborhoods which were ruined were often miserable places.
The South Bronx before the devastation of recent years
was hardly a model community and had it been obliter-
ated as part of a plan which respected both human and
environmental values, that would have been a gain. But
of course what actually happened was that a merely depressed area was turned into a disaster zone. So in many
—but by no means all—cases, what will be proposed is the
creation of new communities, not the rehabilitation of the
old.

There is another reason for emphasizing this point.
America needs more production if it is to meet its obligation to its own people and to the rest of the world. So opposition to a pseudoprogress which makes gains only
because intolerable social costs are imposed upon vulnerable people is not a rejection of economic growth per se.
And since, for all the indignities suffered by the Northeast
and Midwest, those regions are still better off than, say,
the Deep South, one is in favor of new industry developing
the backward areas. But that must be done as part of a
national plan in which all regions can win rather than as
now, following an antiplan in which everyone loses.

That last goal is extremely ambitious. Growth is not
the problem. Indeed it is a precondition for any solutions

if, but only if, it is democratically controlled. For that reason there must be a word of caution which challenges two of the most popular, and very misleading, liberal analogies of the times. Our urban problems are not going to be solved by a "Marshall Plan for the cities." And they will not be overcome by the kind of mobilization used to put astronauts on the moon.

The Marshall Plan was one of those rare instances in which a sweeping government initiative was announced and then put quickly into practice. Small wonder that people who have not carefully examined its history think it provides some magical formula for storming a complex problem. At the end of World War II, European capitalism had been all but leveled. There were hunger and misery and, in Italy and France, mass Communist movements which seemed to be on the eve of an insurrectionary seizure of power. And yet, for all the physical ruin, there was a skilled, modern population; a culture which had pioneered the capitalist mode of social organization; a political structure which, if profoundly shaken, was still intact. So the chief problem was material. If the monies could be found to build, or rebuild, factories, all the other components of a modern economy were in existence.

The money was forthcoming, not the least because of Cold War fears of Communist take-over. To be sure, the funds were spent in a sophisticated conservative way— the point was to restore European capitalism and to head off, not simply Communism, but radical democratic change as well—but there still was a remarkable commitment and it worked. It is interesting to know that one reason for the success was that American law required the European recipients to plan, i.e., to do what American lawmakers abhor at home. The moon shots were not at all as complicated as the Marshall Plan, in great measure because there were no people—and therefore no politics —on the moon. Getting from earth to space was primarily an engineering problem.

The cities of the Northeast and Midwest—and the depressed areas in what is euphemistically called the Sun

Belt—are not the Europe of 1945–46 or the moon. Dealing with their problems demands solving complex economic, social, political and cultural issues. Mere money is not enough. As was noted earlier, the federal funds going to the big cities increased in the seventies, not because something was being done but because the government decided to socialize some of the costs of urban disintegration. A personal anecdote might make this very important point clearer.

In 1964, I spent fourteen days working day and night with the task force, chaired by Sargent Shriver, which developed the original plan for Lyndon Johnson's "War on Poverty." The very first time I met Shriver I told him that the president was only providing "nickels and dimes" for the task. "Oh, really," Shriver responded, "but I haven't ever spent a billion dollars before. Have you?" I was properly chastened for not having understood the value of the considerable monies which were being invested in the program. But as time went on, I realized that there was a deficit which was more important than insufficient funds: if the president had provided $10 billion, the antipoverty planners would not have been sure how to spend it. America, I would argue, has been, and still is, running a programmatic deficit which is more serious than the federal debt.

Therefore I see two broad problems in defining a strategy for cities. There is the task of mobilizing a political coalition effective enough to carry through the necessary program—and the task of defining that program. That second part of the challenge is best served by a candid admission that there is no single answer, no miraculous Marshall Plan or moon shot for the cities. There are some obvious incremental reforms; there are some clear principles for more radical innovation; but there is much that is tentative and experimental. A humility in the presence of this complexity is not, in this case, a "spiritual" virtue unconnected with daily reality; it is the political precondition of being able to do anything at all.

The first measures which would begin to do justice to

urban America are not, however, basic new departures. Almost all of them are already part of the program of the democratic Left and have been so for a long time. Too long a time.

One series of changes might be grouped together under the concept of making the nation whole. The United States pays a high price in economic and social dislocation for its federal system. It is precisely the existence of so many different political jurisdictions that makes it possible for them to compete with one another in antisocial policies. Therefore it is crucial that we abolish these differentials. There are four areas in which the case for such action is particularly compelling: poverty, taxes, health policy and corporate plant location.

The case for a national poverty policy is so persuasive that even Richard Nixon, who did so much to harm the big cities, recognized it when he proposed to federalize welfare mimimums in the Family Assistance Plan. As the analysis has already made clear, one source of the poverty problem in New York, Detroit, St. Louis and many other cities is that they have become custodial centers—reservations—for poor people uprooted from the fields of the South, in part because of the perversities of federal agricultural programs. There are similar interconnections in almost all of the American economic underworld, which is a national phenomenon. Indeed, it is also international, as a city like Los Angeles has learned in recent years when the burgeoning population and miseries of Mexico began to flow across the border.

Under the present system, the cities with the most humane welfare programs are made to bear a disproportionate burden of miseries from other parts of the country. Yet, a major and federalized program, food stamps, has demonstrated that a system of equal benefits for all in the nation can work out very well in practice. It is also of considerable moment that a program for federalizing welfare levels would not only help the big cities which are the focus of this chapter. It would also bring even more assistance to the South, which has a higher percentage of its population in poverty, than to the Northeast and Midwest. Indeed, the Southern reactionaries fought the Nixon Family Assistance Plan precisely because they were fearful that it would do too much for the black and white poor and therefore subvert an economy based on cheap labor (and therefore on economic backwardness). Thus, the demand for the federalization of antipoverty financing is truly national in impact and provides the basis for bringing together the people of the big cities and the poor and low-paid workers of the (misnamed) "Sun Belt."

Tax policy is a similar case in point. Tax inducements, we have seen, are one of the chief arenas of competition for states competing in lower social standards. And yet, as *The New York Times* reported in 1978, it is not at all clear that these legal bribes really motivate business to move into an area. So these tax inducements may or may not be the prime reason for corporations irresponsibly leaving one area and moving to another; but they most certainly cost the states and municipalities offering them foregone revenues, and they contribute to tax injustice in general.[4]

The ideal solution in this area is probably too radical for the foreseeable future. (It also relates to the issue of wealth distribution discussed in much greater detail in the last chapter.) A truly progressive federal income tax is, potentially, the best source of all governmental funds. All other taxes—including levies on corporations, which tend to be passed on to consumers—are reactionary by comparison, and subject to the kind of manipulations that have been described here. Ideally, a progressive income tax should be the *only* tax in the entire nation. All other levies—Social Security, corporate taxes, property taxes, sales taxes—should be abolished. Washington would then return to states and localities monies that it collected on the basis of a formula weighted for poverty and other social problems as well as for population. The basic mechanism is no more visionary than that proposed in Nixon's New Federalism, with one extremely important amendment: the proposal depends crucially on making the income tax base genuinely progressive.

This proposal goes squarely against the major—and reactionary—trend of the recent past. Between 1953 and 1975 the average family's federal income tax went up by 26.3 percent—but it paid 436.4 percent more in Social Security levies, and 553.3 percent more in state and local income taxes. Social Security is notoriously regressive and in 1974 state and local taxes cost a family with $5000 a year 11.3 percent of that sum and a $50,000-a-year family, 7.8 percent. So the radical reform urged here would, among many other things, make the tax system more just as well as eliminating the ruinous tax wars between the regions.

If that is too ambitious a program for immediate passage, there are important steps that can be taken in this direction. Unemployment and workmen's compensation payments can be federalized, with uniform national benefits. Social Security and health programs can more and more be financed by general revenues from progressive taxes. States can be given federal inducements to adopt progressive state income taxes, as Congressman Solarz has urged. In all of these cases—and most dramatically when one talks of a single, progressive federal income tax —measures which would benefit the cities by eliminating the tax wars between the regions would also help the majority of people outside of the Northeast and Midwest.

The third plank of a program to make America one nation is national health. That, obviously, is something which is not simply important for the cities. Indeed, it could probably be called the single most significant legislative proposal being made by the democratic Left today. Clearly, as chapter 2 showed, national health is a critically urgent priority in and of itself. However, it also has a component which touches very importantly upon the cities. In New York, for instance, the municipal payments for health care were a major factor in the fiscal crisis of the mid-seventies.

Fourth. Limitations must be placed on the right of corporations to leave an area without any thought of the social consequences of their actions. A bill originally proposed by then Senator Walter Mondale and by Congressman William Ford takes some first steps in this direction. Under its provisions, any major corporation proposing to move a plant or office would have to give three years' notice. Its plans would then be reviewed by and even subjected to public discussion and review. If it were found that the departure was not economically justified, then various federal benefits—investment tax credits, accelerated depreciation, a deduction for the cost of moving—would be denied. If the decision was economically justified, some measures of support for the affected regions would automatically come into play.

This is only a first step. It concedes the right of major corporations to move on an individual calculus, insisting only that there be some demonstration of economic and social rationality when that is done. But as long as the corporations are behaving in their normal, profit-maximizing way, they will devote all of their energies and talents to subverting any such interference with their freedom to be irresponsible. The grim history of business capture of regulatory agencies speaks for itself in this regard. Corporate egotism might, however, be further restrained if one went a major step beyond the Mondale-Ford bill and legislated employee and public representation on the boards of directors of all major companies. If those groups had a majority on the board, one would be speaking of a major change in American society moving in a clearly socialist direction. But short of such a transformation, it would be valuable to have employee and public directors who, even if in a minority, could break the cloak of secrecy which now surrounds the profoundly social decisions of the elite in private boardrooms.

So there are ways to make America whole, like federalizing poverty programs, health and taxes and restricting the right of major corporations to make unilateral, and antisocial, decisions about plant location. These measures have, to one degree or another, been on the agenda of the mainstream democratic Left for some years and they do not involve any radical shift in the organization of the society. By moving in the direction of a truly united nation, they would help the majority of people in every section of the country—and they would particularly aid the great cities which have been injured by the fragmentation of American social and economic life. But even these modest reforms will only work if full employment, the precondition of all social progress, is achieved. Indeed, building decent communities for all Americans—whether rehabilitating the old or creating the new—is one of the essential tasks which makes full employment possible.

Still, all of the proposals up until now are, in a sense, negative. That is, they seek to deal with the perverse governmental priorities which wreaked so much havoc in the great cities; they would keep us from acting destructively. But important as that is, it is only the beginning of a beginning. Clearly, there must be positive proposals to build human environments which are not only much better than the urban lunarscape of a South Bronx, but which also end an energy-wasteful and alienated suburban sprawl.

That means there must be national urban and land-use planning.

That the political Right is critical of such a notion goes without saying. But there are also significant, and even useful, objections from the Left. Analysts like Jane Jacobs have argued that spontaneously evolved, sloppy neighborhoods are more humanly functional than the grandiose vision of planners. The bulldozers of the "urban renewal" movement of the fifties and sixties, they said, tore down vibrant communities to make way for express highways (leading to suburbia) and revived "downtowns" as isolated enclaves of profitable department stores, shops and office buildings surrounded by slums and empty lots.

There is considerable truth in this indictment.

As the National Commission on Urban Problems—chaired by the distinguished liberal Paul Douglas of Illinois—put it in 1968: ". . . over the last decade, government action through urban renewal, highway programs, demolitions on public housing sites, code enforcement and other programs has destroyed more housing for the poor than government at all levels has built for them." And yet, Jane Jacobs's theories overgeneralized the evidence. The charm of the old neighborhoods was romanticized; the social problems and the dilapidation were skimmed over. More to the point, Jacobs's basic analysis rested on a nostalgia that has no future. It was not the city planners and architects who made such a shocking mess of the great cities, though they sometimes did commit arrogant errors. The massive, and interpenetrating, trends of government policy and economic and technological change described in the last section were the core of the problem. That sorry past tells us something very important about what is to come.

If one relies on spontaneity against planning, the "spontaneity" of corporations, aided and abetted by the government, will continue to prevail. There will be a coherent and antisocial thoughtlessness, not the creativity of families in neighborhoods; the human dimension, which rightly concerns people like Jane Jacobs, will be purposely ignored. But, then, it is not necessary to counterpose a Plan, taken as the abstract decree of an insensitive bureaucrat, to the face-to-face relations of the living community. More and more, those face-to-face relations will only survive if truly democratic planning provides a life-sustaining context for them. The Bedford-Stuyvesant restoration in Brooklyn is a case in point.

In the mid-sixties, the Bedford-Stuyvesant section of Brooklyn was on the well-greased road to economic and sociological hell. The white middle class which once lived in attractive brownstones had long since departed. The blacks, who had come during the Depression and found jobs in the Brooklyn Navy Yard during World War II, now lived in a deteriorating neighborhood with bleak employment prospects. A 1967 New York University study said, "Bedford Stuyvesant is more depressed and impaired than Harlem—i.e., fewer unified families, more unemployment, lower incomes, less job history . . ."

At this point, Senator Robert Kennedy became interested in Bedford-Stuyvesant. His plan was to use federal monies to stimulate investment and to tap the energy of the people in the community. He got a community development law passed and mobilized the support of the conscientious rich in New York: Thomas Watson of IBM, William Paley of CBS, Benno Schmidt of J. H. Whitney, George Moore of First National City Bank. And in a series of tumultuous meetings, he managed to put together a community-based organization to run the project.

Kennedy was murdered in 1968 but his plans were carried out. The result is extremely instructive with regard to the potential, and the limits, of restoring older neighborhoods. What made Bedford-Stuyvesant different—apart from the political support of the Kennedy family and its friends—was that patrimony of magnificent brownstones. Young people in the neighborhood were hired to help rehabilitate them and the streets of the area are now among the most charming in all of New York City, reminiscent of fashionable, high-rent areas like Greenwich Village and Brooklyn Heights. The Restoration Center itself, with a theater, shops, offices, an ice-skating rink, all contained within a brilliantly executed architectural design, is at the heart of the experiment. In the summer of 1977 when power failed in New York City, there was looting and burning in the areas around Bedford-Stuyvesant, most notably in the Bushwick section. But Bed-Stuy itself was remarkably calm.

However, problems begin to emerge when one looks at the attempt at economic development within Bedford-Stuyvesant. Over ten years of effort, supported by some of the most prestigious businessmen in the nation, yielded only one major plant, an IBM operation which employed four hundred workers at its original site and will have five hundred at a new location. But in order to keep IBM in the neighborhood, the Restoration Corporation had to mount a massive effort and to manipulate its many connections in places of power. So Franklin Thomas, who headed the project for its first decade, is quick to agree that it is impossible to solve the problems of a neighborhood, particularly a poor neighborhood, on the basis of its own resources.

I would generalize. Wherever possible, living communities should be restored. When, as in Bedford-Stuyvesant, there is a marvelous heritage, like the brownstones, planning must build on that fact, not obliterate it. When, as in the South Bronx, no such physical heritage exists, it may well be necessary to begin all over and/or to disperse at least some of the people in completely new communities. But in either case, there is no alternative to national planning—except more of the antisocial plan that we have been so carefully and so thoughtlessly following for several decades now.

If the spontaneity of neighborhoods, in and of itself, can contribute to, but not solve, the urban crisis, trickle down, the ideology of the American rich in this and almost every other area, has almost nothing to offer.

In 1977, a "key member of the White House domestic staff" started the trickle-down philosophy in a *Wall Street Journal* interview. "We presume in this administration that government simply doesn't have the resources to create long-term employments in these [older city] areas . . . So, to reverse the tide, we must find ways to make the private sector change its locational preferences. With the right kind of incentives—insurance, low interest loans and other things we're working on—we are convinced we can induce the private sector to make business decisions it would not make without these incentives."

That theory has been behind all government housing programs since the Taft Ellender Wagner Act of 1949—and it has not worked. It was a centerpiece of Great Society efforts in the sixties, and it didn't work, even though many major corporations thought for a while that they might make big profits by acting with a social conscience (as chapter 4 detailed). For instance, in Lyndon Johnson's 1968 State of the Union address, he talked of a "new partnership" between government and industry. It had already been tried. In March of 1967 a program was announced to put 25,000 to 40,000 slum unemployed to work in six months and to find work for between 100,000 and 150,000 in fifty cities in the course of the fiscal year. Nine months later, this effort had produced 6900 jobs—and 6600 people had completed the program but did not find work. So *The Wall Street Journal* called the new program "failure warmed over" and noted, quite accurately, that the incentives were not attractive enough to get business to go into the slums—to put plants there or find people there.

One can generalize. The profound structural harm done to the cities of the Northeast and Midwest—their people and their industrial infrastructure—has put them at such a disadvantage that the federal incentives required to get the corporations to come back would have to be so massive that direct, planned expenditures would be a much more efficient, and certain, way of proceeding. One scholarly study rightly spoke of the "devil's dilemma" which confronts cities trying to woo business back: ". . . they must adopt spending policies which adjust services to the reality of a diminishing population and resource base while enhancing their attractiveness to private investment." That is, the metropolis must cut back on the people and spend for corporations. That is not only an unsolvable dilemma, it is a program for meanness.

But then, even when a neighborhood seems to reverse direction, moving from decay to revitalization, that is not necessarily an unambiguous good. It may be a case of "trickle up." In 1978, a National Urban Coalition study showed that the "new pioneers" who were coming into run-down areas and renovating them were often middle-income families who displaced the poor, and particularly the aging poor, when they begin to restore the broken-down houses. In theory, when buildings become decrepit enough, they are supposed finally to become available to those at the bottom of the society. In practice—and the Georgetown section of Washington, an ex-slum turned into a fashionable, high-rent district is the most famous example—the process fairly often makes structurally sound housing in the central city cheap enough for professionals. Here again, the market faithfully transmits the fundamental inequities of the society.

So the only way that the nation will get a decent, livable urban environment is through national planning. That one sentence is the core of the final basic proposal of this chapter. To be sure, there will be some few details added to it, mainly suggestions about possible directions for that planning. But the truly radical point is to persuade America to decide that it has to plan and to begin to do so. For if one is committed to democratic planning, if it is of the essence that decisions about urban life that have been made behind people's backs be brought into the political arena, it is impossible to predict what the people will freely choose for themselves. What is critical is that they do choose. That will take time. One is talking about several years, perhaps five years, of examining the complex interconnections between job location, transportation, energy innovation and the rehabilitation, or creation, of livable cities.

The truly radical first step is to establish the process whereby the next steps can be taken. That should involve the society at every level. The president and the departments of the executive branch should make their proposals for the urban and land-use future; a Joint Congressional Committee should hold hearings; there should be inputs from people in communities across the nation, and any significant group of citizens should be given the technical resources to develop their own plan(s) or counterplan(s). (This important point will be expanded in chapter 10.) But if one is looking for the widest possible consensus, that does not mean that this mountain should labor to produce a traditional American mouse: a statement of innocuous "goals." The point is to produce legislation elaborating a plan and committing funds to it over a substantial period of time.

This chapter has already suggested a few of the directions such a planning process might take. For instance, the rehabilitation of existing neighborhoods—but not only for middle-class "pioneers"—is an obvious priority. So, too, is the concept of a certain decentralization of the population. That notion has acquired a bad name since it has been urged in a callous fashion and seems simply to perpetuate the existing trends toward urban sprawl. Thus, one expert, Jay Forrester of MIT, told an interviewer that it was necessary to demolish low-income housing in the central cities in order to get the poor to leave. His argument was that federal spending would simply not motivate the middle class to come back, which has some real truth to it. But when asked what would happen to the poor thus exiled from their usual slums, Forrester replied that this was a question that "the model is not designed to answer."

That cruel indifference—which has also surfaced in proposals to "shrink" New York City—is obviously not what I have in mind when I speak of decentralization. One may want to demolish housing in areas where it is not, and cannot become, viable; one may want to reduce population density for reasons of simple humanity. In *The Other America*, one of the central points I made with regard to the ghettos was that they were impossibly jammed with people. But one can only proceed in this fashion if clear and prior plans have been made to relocate people to much better places.

Strangely enough, one of the best statements of this theme was made by a conservative, former President Dwight D. Eisenhower, writing in the *Reader's Digest* in 1968. In keeping with the preoccupations of the late sixties when urban riots were common, Eisenhower's analysis was entitled, "To Insure Domestic Tranquillity." The urban crisis can't be solved, he said, by "stacking people vertically in new high rise apartment complexes." So density must be reduced by locating people in new towns with new jobs, mass transit facilities, and with an integrated population. There were black militants in those days who regarded such schemes as an attempt to dilute the potential political power of minorities concentrated in areas like Harlem or Chicago's South Side. Their fears were understandable, yet what has happened since—with blacks winning city hall in central cities on the verge of bankruptcy—does not really resemble "power."

Kenneth B. Clark, the black psychologist, was much closer to the truth in the late sixties when he argued that a "systematic, voluntary redistribution of ghetto populations" might well be necessary. Clearly this concept has nothing to do with the American "relocation program" of the past several decades, i.e., with moving the better off to new homes and leaving the rejects to rot in the central cities. Rather the point is, as Eisenhower grasped, to create new communities. Insofar as the private sector has engaged in building what are euphemistically called "new towns," it has simply given a European socialist name to the building of capitalist bedroom communities to which the middle and upper classes can flee at night. That, clearly, has nothing to do with what is being urged here.

However, the recent European experience is relevant to the United States. It would be foolish to suggest that the Old World has solved its urban problems, yet there is no question that it has done a better job than the United States in large measure because Europeans engage in systematic planning. In Britain, for instance, a licensing requirement has kept many plans from participating in the "Drift to the South." And in France there has been a policy of planned decentralization where tax incentives and disincentives have oriented business away from Paris and toward eight other cities.

But isn't it true that the new cities and towns of Europe have had problems with overly neat, unimaginative planning which left the human dimension out? Of course. Ada Louise Huxtable, the former architecture critic of *The New York Times*, wrote in 1978 of the "monumental superkitsch" which sometimes appeared in the French new towns. The decentralization program, Huxtable wrote, had been decided upon in the late fifties; the master plan was adopted in the mid-sixties. Some of the towns were based on existing suburbs; others were built from the ground up. All of them were integrated into permanent green spaces and designed to counter the "normal" tendency of development to move to the west of Paris. The result, Huxtable wrote, was "future shock," communities without soul.

In part, that judgment rested upon the kind of romanticism which is also found in Jane Jacobs. "It may be," Huxtable said, "that a city is simply an act of God rather than an act of architecture," a fact incarnated in Paris, "the most beautiful and urbane city in the world." But Paris was not, and is not, an act of God. It was in part a product of the *ancien régime* which created marvelous public spaces for kings and nobles which were taken over by the Revolution. It was also a consequence of the work of a dictatorial city planner, Baron Georges Haussmann, who was at least as autocratic, and much more tasteful, than Robert Moses. And finally, the social mix of Paris was a function of one of the most class-ridden societies in Europe.

And yet, if Huxtable's history is bad, her warning should be taken to heart. It is not easy to create a living social organism consciously. There will be mistakes in the process, of course. But, and this is to be emphasized, none of them will be as horrendous as the South Bronx. And, second, there is no alternative in America to the South Bronx unless the nation engages in planning on a European scale *as a first step.* The trends, the supposedly impersonal economic forces, can be, and are, shaped by conscious political decisions. Our problem is not that we have been intervening into automatic processes but that we have been doing so with a minimum of social decency and plain intelligence. As Jay Forrester put it, "Many people recoil at the thought of anyone's designing a social system. But we have no choice. We already live in social systems that have been designed—by national or state constitutions, laws, tax regulations and traditions."

America has been living a myth for decades. In the name of individualistic choice the nation has submitted itself to economic and technological forces much more authoritarian and inhuman than most bureaucracies—to a kind of Adam Smithian Stalinism. A society which thought it was opposing planning followed a rigid, coherent and antisocial governmental plan which maximized corporate profit and the welfare of the rich and destroyed great cities in the process. The results have been most destructive for the poor and the minorities, of course, but every American suffered.

There are, this chapter has clearly demonstrated, no easy ways in which to resolve a failure which required billions of dollars of federal spending to effect. But a new beginning could be made when it is discovered that democratic planning of where and how we live is the only hope for freedom in the late twentieth century. If we do not act in this way, then the Appalachian pattern of systemic decay, which has already spread from the mountains to a third of the nation, will become the norm for the entire country. It sounds utterly farfetched to speak of the United States of Appalachia as a serious possibility in the middle distance. But then, if one had told New Yorkers in 1970 that major portions of the city were to suffer an Appalachian fate, they would have scoffed. Only it did happen here.

Notes

1. Auletta: *The Streets Were Paved with Gold*, pp. 253, 39, 218. Caro: *The Power Broker*, pp. 928–29. Urban theory: Don Martindale, p. vi. Jobs in New York: Bureau of Labor Statistics, *The New York Labor Market*. Northeast income: Vaughan, tables 2-5, p. 31. Chicago: "How Federal Policies Are Hurting the Cities," *Business Week*, December 19, 1977. New England: George Sternlieb and James A. Hughes, in *Toward a National Urban Policy*, pp. 44–45.

2. Sternlieb and Hughes: Op. cit. supra, pp. 1–3. Rand: Vaughan, p. 9. Northeastern policy makers: *Revitalizing the Northeast Economy*, p. 40. JEC: Quoted in Vaughan, p. 10. CEA, 1968: p. 139. *London Economist:* "What Next New York?" March 25, 1978.

3. Rand: Vaughan, p. xiii. Department of Transportation: *A Prospectus for Change in the Freight Railroad Industry*, p. 102. *London Economist:* "At Last an Urban Policy," April 7, 1978. Sternlieb and Hughes:

Op. cit. supra, p. 9. Railroad subsidies: Harrington, "How to Run a Railroad." User taxes: Ibid.; Department of Transportation, op. cit. supra, p. 106. Penn Central: Albert Karr, "Operation Pothole," *The Wall Street Journal,* January 31, 1978. Norfolk and Western: Harrington, op. cit. supra. Kennedy: *Congressional Record,* May 18, 1977, p. S7842. Hirsch: *Social Limits to Growth,* p. 18. Moynihan: *Congressional Record,* February 27, 1977, S10829 ff. Federal grants: Pechman, ed., *Setting National Priorities: The 1978 Budget,* pp. 19 and 295. Wood: *Toward a National Urban Policy,* p. 37. *Business Week:* "How Federal Policies . . . ," op. cit. supra. Rand: Vaughan, p. ix. Sun Belt: David C. Perry and Alfred J. Watkins, "Saving the Cities, the People, the Land," *The New York Times,* February 27, 1978. Public relations: Lindblom, p. 78. Academy for Contemporary Problems: *Revitalizing the Northeast Economy,* pp. 53–54. Canada: "A U.S.–Canada Rivalry," *Business Week,* July 24, 1978. France: Paul Lewis dispatch, *The New York Times,* March 22, 1979. Academy: Op cit. supra, pp. 160 ff. Net gain: Ibid., p. 105. Congressional committee: Quoted in Castells, pp. 386–87. Los Angeles smog: "The Billowing Cost of LA Smog," *Business Week,* August 7, 1978.

4. *The New York Times* on tax policy: "States Wage War for New Industry," NYT News Service, *St. Louis Post-Dispatch,* July 30, 1978. State and local taxes: Advisory Commission on Intra-Governmental Relations, table 27, p. 44 and table 28, p. 45. Harrington: *Newsletter of the Democratic Left.* Jane Jacobs: *The Death and Life of Great American Cities,* p. 67. New York University study: Harrington, "The South Bronx Shall Rise Again," p. 78. White House staffer: James M. Perry, "Mr. Carter's Urban Plan," *The Wall Street Journal,* August 9, 1977. LBJ plan: James Gannon, "LBJ's Job Plan," *The Wall Street Journal,* January 22, 1968. Devil's dilemma: *Revitalizing the Northeast Economy,* pp. 136–37. National Urban Coalition: *City Neighborhoods in Transition,* passim. Forrester: quoted in Kain, p. 242. Clark: "The Negro and the Urban Crisis," p. 135. Europe: Peter Hall, "National Urban Policy in Europe," in *Toward a National Urban Policy;* George Wynne, ed. Huxtable: "The New French Towns," *The New York Times.* Forrester: "Overlooked Reasons for Our Social Troubles," p. 191.

7

The Nonpeople

The eyes are organs of society as well as of the individual human being; most people see only what their times and culture permit them to see.

Poverty is an obvious case in point. In the fifties, when domestic conservatism was reinforced by the widespread conviction that criticism of America played into the hands of the Soviet enemy, the poor hardly existed in the national consciousness. In the sixties, upper-class conscience in the Kennedy administration was awakened by the mass movement of blacks led by Martin Luther King, Jr. When Kennedy was murdered, the New Deal alumnus Lyndon Johnson took up the theme and poverty was officially rediscovered. In the seventies one could not simply return to the social blindness of the fifties—the sixties made that impossible—so sophisticated analysts had to define the poor out of existence. This was difficult given the obvious fact of the ruins in the central cities where so many of them lived. But it was done.

This is not to suggest a callous conspiracy to falsify the computer printouts. The social development of the national eyesight is a more subtle process than that. Rather, the vantage point of vision was changed. Government focused on inflation and capital formation rather than on full employment and the plight of the most vulnerable citizens. From that perspective the world looks different than it did in the sixties. The lights and the shadows trade places. Then there are crass mechanisms at work, too. Those who proved that poverty was an issue were heeded and rewarded during the Kennedy-Johnson years; those who showed that it was an exaggerated issue earned the gratitude of the powers that be in the Nixon-Ford, and even the Carter, years. If the fact of misery could be rendered invisible, then mean-spirited policies, which were deemed necessary for practical reasons, could be followed with good conscience.

Consider a revealing incident in 1978 as an illustration of this trend. Late that year the results of several Health, Education and Welfare studies on guaranteed income experiments were released. They showed that people who were paid whether they worked or not worked less and that people who were supported at 90 percent of the poverty "line" had a higher rate of marital breakup than ordinary families which earned their own daily bread. At this point, Senator Daniel Patrick Moynihan spoke up. He had been a member of Lyndon Johnson's antipoverty task force and, as a White House counselor, had persuaded Richard Nixon to come out for a guaranteed income in the form of the Family Assistance Program. But in 1978 he seemed to recant. "We must now be prepared to entertain the possibility that we were wrong," Moynihan said. Commentators were quick to seize upon this defection and to cite it as proof that the guaranteed income, which had once been supported by Milton Friedman, Richard Nixon and George McGovern, was an idea whose time had gone.

In fact Moynihan and everyone else overreacted to the data. The reduction in work hours was quite moderate (four hours a week) and occurred among predictable people (wives in two-income families; teenagers). And the marital breakdown figures were ambiguous since those families which had received 140 percent of the poverty line, rather than 90 percent, did not dissolve in a statistically significant number. Yet Moynihan had been quick to concede the worst possible reading of the data. Ten years earlier Moynihan himself would probably have been emphasizing the same facts which I concentrate upon.

Two days after Moynihan made his attention-getting reversal on family assistance, Henry Aaron, as an assistant secretary of HEW, offered a much more sober and serious evaluation of the new figures. "Increases in income maintenance payments for *all* low-income families with children," he said, "would not cause large reductions in work effort among prime-age men or female family heads, nor would they cause much outright withdrawal from the labor force." Moreover, if there were job creation efforts—which every Left proponent of a guaranteed income, including this writer, had insisted on for years— total hours worked would increase. And finally, Aaron said that there were "serious questions" about the family breakdown statistics as applied to any real-world welfare plan. This was a far, far cry from Moynihan's assumption that the data showed that a guaranteed income would "produce substantial reductions in work effort" and would weaken family ties.

Still, a new "truth" had been established: guaranteed incomes do not work; they are dangerous to productivity and marriage. But then this is not the only recent revelation in this area. In 1975 the Congressional Budget Office took up some ideas which had been launched by Nixon's Council of Economic Advisers and, by means of a complex argument, showed that at least half of the people defined as poor were not. Earlier Richard Nixon had convinced millions of Americans that the sixties had erred in "throwing money at problems" in permissive, ill-conceived and counterproductive programs that weakened the moral fiber of the nation. All of these theories, I will show, do not stand up to the test of rigorous criticism. Yet they are the lenses through which people now look at American society.

The first task of analysis, then, is to restore the country's eyesight, to allow it to see the poor. I would prefer to do that in the mode of documentary, evoking the visible reality of the slums and ghettos and rural hovels. But that would not be convincing in these statistically obsessed times. So it is necessary to present the numbers and to deal with the attempts to show that the poor are hardly with us any longer. Then the related myths about the prodigality of federal programs will be disputed. With the nation's rose-tinted glasses thus removed, it will then be possible to talk about the policies which could end the outrage of poverty in the richest economy humankind has ever known.

In the process, the issue of racism will inevitably come to the fore. This does not mean that poverty is exclusively, or even primarily, a fate that afflicts the minorities. The latter are, to be sure, disproportionately poor—but white "Anglos" (non-Hispanics) are still the majority in the other America. Blacks are 12 percent of the population and 31 percent of the poor; Hispanics are 6 percent and 11 percent respectively.* Those statistics register discriminatory rates of poverty—but they still leave more than 50 percent of the poor who are neither black nor Hispanic. So poverty is not simply racism—but racism cannot be understood without relating it to its structural economic roots. This is where I take these themes in tandem.

Let us now begin to open our eyes and see the nonpeople who are poor.[1]

—— I ————————————————————

The official government definition of poverty—setting what is erroneously known as the poverty "line"—is based on money income. In fact, there are a whole series of poverty lines, which vary according to family size, rural or

* I am using official figures which will be dealt with in some detail later on. For now it should be noted that there is a systematic undercount of the poor which is probably most pronounced for Hispanics, many of whom are "undocumented" and do not want to be identified in any way by the government.

urban location and other factors. What is known as the poverty "line" is the figure for an urban family of four. It is computed by taking the cost of an "economy" food budget and multiplying it by three (a 1955 study showed a 3 to 1 ratio between food budget and total budget). For couples and single persons the multiplier is higher.

There are many people, including this writer, who feel that this method *understates* the number of the poor. It is based on the consumption patterns of 1955 and the dietary criteria of the mid-sixties. Thus, even though the numbers are adjusted to reflect inflation, they do not take into account the way adequacy should be defined upward in a growing society. This definition is obviously relative, in the sense that the American poor are well off compared to, say, the people living their lives on the streets of Calcutta. But it is hardly arbitrary since anyone who is below his or her appropriate poverty line will have to choose among necessities as this society defines them. If, however, poverty is defined as one-half of the median income or less, then the number of the poor has remained constant for the last quarter of a century.

For the moment, all the complexities of definition will be put into parentheses. Who is poor according to the official figures?

There is a familiar, pernicious stereotype as to who the poor are and it is widely believed in the United States. They are mainly black, lazy, welfare recipients who are shunning work. In point of fact, every element in this definition is wrong. In 1977, the poverty "line" for an urban family of four was $6191 (the median income for the nation was $16,010). In that year, as we have already seen, the majority of the poor were white non-Hispanics—but the poverty rate for the 18 percent of the people who were either black (12 percent) or Hispanic (6 percent) was much higher than for white "Anglos." Among the Anglos 8.9 percent were poor, while the incidence of poverty for blacks and Hispanics was 31.3 percent and 22.4 percent respectively. The other America is, in short, an integrated, but a distinctively discriminatory, place.

It is also a world in which more than half of the people are either too old or too young to work. On the official (understated) figures only 13 percent of Americans over sixty-five years of age are poor, which represents a significant gain brought about by increased Social Security benefits and Medicare. And 41 percent of the poverty population is under eighteen years of age, which is a particularly disturbing number since it shows that the poor are younger than the rest of us (only 29 percent of our people are under eighteen). The teenagers in this group are the ones who suffer the catastrophic rates of unemployment—40 percent, 50 percent, 60 percent in some ghettos and slums—and they are likely to be the mothers and fathers of the next generation of the poor. For now, however, let me simply note that the stereotype of the lazy poor is obviously contradicted by the fact that more than half of the other Americans are not even in the labor market.

But what of those who could work? Slightly less than half of poor families are headed by a worker. Almost *all* of those family heads worked during 1976—and roughly 40 percent of them worked fifty to fifty-two weeks. When one looks at husband-wife families—i.e., abstracts from one of the most problematic categories, families headed by a woman—60 percent of the men worked all year. It is true that those female-headed families—in which the woman typically has many children to take care of and few qualifications on the labor market—tend to rely on welfare. In more than half of them there are no workers at all, and less than 5 percent of those female heads of family work all year. But it is clear that these statistics represent the impact of a cruel necessity and the lack of marketable skills rather than laziness.

So the typical poor person is neither black nor lazy nor both; neither is he or she a welfare recipient. Of the impoverished who live in families (who are about 80 percent of the poor), only 38 percent are totally dependent upon public assistance. They do not receive the tremendous largesse that the public often imagines, since their mean income in 1976 was $3239—or approximately half of the poverty "line." The poor who are "unrelated individuals" are much more welfare dependent. Almost 60 percent of them receive all of their income from transfer payments —but then about two-thirds of that total are over sixty-five years of age, i.e., belong to that welfare group to which the people are most sympathetic. Adding all these numbers together, only about 50 percent of the other America is dependent on the government for all of its income.

If the poor do not conform to the popular stereotype, neither are they a permanent underclass as some left-wing analysts have suggested. In a longitudinal study of five thousand families, it was discovered that 21 percent of the total population was poor in at least one year between 1967 and 1972, but only 2.4 percent were poor in all six years. This suggests that poverty is a dynamic phenomenon with a huge "at-risk" population which moves in and out of the other America. One factor which intensifies this process is, obviously, the business cycle. In both 1973–74 and 1974–75, there were significant increases in the poverty population (by 1.3 million and 2.5 million respectively); in 1975–76, which was a time of (feeble) recovery, there was a decrease of 900,000.

Finally, this brief sketch of the characteristics of the poor as revealed by the official statistics should note some of the larger trends. Among other things these raise the question of whether the antipoverty efforts of the sixties were, as people like Richard Nixon imply, a complete failure. The answer is complex—the real dimensions of the federal programs will be treated later on—but an initial response can be made.

In 1962, when *The Other America* was published, I estimated that the poor numbered between 40 and 50 million. I reached that figure using very rough criteria and more than a little intuition. In a retrospective analysis based upon the much more sophisticated methods now in use, the Department of Commerce concluded that in 1959 (the base year for *The Other America*) there were 39,490,000 below the poverty line; using the standard of

125 percent of the line—which is nearer to reality, in my opinion—there were about 55 million poor in 1959. Later research, then, confirmed my rough approximation. In 1976, the government said, about 25 million were living in the other America on the official count, thirty-five and a half million if you took the 125 percent measure. The figures are clear enough—but they do not interpret themselves.

One way of reading the trend would be to note that more than fourteen million people had been liberated from poverty. Yet if one looks behind the figures there are some disturbing facts. There were fewer poor people in 1969 than in 1976. Significant progress began in 1962 and lasted for seven years during which there was an annual decline in the poverty population. In 1970, 1971, 1974 and 1975 the number of the poor increased; in the other years of the seventies there was a decrease, but the entire period, 1969–76 saw no significant change in the situation, only ups and downs. This emphasizes a point made earlier: that poverty is a structural problem inextricably tied up with the basic economic rhythms of American society.

One of the major successes of the Kennedy-Johnson years illuminates this point. As the jobless percentage fell between 1962 and 1969, there was a sharp decline in the poverty of families headed by a year-round worker; more than five and a half million such families were poor in 1959, about two and a half million in 1976. Two chastening comments are, however, in order. Here again the advance was made between 1959 and 1969 and there have been no real gains since. And, second, it is still an outrage that there are two and a half million families whose head works all year and yet cannot lift his or her dependents out of poverty. Moreover, for these women heads of large families who are able to work, the pay which they can obtain is, in some cases, less than the payments they receive from Aid to Families of Dependent Children. If they act according to the approved profit calculus of the society, these women will not work. And a good number do not for precisely that reason.

The other group which made significant gains during the Kennedy-Johnson years, and even continued to advance under Nixon and Ford, is composed of people over sixty-five years of age. In 1959, fully one-third of the aging were poor; in 1976, 13.2 percent. That last figure represented an improvement over 1969, the one major category where that is the case. The reason is that a Democratic Congress forced Social Security increases—and a system of indexing—upon a reluctant Nixon administration which was, however, quick to take political credit for the change once it was put into effect.

If the working poor made gains between 1962 and 1969, and the aging poor throughout the period 1959–76, the case of families headed by a woman offers pessimistic data. To be sure, the poverty *rate* in such families declined, from 40.2 percent in 1959 to 28 percent in 1976, but the total increased from 8 percent of the American population to 11 percent, and therefore the absolute numbers went up slightly between 1959 and 1976 (by about 230,000). This meant that while the other major categories were making gains, this one stagnated and therefore significantly increased its proportion of the other America. In 1959, families with a female head and no husband present were 14.9 percent of the poor; in 1976, they were 26.7 percent. Even more ominously, the number of impoverished children in such families rose sharply. In 1959, 24 percent of the children in the other America had no father in the household; in 1976, 55 percent. And one of the main reasons why such units were immune to progress even in the good years is that many of these mothers can't work and those who can need genuine full employment before their prospects on the labor market become competitive with welfare payments in the more humane states.

In all of this statistical analysis, I have been purposely making a simplifying assumption: that money income accurately defines poverty. The neoconservatives and disillusioned liberals of the seventies (who were often one and the same people) question that proposition in order to reduce the number of the poor, a theory which will be dealt with shortly. But there is another objection to my procedure which comes from the Left and is valid. Poor people lack money, of course—but they are also deficient in political power, legal defenses against charges of wrongdoing, friends, organizations and just about every aspect of social life. So even if all of these people were miraculously lifted above the poverty "line" in terms of money, that would not necessarily change their subordinate, miserable place in the society.

Still, using the sophisticated analytic tools and the improved data of recent years, we can come to an approximate definition of poverty which is almost totally at variance with popular stereotypes. The poor are by a majority white; most who are able to work do so; only half of the poor rely on public assistance for all of their income and most of those people are either too old or too young to work. In the brief period 1962–69, under the Kennedy and Johnson administrations, all major categories of the poor, except families headed by a woman, made significant, if modest, gains. Since 1969, under the Nixon and Ford administrations,* only people over sixty-five have continued to advance, mainly as a result of increases in Social Security benefits. The failure of the Nixon-Ford years to improve the position of the non-aging poor was primarily a result of the stagflation characteristics of that period.[2]

II

It is now time to take this approximation and refine it by adding some figures which demonstrate the discriminatory nature of poverty in America. Poverty is integrated —but it is also racist.

In what follows, I will focus on blacks. They are by no

* There is a considerable time lag in federal statistics. At this writing figures on the Carter administration are too fragmentary to generalize.

means the only people who suffer from the double indignity of poverty and discrimination. The poorest people in the land are the descendants of its original inhabitants, the Native Americans. The Hispanics, as we have seen, have a poverty rate three times that of "Anglos" (non-Spanish whites) and that number surely understates the problem. Given the fact that so many Mexican-Americans are undocumented, and therefore must flee the census taker, we literally do not know how many such people there are. But we do know that undocumented workers are often among the poorest of the working poor because they are afraid to bargain for themselves or engage in attention-attracting militance. There are similar problems with at least some Asian-Americans and people from the Caribbean.

But even though the discrimination mechanisms affect groups which are not black, I will focus on the latter. First, the data are most abundant in this case as a result of the civil rights struggles of the fifties and sixties. Second, the mechanisms of economic discrimination against blacks are the same ones which affect Hispanics, Native Americans, Asian-Americans and others. Since the Civil Rights Act of 1964, formal and overt discrimination has been illegal, but social and economic discrimination has been a pervasive fact. As a result of the indignities suffered under the old system of open prejudice, and also because of the time when they arrived in the urban labor market, the minorities tend to be concentrated in low-paying jobs which are particularly vulnerable to the business cycle. They are, in the classic phrase, the last hired and the first fired.

Thus, the position of blacks in 1976—which was, speaking very relatively, a "good" year of the recent past —is paradigmatic of that of all minorities. Only 25 percent of them were in white-collar occupations, and only 8.5 percent in the professional and technical jobs where the money is to be made in the white-collar category. For whites, 45 percent were white collar and 17 percent professional and technical workers. At the bottom of the social structure, in the service category where the lowest-paid workers are to be found, one discovers 12 percent of the whites and 27 percent of the blacks. It is this occupational structure which guarantees lower pay for blacks and rates of unemployment roughly twice that of whites.

Does this mean that there has been no progress at all for black Americans (and by implication for all of the late-arriving minorities)? No, it does not. But the statistics do show that the progress has been intolerably slow and became ominously ambiguous in the late seventies.

Here is how two of the leading scholars in the field, James D. Smith and Finis R. Welch, summarize the data: ". . . although by historic standards the gain of the Sixties is truly prodigious, the absolute magnitude of the change is not overwhelming." Between 1890 and 1940, the black/white ratio was stable. Then, with the full employment achieved during World War II, blacks made the most impressive gains they have ever recorded, improving their relative position by 12 percent. Between 1960 and 1972, further progress took place, but not at the rate of World War II. The black percentage of white income rose from 57 percent to 62 percent. If these percentages would persist—which will not happen if the economy remains in deep, structural trouble—then new black entrants to the labor force would be on the same footing as whites in the year 2000 and it would be 2040 before there is full racial parity.

There are, it should be noted, good reasons to think that even this slow progress will not continue. Schooling yields blacks the same earned rate of return as whites, and this has been an important avenue of upward mobility. But if, as the next chapter suggests, schooling is going to provide declining returns, particularly to college graduates, this trend could become perverse. Blacks would win college degrees in large numbers just when those degrees are devalued. At the other end of the scale, the Council of Economic Advisers' 1978 Report notes that the black teenage population is increasing much faster than whites with the results that the tighter labor markets of the mid-eighties (when the baby "bust" starts looking for jobs) will least benefit those who most need opportunities.

Indeed, some of these negative trends were at work in the seventies. In 1974, for instance, the ratio of black to white income inclined during the recession, falling back to 59.7 percent. That is a familiar enough pattern: as the "last hired and first fired," blacks, and all minorities (and women), are particularly vulnerable to the business cycle. Thus, so long as stagflation remains in force, there is an important racist consequence. But then, the black losses continued even during the "recovery" of the late seventies. In 1978, median black family income dropped to 57.1 percent—the lowest figure in twelve years. The structural racism of the American economy, which seemed to have ameliorated during the sixties, thus came back with a vengeance in the seventies and will, unless there are radical policy changes, persist in the eighties.

There is an important policy conclusion to be drawn from this analysis. Programs specifically aimed at helping minorities—affirmative action, job training, remedial education and the like—are both valuable and necessary. But the inferior position of minorities is now primarily a result of massive economic and social structures which are relatively impervious to such ameliorative programs as long as the economy functions with high rates of unemployment even in "good" times. That, as we have seen, was precisely the hallmark of the seventies, and it will characterize the eighties, too, unless there are significant changes in the society. From this perspective, full employment, which would be of enormous benefit to the white, nonethnic majority, would be of even greater worth to the minorities. It was this understanding which motivated the Black Congressional Caucus to make passage of the Humphrey-Hawkins full employment bill a central priority. Unfortunately, the version of that bill finally passed in 1978 had been seriously compromised and did not have the power of the original text. Still, there is now a legal basis for demanding full employment, something which the Employment Act of 1946 did not provide.

This, however, is not the place to discuss antipoverty
—and antiracist—policies, which will be taken up later
on. For now, the initial definition of poverty is completed
by taking account of its structurally racist features. It is,
to repeat, an integrated, but discriminatory, phenomenon.[3]

III

There are sincere, and even, good people who would
argue that the previous section is preposterous. It is, they
would say, based on statistics which fundamentally over-
state the problem. As a result, the liberals among them
add, Americans become disillusioned with government
programs because they think that all of the efforts of the
1960s did not change anything. So, they conclude, the exaggeration of the dimensions of the other America actually plays into the hands of the conservatives.

This point of view had been germinating for a long
time, but it did not really come out into the open until
1976. In that year, President Ford's Council of Economic
Advisers announced that it had serious doubts about the
poverty statistics because they did not count in the value
of in-kind income (Medicaid, food stamps) received by the
poor. Then Edgar K. Browning pursued this line of
thought in an article in the *Public Interest* and concluded: ". . . there is practically no poverty—statistically
speaking—in the United States today and indeed there
has not been for several years." Browning's essay was,
significantly, titled, "How Much More Equality Can We
Afford?" In *The New York Times*, Harry Schwartz quoted
these studies and chided the government for publishing
"misleading" figures. "Is Poverty Abolished?" Schwartz
asked.

Shortly thereafter an official federal agency, the
Congressional Budget Office (CBO), capitulated, adopting
the critics' point of view and reducing the number of poor

families by 4,275,000. It did so in the name of the liberal fear that exaggeration of the poverty problem causes disillusionment with federal efforts to cope with it. There are, the CBO argued, three levels of poverty. First—and this number is rather shocking, although the analysts did not linger over it—the "natural" workings of the American economy, uncorrected by any public programs, leave one-quarter of the people poor. If one then takes account of cash transfers, that cuts the poverty population in half and yields the official figure, according to which 13.5 percent of families were poor in 1976. However, if the cash value of in-kind goods and services received by the poor is computed and added to their actual cash income, there is a drastic reduction in their number. If Medicare and Medicaid benefits are excluded, but the other in-kind programs are counted, poor families now drop to 11.3 percent of the American total. If Medicare and Medicaid are added, the percentage goes to 8.1 percent and those 4,275,000 families miraculously disappear from the other America.

In 1978, the statistical attack upon the poor was stated at book length in Martin Anderson's *Welfare: The Political Economy of Welfare Reform in the United States.* Appropriately published under the aegis of the (Herbert) Hoover Institution, it argued that "The 'war on poverty' that began in 1964 has been won. The growth of jobs and income in the private economy, combined with an explosive increase in government spending for welfare and income transfer programs, has virtually eliminated poverty in the United States." Anderson's analysis was scholarly in superficial form and utterly polemical and tendentious in substance. It was immediately picked up by conservatives—and even by some who are not conservative—as a statement of established fact.

How, then, does one evaluate this radical—rightist—critique of the very concept of poverty?

First, the CBO's point about in-kind income is completely legitimate. There is no point in overstating the problem of poverty, not the least because, as the CBO study itself notes, that leads to the pessimistic conclusion that all governmental programs are failures. There is no question that an accurate statement of the actual conditions of the poor would take into account the value of food stamps, Medicare, Medicaid and the like. What is profoundly disturbing about the CBO analysis, however, is that it looked *only*—and much too casually—at this one possibility of an overcount of the poor and did not even mention the equally real possibilities of an undercount. This one-sided approach suggests that only those data were considered which would corroborate the conclusion that there are not nearly as many poor people as we think.

For instance, the CBO must be aware of the fact that the official definition has been under attack for years on the grounds that it sets the poverty line too low. A Health, Education and Welfare study showed that, by raising the multiplier in the poverty definition from three times the cost of the food component to five times, and by using a "low cost" rather than an "economy" food budget, one-third of the American people were poor in 1974. A similar computation by Molly Orshansky, the expert at the Social Security Administration who designed the original definition of poverty and is unhappy with it, increased the poverty line by roughly $3000 in 1974, yielding a poverty population of 55.4 million instead of the official figure of 24.3 million. Other critics have pointed out that the "indexing" of costs in the poverty budget, for technical reasons having to do with the prices paid by the poor, also understates the problem.

The CBO is obviously not required to accept the assumptions used by HEW, Orshansky and other experts who see a poverty undercount. But in a serious study purporting to correct "misleading" data, these critiques should have been mentioned and evaluated. Neither was done. Even more shocking was the failure to note the problem of the census undercount of the poor. It is admitted by every government agency involved that our official population figures fail to count a significant group of undetermined size. Estimates vary from four million to more than ten million. These millions do not show up in the statistics because they are so marginal that they do not have jobs, Social Security numbers, permanent addresses, phones, etc. A portion of them are obviously "undocumented" people who do not want to be identified by any federal agency.

In other words, it is fair to assume that a majority—perhaps a very large majority—of the uncounted people in the United States are poor. If one is truly interested in a precise description of the extent of poverty, this problem has to be confronted, even if only in the form of sophisticated estimates. Here, again, the CBO ignored important, and well-known, data which would be damaging to its major conclusions.

Finally, there is a defect in the very method of computing "in-kind" income. It assumes that a good or a service which is obtained through a governmental bureaucracy, on terms which it sets, is "income" in the same way as money in the pocket of a nonpoor citizen. That is as questionable as the notion of Social Security "wealth" analyzed in chapter 5. To state simply one huge difference between regular and in-kind income: the latter involves the recipient in a psychology and a social reality of dependence, the former can be a means to independence. Second—and the CBO itself briefly alludes to this problem—by valuing Medicaid and Medicare services at the cost which the federal government pays, the CBO makes a series of extremely questionable assumptions. It takes the most inflated single item in the consumer price index of recent years, where cost reflects high incomes for doctors and a wasteful system of health delivery rather than value received by the patient, and uncritically accepts it as determinant of what people get. Third, and related, it ignores the widely documented fact that people who patronize Medicaid "mills" often receive unnecessary, and even harmful, care which hardly increases their living standard. In late 1978, for instance, a House subcommittee reported that the incidence of surgery for Medicaid patients was 70 percent higher than for the population as a whole. And finally, this analysis does not notice that the largest payments in the medical category are for terminal care, thus making it possible, given this statistical approach, for a person to achieve extreme upward social mobility by suffering a long and costly final illness.

I have gone into these somewhat technical matters for a reason. I do not think the CBO scholars are liars even though I do believe that their research is an assault upon the poor which is more effective than a fist or a club. I read this tendentious, one-sided study as a sincere refraction of a period in American life when the society once again wants to ignore the poor, and honest scholars unconsciously adopt that prejudice in their work. This is, in short, a radical instance of that social blindness which I analyzed at the opening of this chapter.

There is a related distortion of the truth which is more influential than the CBO's analysis. The latter has reached scholars and relatively sophisticated *New York Times* columnists. But another stereotype, even more damaging to the cause of the poor, is widely accepted by average citizens. In dealing with it, some surprising data which touch upon those in-kind transfers will surface as it is established that the social programs of the sixties did much, much more for the nonpoor than for the poor.

First the popular stereotype should be summarized. In considerable measure it was shaped by the interview which Richard Nixon gave to Garnett D. Horner of the *Washington Star* and which was published on November 9, 1972, the day after Nixon's landslide reelection victory. The White House had carefully reviewed the transcript and approved it for publication. The interview thus had the status of a serious presidential declaration. "This country," Nixon told Horner, "has enough on its plate in the way of new spending programs, social programs, throwing dollars at problems . . . I don't believe that the answer to the nation's problems is simply massive new programs in terms of dollars and in terms of people."

Then came the central theme: "What we have to realize is that many of the solutions of the 60s were massive failures. *They threw money at problems and for the most part they failed"* (emphasis added). That italicized sentence was clearly intended to stand as a conservative indictment of the New Frontier and Great Society. More to the point, it aptly summarized, and reinforced, the prejudice of the average American. And clearly a major focus of the irritation expressed in that statement is the antipoverty program—and, one suspects, the various efforts to aid black Americans. In fact it is not true that the sixties "threw money at problems"—that there was wild, innovative and extremely costly spending—or that the programs of that decade ended up in failure. I have documented the reality which contradicts this stereotype in *The Twilight of Capitalism.* But on the basis of new data I can now more precisely apply the generalizations of that study to the specific issue of poverty. Richard Nixon, it can be shown, was as wrong on his facts as he was widely believed. The reactionary illusion which he fostered has to be cleared up before there can be any intelligent discussion of, or policy making about, poverty in America.

To begin with, there was no radical increase in federal spending and, in particular, the amount spent on "welfare" did not grow by leaps and bounds.

When estimating the percentage of gross national product spent by Washington, it is important to compute that figure on the basis of "full employment" GNP. If one looks at actual GNP, the fluctuations will primarily reflect the ups and downs of the business cycle, not changes in federal policy; e.g., the Republicans in the early seventies paid out $15 billion more in unemployment compensation than the Democrats did in the sixties and the joblessness which imposed this cost also reduced GNP and tax revenues. Therefore, if one wants to isolate the intentional impact of the Great Society as contrasted to the Nixon years, one uses a hypothetical "full employment" GNP in order to make the years comparable. On this basis, Lyndon Johnson spent slightly less of a percentage of full employment GNP in 1965 than Dwight Eisenhower did in 1955 (18.1 percent as contrasted to 18.2 percent). In 1977

—a Carter year which, however, followed Gerald Ford's priorities in the main—the government was spending 20.1 percent of full employment GNP.

These numbers, Charles Schultze pointed out in 1976, *overestimate* the federal portion of the economy. The prices Washington pays for goods and services rise faster than the average of prices on the consumer price index. Over the past twenty years, they have outstripped the CPI by 1.0 percent to 1.3 percent annually. Therefore the stable percentage of GNP between 1955 and 1965 meant that the government's share of real output was falling. And the increase between 1965 and 1977 merely compensated for the high prices of federal goods and did not represent any objective growth in the share of output.

We can thus formulate a first, somewhat gross but essentially accurate, statement on federal intervention: *Between Dwight Eisenhower and Jimmy Carter the federal portion of real output has not changed at all.* That statement, it should be immediately noted, is somewhat deceptive. In the twenty-two-year period between 1955 and 1977, the composition of government outlays changed even if the totals did not. There was a significant shift from military to domestic spending. In 1955, government payments to individuals were 3.2 percent of full employment GNP; in 1977, 8.4 percent. And social investments and services went from 0.6 percent to 2.1 percent. Here, it would seem, there is room for Nixon's assertion that the sixties "threw money" at problems, for those percentage points represent tens of billions of dollars. So it is necessary to be more precise about where those funds went. Were they, as Nixon argued, lavished on failures?

The answer is no. More than 50 percent of the domestic increase went to Social Security (higher benefits) and Medicare. Those two programs are widely supported by the American people and, for all of their faults, have resulted in a real increment in the well-being of people over sixty-five years of age. In 1977, for instance, Federal monies spent on retirement, disability and unemployment amounted to $144.7 billion, while Aid to Families of Dependent Children and Supplemental Security Income (SSI)—for the aged, the blind, the severely handicapped —received $12.3 billion and Medicaid $9.4 billion. In other words, the funds for "welfare" were only a fraction of those spent on popular and effective programs. Schultze synthesized these figures quite neatly. If, Schultze said, one takes all of Washington social grants to state and local government ($20.8 billion in 1977) and all of its payments to low-income individuals ($30.9) and contrasted that total to the amount that would have been paid had there been no increase whatsoever from 1965 on, the difference between them is $34 billion. That is 1.7 percent of GNP and it is the sum which is in dispute when people debate welfare. The increase over a decade is, one should note, roughly one-fourth of what is spent on retirement, in any one year.

Schultze himself—and in 1976 he was an exceedingly moderate liberal on such questions—says that the money thus in contention is of "modest size." "It is," he continues, "probably the perceived lack of equity and efficiency in the structure of these programs, rather than the real burden on the taxpayer, that is the underlying cause of the dissatisfaction." The source of this illusion will be treated in more detail shortly. For now, another startling and related fact must be documented. Henry Aaron has done an excellent job of showing that "in dollar terms, most of the War on Poverty was a by-product of programs intended primarily for the middle class." A portion of one of Aaron's charts illustrates his point brilliantly.

"Merit wants," as Aaron defines them, are expenditures designed to enhance earning power, like job training. Note that the rate of increase in programs not exclusively for the poor roughly paralleled that of the programs for the poor—and that in 1976 the United States was paying out much, much more for the nonpoor than for the poor. Another study reinforces this point and makes it more precise. In 1970, as chapter 5 noted, in-kind programs reached people in inverse relation to their need, i.e., a family with $25,000 a year received $1965 in

Federal Expenditures on Human Resources as
a Percentage of Total Budget Outlays, by
Broad Categories, Selected Fiscal Years

EXPENDITURE

Categories	1961	1969	1975	1976
For the poor				
Merit wants	0.17	2.17	2.34	2.32
In-kind transfers	0.56	1.03	3.46	3.03
Cash transfers	3.93	4.65	3.85	4.03
TOTAL	4.65	7.85	9.66	9.40
Not exclusively for the poor				
Merit wants	0.55	1.45	2.32	2.52
In-kind transfers	2.89	6.93	7.72	8.36
Cash transfers	25.53	24.57	34.96	39.27
TOTAL	28.97	32.96	45.00	50.15

SOURCE: Henry Aaron, *Politics and the Professors* (Washington, D.C.. Brookings Institution, 1978), Table 1A–3, p. 12.

in-kind benefits from government; a family with between $0.00 and $999 received $559. This perverse relationship existed at every level and thus the in-kind payments were uniformly regressive.

Let us summarize. The sixties did not radically expand the federal percentage of GNP—it did not expand it at all in real terms. Second, there were significant shifts from military to social spending, but most of those primarily benefited the middle class, not the poor—and, as Aaron's figures show, the poor began to receive even less in 1976. Third, the amount of money actually spent on welfare is exceedingly modest and the total increment in those expenditures during the sixties is about $34 billion. A considerable portion of that (in Medicaid in particular) went to inflation and waste rather than to improving the real living standards of the poor.

But why, if the facts contradict his thesis at every point, did Richard Nixon find such acceptance for the notion that the sixties had been foolishly and ineffectively throwing money at problems? There are a number of reasons. First, Lyndon Johnson used sweeping rhetoric. It was thus quite possible for the public to believe that the exaggerated intentions stated in the White House were immediately put into practice. The "War" on poverty turned out to be a skirmish. Yet many people were convinced that we had really launched the "unconditional" effort which Johnson proclaimed in his 1964 State of the Union message. Second, and related, the working people and members of the lower and middle class felt that they were being "volunteered" by the government to make contributions to the poor. As chapter 5 documented, they were right in a very important sense: those in the middle of the income-wealth structure pay more than their fair share for the transfers and programs provided to those at the bottom. But rather than becoming angry with the shirkers at the top and demanding that the programs be financed in a progressive way, the middle stream became hostile to the programs themselves.

Third—and this point bears significantly on the next section—the theorists and agitators of the War on Poverty often talked as if this campaign was something which the affluent majority was doing for the deserving poor. Only the majority was not affluent and knew it, and the whole undertaking actually did more for the nonpoor than for the poor. But the people, and particularly that middle stratum, did not know that, and the idealistic arguments which were supposed to mobilize them on behalf of the other America often convinced them that they were being used. For these, and many other, reasons a good many Americans wanted to believe the falsehood which Nixon sponsored.

So it is that the first step in convincing America to confront the problem of poverty—in rescuing the poor from the invisibility to which the seventies once again tried to consign them—is to debunk the tough, hard-nosed and cynical untruths which are at the heart of our reactionary folklore about the New Frontier and the Great Society.[4]

IV

What, then, should be done?

I am afraid that once again the answer is that there must be significant structural changes in the American welfare state—which is the most minimal welfare state in the advanced world. I say that I am afraid that this is the case because, as I write at the end of the seventies, the American people seem to be in a mood to march to the rear on this issue and it is difficult to conceive how they can be persuaded to do what is necessary. In what follows, I will not confront that larger political problem, leaving that question to chapter 9, which will treat the matter in an overall fashion and not just in terms of poverty. But I will try to show how political considerations must play a role in the very design of a program to end the other America.

The American welfare state, as Norman Furniss and Timothy Tilton have pointed out, is based on a minimalist full employment policy, government-business collaboration and social insurance on actuarial principles. Its beneficiaries are, disproportionately, the well-off and its vision is one of "rugged individualism within the context of balanced growth and protection of corporate interest." In the late seventies, the profound conservatism of this arrangement became more and more apparent as a Democratic president, theoretically the political heir of Franklin Roosevelt, moved to sacrifice the well-being of the most vulnerable people in the land in order to fight inflation.

In the "social security state"—the United Kingdom, for

instance—there is a commitment to a guaranteed minimum for all; in the social welfare state—say, Sweden— there is a "solidaristic" wage policy which seeks to equalize incomes.* There is at least one surprising aspect which emerges when one contrasts America to other countries: our cheapness is extremely expensive to maintain. In the seventies, the Department of Health, Education and Welfare discovered that a universal income support program for everyone below 150 percent of the poverty "line" would reduce administrative costs by $3 billion. It takes a lot of effort—and money—to keep the national fist tightly closed.

In all of this, the toleration of high levels of unemployment is, as chapter 3 showed, a key structural limitation of the American welfare state. During the postwar period there is, as has been noted, clear evidence that the United States has allowed an unemployment rate roughly twice as high as in the European welfare states. And it has already been documented that the government—under Democrats as well as Republicans—is officially raising the definition of the amount of joblessness which is necessary for this economy. Earlier, I made the general argument that full employment is the precondition of *all* progressive programs in the United States. In outlining an antipoverty program, that fact will emerge in greater detail in one specific area.

However, before getting down to cases, one more important generalization must be made. Poverty, we have seen, is both integrated and discriminatory. Therefore any attack on the economic and social determinants of racism must deal with this critical issue. There is obviously a

---

* In 1978, a private American consulting firm hired by the "bourgeois" (coalition) government of Sweden analyzed that economy in a way which, to the great annoyance of the conservatives who had engaged the group, corroborated the principle themes of the labor and socialist movements. Among other things it discovered that the solidaristic wage policy, which favors the least well-off, was anti-inflationary in that it had held down remuneration in the most advanced sectors and thus made Sweden more competitive there.

need for special, focused programs which combat the consequences of both de jure and de facto racism, through affirmative action and other means. But even as I insist upon that point, I will not explore it any further. For one thing, it does not relate to the crux of an antipoverty strategy. More important, in both political and economic terms the greatest single blow against racism in America would come from a planned, full employment economy which would disproportionately benefit those at the bottom, where the minorities are so outrageously numerous, and would also improve life for everyone else. Paradoxically, the most important action that can be taken in favor of nonwhites and non-Anglos is a program which will help white Anglos as well.

Moreover, a full employment strategy in the fight against poverty is also critical for groups which are not even in the labor market, i.e., for the aging and the welfare-dependent poor. But before turning to those two subgroups I will first develop my basic theme in relation to those whom it most obviously and immediately touches: impoverished families headed by a worker.

One of the profound, structural limitations of the American welfare state, we have seen, is its toleration of levels of unemployment which are double the European rate. That fact is in turn related to another structural aspect of the American system: the mystical attachment to the private sector. Since this country normally only nationalizes bankrupt enterprises, like the Penn Central Railroad, or inherently unprofitable functions, like mail delivery, the public sector is seen as an area of waste and inefficiency. Since the public sector (with occasional exceptions like TVA) is designed to lose money, this is hardly a surprise and it does not establish the principle of the inherent superiority of the private sector. But the fact of the matter today is that the private sector, with its calculus of profit, will not provide decent jobs for the working poor and the unemployed. Devastated areas, like the South Bronx, are simply not attractive to private capital.

David Perry and Alfred Watkins noted a crucial aspect

of this process in 1978. As business flees to the Sun Belt, it leaves behind a poverty based on unemployment—and it helps create a Southern poverty based upon cheap labor. Thus it is that the percentage of ghetto populations in the South with incomes less than the Bureau of Labor Statistics minimum adequate budget is higher than in the North. Corporate priorities are thus part of the problem, not its solution. Moreover, the existence of this poverty-wage private sector places a fundamental limitation on all government programs, those intended to provide work as well as those which fund welfare. Neither welfare benefits nor the wages of jobs created by public-service employment can be higher than the minimum wage jobs of the private sector. Here, for example, is Hubert Humphrey arguing for his full employment bill in 1977, and talking about the jobs which would be created by the government: "These positions would be temporary, confined to the lower levels of skill and pay, be subject to careful screening to prevent crossover from private employers . . ." Business, in short, would establish the pay levels in federally funded employment.

President Carter agreed. In his 1977 welfare message he said, "The new program will . . . Ensure that work will always be more profitable than welfare and that a private or non-subsidized public job will always be more profitable than a special federally funded public service job." The private sector is, of course, enthusiastic about a principle which defends its special privileges. Thus, Felix Rohatyn, one of the new breed of corporate socialists, i.e., of the private-sector technocrats who want the government to pay business a premium for minimal social decency, said that the solution to poverty and urban blight was through "marrying Federal financing to private employment."

The problem is that if one accepts the principle that government intervention is only justified when it meets private criteria of profitability—and indeed, promotes the profits—then full employment will never be achieved and poverty will not be abolished. The plight of the poor in decaying central cities and rural backwaters is systemic and they are out of the industrial mainstream in considerable measure because industry has made a conscious decision not to go where they are. The answer to this situation is not to locate more socialized losses in the slums, for that would make the people there vulnerable to political attack and it would reinforce the stereotype that the poor are lazy and unproductive people. The proper response requires government to locate some of the *profitable* public jobs in the poverty areas. If that were done, if, for example, the South Bronx became a center for producing a new solar technology, then the private sector would follow in of its own accord, attracted by the various markets which the federal action would have opened up. I am talking, then, about a mixed economy strategy in which there is a very real role for corporations—but not the dominant, determining role they now play—and in which public enterprise would be a critical, but not exclusive, component.

In the chapter on the urban crisis I have already shown that there must be regional planning, that job openings cannot be determined solely on the basis of individual, uncoordinated and profit-motivated decisions. There must be, as *The New York Times* said in 1968, "a national migration policy to direct the flow of people which now eddies haphazardly from rural backwater to city slums . . ." Without going into any detail with regard to an exceedingly complex question, this issue poses the problem of America's policies toward the Third World as well as our internal population flows.

In the spring of 1978, General Maxwell Taylor told the House Committee on Population that by the year 2020, demographic pressures could cause an "invasion from Mexico to regain the territory lost to the Yanquis in 1848." The Soviet Union, Taylor said ominously, might exploit this situation. And several months later, William E. Colby, the former director of the CIA, said that Mexican population growth was more of a menace to the United States than was the Soviet Union. By the end of the century,

Colby said, the number of "illegals" in this country would reach twenty million, i.e., it would equal the present population of the state of California. Both Taylor and Colby were being fanciful and alarmist, yet they were talking about real trends. The poverty to the South of the United States is a problem not totally dissimilar to the poverty within the United States. One function of full employment policy—as I documented at length in *The Vast Majority* —would be to permit this country to act decently toward the wretched of the earth. And, we might add in the present context, to help us solve some of our own problems.

The structural changes required to help the working poor thus involve planning—including publicly owned social investments located so as to deal with internal migration—for full employment, profitable public-service jobs at good wages and the like. With such macroeconomic policies, it would then be possible for the country to do what it has been trying to do, without too much success, for some time: to target job programs specifically for particular groups of workers. Under present high, chronic unemployment conditions, Comprehensive Employment and Training Act (CETA) slots often go to the most qualified workers who would have otherwise been laid off by state or local government. If, however, there were full employment, there would not be any ferocious competition for such openings and they might even reach those for whom they were intended.

It is, then, clear that full employment is a necessary condition for ending the poverty of the working poor. It is not so clear, but quite true, that such a policy must have a "solidaristic" effect, i.e., it must raise the *share* of the bottom fifth in income and wealth if it is to succeed. In 1976, the lowest fifth of the American population had 5.4 percent of total income; the highest fifth (which began at $23,924 in that year) had 41.1 percent; and the median income was $14,958. One of the useful definitions of poverty is that it is equal to half of median income or less (when the general public is asked by survey takers how it would define poverty, this is where it tends to come out).

But it is simply impossible under present, or foreseeable, circumstances for 20 percent of the people to reach half of median income, when they have a mere 5.4 percent of total income. Thus, the society must become *somewhat* less antiegalitarian if poverty is to be brought to an end.

This point is not a digression from the emphasis on full employment; it is a further confirmation of that priority. We know that the only time in recent history when significant relative progress was made by those at the bottom —when the shares shifted for the poor and the minorities —was during World War II when joblessness dropped to 1 percent. If, as chapter 5 showed, it is exceedingly difficult (though highly desirable) to legislate a redistribution of wealth, full employment tends to have that effect. It is a critical priority for the poor as well as for the rest of the society.

This point even extends to the dependent poor who are not in the labor market.

We have already seen how the low wages of the working poor establish the upper limit of benefits for the welfare poor. If the poverty of working poor were abolished through full employment (and the share of income of the bottom quintile increased) that would automatically generate higher federal revenues to pay for the higher welfare benefits which would then be politically possible. Conversely, if there is chronic joblessness, as in recent years, that undermines the political and economic basis of minimal decency toward the dependent poor.

Let us assume that the economic conditions were propitious for changing the welfare system. What should be done? First, it is critical to establish federal, universal programs for the poor. The existence of fifty different programs, jointly funded by states and Washington but run by the states, has, as we saw in the chapter on the cities, penalized the most humane areas by making them an inviting place for the poorest people and the unemployables. This, as we have seen in the case of the New York City crisis, is a major factor in the collapse of many of the cities in the Northeast and industrial Midwest. We know from the food stamp experience—the one truly national welfare program—that this federal approach can be extremely effective.

In saying this, there is no point in overstating a case. Families headed by women, that most intractable subgroup of the poor, the one most resistant to change, are not simply a product of poverty. There are other factors at work as well and some of them are even positive, e.g., when a rise in female income makes independence possible for some women whose dependence otherwise would have forced them to maintain a marriage they could not abide. That last effect, for instance, may have been at work in some (but only some) of the cases in the guaranteed income experiment discussed at the outset of this chapter. The abolition of poverty would end a part of this problem but not necessarily all of it. Above all, the existence of full employment and a minimum income above the poverty line would make it possible for the young people in those female-headed families to make the transition into the larger society. In their case, one suspects that the gains would be major and unambiguous. It will be remembered that they account for more than half of the youthful poor, so this is an extremely significant possibility.

But does this then mean that a guaranteed income is the proper means of providing a uniform, federally financed welfare system? Yes. Henry Aaron's testimony before the Moynihan subcommittee made it clear that such a program, so long as it was part of a government effort to provide jobs for all who needed them, would not significantly reduce work effort or promote family breakup. And it would have the enormous merit of finally getting the United States committed to that national minimum which has prevailed in most of Europe for a generation now.

The third major group of the poor, the aging, are in one sense the easiest to help—and in another sense, the hardest. Nixon's contemptuous remark about "throwing money" at problems overlooked the most obvious single case: when people do not have enough money, throwing them some (which was not what the sixties did, as we have seen) will solve some of their difficulties. The increased Social Security benefits which were forced upon Nixon by a Democratic Congress—which Nixon took credit for in a letter mailed to 24,760,000 beneficiaries on the very eve of the 1972 elections—have had a measurable and positive impact upon those who received them. The poverty of the aging could thus be abolished, insofar as it is merely a matter of money, by universalizing Social Security benefits and fixing them at a nonpoverty level.

Once more, I do not want to claim too much. The poverty of the aging is not simply a matter of income. It also has to do with isolation, irrelevance and all the other anxieties the old suffer in a nation which worships youth. It is better to have an adequate pension and feel useless than not to have one and feel useless. But it is clear that the measures advocated here will only solve some of the problems of this (and every other) group.

Still, there are some solutions and I have outlined a few of them. Modest as that undertaking has been, it has emphasized the essential: that poverty is a structural problem in American society. It is maintained because of the prejudices and stereotypes of the people, which are sometimes cruelly fostered by leaders like Richard Nixon. It is rooted in systemic injustices like unemployment, underemployment, the functionality of low wages for the private sector, regional imbalances and the like. Between 1962 and 1969, progress was made in reducing the other America but since then there have been no real and enduring gains. The poor have suffered the most from the stagflation of the seventies and as the decade ends there is every sign that they will be further sacrificed by politicians who will volunteer them, rather than the corporate rich, to do frontline duty in the anti-inflation campaign. In addition to the integrated evil which these trends effect, they also have the tragic consequence of reinforcing the historic racism of American society, of hurting the black and the brown and the other minorities in a disproportionate way.

There are solutions to this outrage—but they, like all of the solutions described in this book, require structural change in American society. And they will benefit not simply the poor but the apprentices to the middle class on the nation's college campuses, the unlikely victims of the crisis who are the subject of the next chapter.[5]

____ Notes ____

1. Moynihan: Chapman, "Poor Laws"; Release, Moynihan office, November 15, 1978. Aaron: Release, November 17, 1978 (HEW). CBO: *Poverty Status of Families*, passim. Race of the poor: *Money Income and Poverty Status of Families*, p. 3.

2. Poverty definition: CBO, *Poverty Status*, p. 5. Poverty as percentage of median income: Rivlin, "Income Distribution—Can Economists Help?" p. 4. Poverty statistics: *Money Income . . .* , op. cit. supra, p. 4; *Characteristics of the Population Below the Poverty Level: 1976*, pp. 25, 108, table 37, p. 144. Longitudinal study: George Carcagno and Walter Corson, "Welfare Reform," in Pechman, ed., *Setting National Priorities: The 1978 Budget*, p. 259. Poverty population statistics: *Characteristics*, op. cit. supra, table 1, p. 15. Kennedy-Johnson years: Ibid., table 5, p. 25. Aging: Ibid., table B, p. 5. Women: Ibid., figs. 4 and 5, p. 4; table B, p. 5.

3. White-black occupations: *Money Income*, op cit. supra, table 26, pp. 140 ff. Smith and Welch: "Black/White Male Earnings and Employment, 1960–1970," in Juster, ed., p. 233. CEA, 1978: p. 166. 1974 ratio: CBO, *Income Disparities Between Black and White Americans*, p. 7. 1978 figures: Alfred J. Malabre, Jr., "After Shrinking, the Gap Widens," *The Wall Street Journal*, March 6, 1979.

4. CEA, 1976: Chap. II. Browning: *Public Interest*, Summer, 1974, passim. Schwartz: *The New York Times*, October 19, 1976. CBO: *Poverty Status of Families Under Alternate Definitions of Income*, passim. Anderson: *Welfare*, p. 15. HEW: *The Measure of Poverty*, pp. 626 ff. Orshansky: Harrington, "Hiding the Other America." Surgery: "Welfare Bota $ En Cirugia," *El Diario* (New York), December 21, 1978. Schultze: In *Setting National Priorities*, Owen and Schultze, eds., pp. 330–31. Composition: Ibid., table 8-6, p. 334. On social spending increment: Ibid., p. 345. Aaron: *Politics and the Professors*, table IA-3, p. 12. In-kind income: Eugene Smolensky et al., "Distribution of Economic Well Being," table 3, in F. Thomas Juster, ed.

5. Furniss and Tilton: *The Case for the Welfare State*, pp. 15 ff. Ad-

ministrative cost: Ibid., p. 82. United States and Europe: Tufte, Fig. 4-2, p. 93. Perry and Watkins: "Saving the Cities," *The New York Times,* April 27, 1978. Humphrey: *Congressional Record,* May 20, 1977, p. S8243. Carter: *Congressional Record,* September 7, 1977, p. A14237. Rohatyn: "Indeed, 'the Moral Equivalent of War,'" *The New York Times,* August 12, 1977. *The New York Times* on migration: Editorial, February 3, 1968. Taylor: "Over Population," AP dispatch, *Burlington Free Press,* April 20, 1978. Colby: "Invasion *de los* Ilegales," UP, *El Diario* (New York), June 7, 1978. CETA: John L. Palmer, "Employment and Training Assistance," in *Setting National Priorities: The 1978 Budget,* Pechman, ed. Quintiles: *Money Incomes in 1976 . . . ,* table B, p. 2. Food stamps: Kotz, *New Republic.* 1972 Social Security: Tufte, p. 32.

8

Revolution
Without Change

In 1965, Lyndon Baines Johnson went back to a one-room schoolhouse near his home in Texas and signed the Elementary and Secondary Education Act into law in the presence of his first teacher, Miss Kate Dietrich. He said, "As President of the United States, I deeply believe that no law I have signed or will ever sign means more to the future of America."

That was thoroughly in keeping with the personality and biography of the San Marcos, Texas, college freshman who had written that "perfect concentration and a great desire will bring a person success in any field of work he chooses. The very first thing we should do is to train the mind to concentrate upon the essentials and dismiss the frivolous and unimportant. This will ensure real accomplishment and ultimately success." That formula had worked for Lyndon Johnson. Why could it not be applied to all the young people in the land, the disadvantaged first and foremost? Train their minds and success would be assured.

Johnson was not alone in that faith. Richard Nixon was another American who had fought his way up from humble, if genteel, beginnings. He attacked many of the Great Society training innovations, like the Job Corps— and yet during his first term the outlays for manpower programs more than doubled, reached $5 billion in 1973. But, then, Nixon's attitude in this area was not so strange since it can be argued that the underlying theory of these federal investments in education was conservative. What both Nixon and Johnson were saying was that the United States could have a revolution in class structure without the inconvenience of changing any established institutions or challenging fundamental inequalities.

There are several misinterpretations of what was just said and it is important to get them out of the way at the outset. It is not being argued that Johnson, or even Nixon, promoted education out of a conscious and manipulative desire to solve some social problems and maintain the status quo at the same time. Both of them—and the majority of the American people who shared their dream—were sincere in advocating a contradictory, and ultimately, impossible program. Indeed, I think that their delusion, and Lyndon Johnson's in particular, was a credit to good faith, even if that faith was, as will be seen, misplaced.

Second, I am not turning the traditional faith upside down and saying that education has *no* contribution, or only a minor contribution, to make to the eradication of social evils. I simply, but emphatically, hold that education, of and by itself, cannot perform the prodigies of change which were expected from it in the sixties and early seventies. If the institutional structure, and especially the class system, remains unchanged, then the social potential of education will be severely limited but it will still exist. If, on the other hand, there are significant changes in public policy of the kind to be described in this chapter, then education, as one very important element in a broad drive for change, can play a major role.

The final misinterpretation of my views has to do with the way in which one talks about education—or, more profoundly, how one conceives its essential value. In the sixties, educational and economic theorists bent on persuading pragmatic legislators to vote funds for schools tended to put their case in dollars and cents. Education was thus defined as an "input" in a "production function" which would yield increased GNP as well as upward mobility for all. Little or no mention was made of the role of learning in enriching the human spirit. How, after all, can you quantify the impact of a poem or a Greek tragedy—or, more to the point, persuade politicians to finance contemplating them?

In what follows, these arguments will be stated and criticized in their own terms in an attempt to show why the neat equations did not lead to the predicted results. That does not mean, however, that I accept the method which conceives of education primarily in terms of its economic effect. On the contrary. If education is seen as one element in a broad and ranging process of social change —if it is relieved of the impossible obligation of making a revolution without challenging established authority— then it can not only acquire a greater social relevance, it can also reassert the value of thought and culture in themselves.

With these three misinterpretations out of the way, it is now possible to make a preliminary statement of the main themes of this chapter. During the sixties and early seventies, most Americans, conservatives as well as liberals, thought that schooling was the key to solving some of the nation's most urgent problems. Two groups, one a minority, the other a majority, were supposed to be the main beneficiaries of the new commitment to learning. Preschool education and enhanced schooling efforts were to help the poor acquire the skills which would bring them into the mainstream of economic life. Since many people thought—wrongly—that the poor were overwhelmingly black, this approach was also going to be central to the attack on racial discrimination in the United States.

The second group which was going to gain from the revolution wtihout change was less obvious than the poor but politically more important: the American working class. The new initiatives would educate the children of

blue-collar workers into the middle class, above all by allowing them the opportunity to go to college. The working
people of the country believed deeply in this promise.
When, for instance, the principle of "open admissions"
(which guaranteed a place in the city university system
for every high-school graduate) was attacked in New York
City during the fiscal crisis of the mid-seventies, the municipal AFL-CIO argued vigorously for this policy which
had been originally established in response to black and
Hispanic militancy. For, it turned out, the children of
white workers had actually gained more from the system
than those who had forced it into existence. More broadly,
it was support from this constituency which made the
enormous growth of higher education politically possible
in the sixties.

Education, then, was to abolish poverty and provide a
road to the middle class for anyone with the talent and
drive to take it. Neither expectation came to pass. In part
that was because, for all the talk, insufficient resources
were put in the service of soaring visions. But in greater
part, it was because both efforts took place in a society in
which the structures which militated against the poor and
working people remained very much intact. There were
gains, to be sure, but the established order of inequality
prevailed against the attempt to transform the class system without disturbing it.[1]

___ I _____

In the post–World War II period, the traditional American faith in the economic power of education seemed to
receive sophisticated corroboration. It came from a theory
about "human capital."

Between 1944–53 and 1969–78, the inputs in the
American economy—capital and labor—increased four
times. But the outputs went up by thirteen times. Why?
There were many factors at work, all of them the result of

popular struggles which made the economy more efficient despite the resistance of those who owned and managed it. Better health and more leisure, for instance; both had a positive impact upon productivity. But one factor stood out above all the others by virtue of its universality. During those years, the American people were becoming more educated. That trend accelerated right after World War II. The per capita education of members of the labor force went up by 8 percent in the forties, 13 percent in the fifties and more than 16 percent in the sixties. These were, of course, the times of a tremendous capitalist boom and of American dominance within the Western camp. It would be hard to imagine a more spectacular confirmation of the conventional American wisdom.

So it was reasonable to assume that education was the decisive "input" in explaining that mysterious growth of output in the economy. If the neoclassical theorists had understood that the increasing productivity of machines was a key element in progress, it was now seen that human beings were a kind of capital too. The education invested in them operated like the modernization of a plant. Moreover, since people's talent is much more democratically distributed than wealth, this discovery had egalitarian implications. As Theodore W. Schultz, one of the theorists of the idea, put it: "With respect to the distribution of personal income . . . changes in human capital are the basic factor reducing the inequality in distribution of personal income. . . . Modifications in income transfers, in progressive taxation and in the distribution of private owned wealth are relatively weak factors in altering the distribution of personal income."

In short, the historical relation between education and productivity was projected into a future which would work like the past. If the society invested more in people —i.e., in education—it would reap vast material benefits. The outlays would clearly be paid for by the increased GNP and the tax revenues which it would bring; social justice was going to turn a social profit. That conclusion, it will be seen, does not follow necessarily from the historical evidence. For one of the main reasons for the disappointment of these high hopes was that the future became increasingly unlike the past. My critique, then, does not challenge the accuracy of this theory in times gone by. It has to do with its present and future significance.

And on this last count I am afraid the evidence is clear: although education may facilitate the rise of individuals, it does not, by itself, change class structure and its productivity yield is declining. In 1974, for instance, Richard Nixon's Council of Economic Advisers commented, "It is striking that there has been no change in the relative inequality of income among adult males. The greater opportunities for schooling at all income levels and the larger subsidies for training less advantaged persons might have been expected to reduce earnings inequality in the past twenty years, but the relation between equal access to training and schooling and earnings inequality is not so straightforward."

Lester Thurow, a brilliant economist of the democratic Left, was even more specific. During the post–World War II period, education has become more equal and earnings slightly less equal. Some would explain this anomaly by emphasizing the part that racial and sexual discrimination played in blocking the predicted trend from working out. To discount for that problem, Thurow examined the data on white males between twenty-five and sixty-four, i.e., on those who were not victimized by either form of prejudice. Between 1950 and 1970, the bottom 60 percent of this group (in income terms) increased its relative share of education by 5 percent—but there was no rise in its share of earnings. More broadly, Thurow points out that the years in which the workers were increasing their education faster than ever—the sixties—actually saw a *decline* in equality.

I take it as established that the expectations of human capital theory have been disappointed in the recent past and present. There are three factors which may account for this fact and they could well be crucial in the future. In analyzing them, one is not simply engaged in a scholarly investigation, for these matters have momentous implications for the schools, the labor market and the society as a whole. First, there is the thesis that the nation never really acted on its human capital rhetoric and that all we have proved is that inadequate inputs will lead to indifferent results. Second, there is the argument that our failures are due to structural factors inherent in the American (capitalist) class structure. And third, there is the idea that the payoff to education declined because of a new situation which was, in part, the result of the past success of investments in human capital.

Did we ever really act on our commitment to give the poor the education and training that would enable them to fight their way out of poverty?* Serious scholars say that we did not and that this fact accounts for the ambiguous results of the whole undertaking. In what follows, I will rely heavily on two volumes which summarize more than a decade of research into these matters: Henry Aaron's *Politics and the Professors: The Great Society in Perspective,* published in 1978; and *The Promise of Greatness* by Sar Levitan and Robert Taggart, which came out in 1976.

Lyndon Johnson declared his "War on Poverty" in January 1964. But with the escalation of the American intervention in Vietnam in 1965, the educational component of that effort declined relative to the total expenditures (which rose, but at a reduced rate). With Vietnam, Aaron writes, "aid to the poor was conveyed increasingly through transfers in kind that alleviated the symptoms of poverty but did not deal with its causes." So if the research shows "no perceptible nationwide effect of the training programs on employment or productivity that is perhaps because the programs were too small in the aggregate." The Job Corps and the Neighborhood Youth Corps, Daniel Patrick Moynihan conceded, "never reached more than a fraction of those for whom they were intended."

---

* This section is clearly complementary to the more extended discussion of poverty in the last chapter. It focuses on the educational component in the antipoverty effort and should be taken together with the material in chapter 7.

Similarly with that landmark educational law which Lyndon Johnson signed in Texas. In 1972, Levitan and Taggart report, there were 66,000 public and 14,000 private elementary schools and 25,000 public and 4000 private secondary schools. In 1974, public authorities spent $79 billion on education, the private sector, $17 billion. Thus, even though Washington's outlays expanded greatly in the sixties and early seventies, the enormity of the system and its problems meant that the government was "trying to feed the multitude with sparse loaves." Moreover, the monies were not necessarily concentrated in the areas of greatest need, in part because those "production functions" abstracted from history did not tell the investors in human capital where to put their money in the here and now. So one of the problems in computing the effect of the federal input into education is that, for all the sweep of the Johnsonian rhetoric, the effort was often both halfhearted and unfocused.

Thus when Levitan and Taggart summarize the various studies of Head Start, the Job Corps and Manpower Development and Training, they conclude—contrary to the judgment of people like Moynihan—that there is no evidence of outright failure. But neither is there proof of real success. Their findings, as well as Aaron's, reinforce a theme which was central to the chapter on poverty and race. The popular belief that there were truly massive—indeed, prodigal—expenditures for the poor simply does not stand up to close examination. Yet, the equally widespread conviction that the monies did not really accomplish anything is also a myth. Even though they were inadequately funded, the programs did have some effect. Finally, it is at least possible that one of the reasons that the attempt to eradicate poverty by means of education and training did not improve the earnings share of the bottom quintile is that the rhetoric was never taken seriously enough.

The second basic theory holds that the problem in this area is to be found in the power of class structure as against education.

The increase in the per capita education in the post–

World War II period did not, we have seen, lead to the predicted rise in either earnings or productivity. Henry Aaron, who is a moderate on policy issues, summarizes the data: ". . . few differences among schools seem to have consistent and socially significant effects on how children do on standardized tests; and performance on standardized tests does not seem to have much to do with subsequent earnings." For Aaron, this result is particularly puzzling since he believes that there is a relationship between income and education. Samuel Bowles and Herbert Gintis provide an explanation for this anomaly which raises a fundamental question: Does improving cognitive skills have anything to do with bettering a group's social class position?

Bowles and Gintis agree with Aaron: there is a strong relationship between earnings and education. But a careful study shows that education is not the *cause* of this relation since performance on tests within any social stratum does not affect the income of individuals within that stratum. Those who make average scores have roughly the same earnings as those who do much better or much worse. It is membership in the particular stratum, not the intelligence or training of the members, which appears to be decisive. The same point applies to IQ. Children from the top social-economic decile have a 42 percent chance of being in the top IQ quintile; those from the bottom decile have a 4.9 percent chance. So, some "IQists" have said, it is class which explains high IQ—and high IQ which perpetuates class.

Here, again, the problem with this argument is that the evidence does not show that it is the IQ which leads to higher income. People with identical IQs from different social classes have different earnings. It is not, Bowles and Gintis rightly argue, the IQ that is decisive, but the social class: ". . . the fact that economic success tends to run in the family arises almost completely independently from any inheritance of IQ, whether it be genetic or environmental." There is also an incredible statistical aspect of the problem which these authors do not mention. IQs are computed on a "normal curve," i.e., the tests are designed to end up with two-thirds of those who take them grouped in the middle and one-sixth located at the bottom and the top respectively. Therefore, if one increases the scores of those at the bottom, there must be a relative decrease for some of those in the middle. This procedure is, I think, severely flawed in and of itself, but aside from that fact, it literally makes it impossible for any change in IQs to alter class structure. Thus, even if IQ were related to earnings, raising the IQ of the poor to get them a better income would require lowering the IQ of the previous middle class and decreasing their earnings.

The main point, however, does not have to do with this statistical sleight of hand. It is that there is formidable evidence that better cognitive development for the poor will not in and of itself alter their relative position in the society. If there were other programs transforming class structure—and those will be identified at the end of this chapter—education could make a major contribution to progress, but only then. In short, the Great Society thesis that the schools would be the battering ram of equality had something fundamentally wrong with it.

Before trying to explain in greater detail why this is the case, it is important once again to clear up an understandable, but very wrong, interpretation of what is being said. There are two distinct issues: Do increased educational investments improve cognitive development? Does improved cognitive development enhance income? That first question was the subject of a lively debate in the sixties, which continues to this day. The "Coleman Report" (The Equal Educational Opportunity Study of the mid-sixties), another analysis by the Rand Corporation and Christopher Jencks's very influential book, *Inequality*, argued that money "inputs" in schools did not really raise the cognitive "outputs." (Aaron summarizes the debate in his study.) That finding satisfied conservatives and radicals. Richard Nixon, for instance, used it to attack the Great Society in the name of a sophisticated agnosticism about the value of its educational programs. Even though I find this dispute important and revealing, it is not relevant to my main point. I am not concerned with the limited (or not-so-limited) impact of schools upon minds, but with the limited impact of minds upon income.

Lester Thurow cites dramatic evidence in this regard. In the sixties, he notes, the president's Commission on Technology, Automation and Economic Progress found that only 40 percent of the work force actually used cognitive skills acquired in formal training programs. The other 60 percent had learned all they needed to know on the job (and even the 40 percent credited some of their ability to that process). This is in keeping with the findings of another researcher in a joint economic committee study: that 80 percent of recent college graduates are underemployed in occupations which had been previously filled by those with lower educational credentials.

In 1979, Christopher Jencks and a number of associated scholars published a thorough, extremely technical statistical study of some of these issues. Family background, they discovered, accounted for about 48 percent of the variance in occupational status among men, and for 15 percent to 35 percent of their variance in earnings. Like Thurow, they concluded that "only a part of the association between schooling and success can be due to what students actually learn from year to year in school." Even in schools which taught specific skills, where one would think that a student with high test scores would do better than one with lower scores, that was not the case. This leads Jencks and his co-workers to an important conclusion: ". . . past efforts at equalizing the personal characteristics known to effect income have been relatively ineffective and there . . . [is] no good reason to suppose that future efforts would be more effective. Thus, if we want to redistribute income, the most effective strategy is probably still to redistribute income." But why, then, this profound limitation upon the power of education in the marketplace? Thurow has provided one of the best answers.

His analysis is extremely sophisticated and complex,

and I will only be able to outline some of its main themes here. The issue it confronts, it should be noted at the outset, is not simply academic, for it touches on an important social phenomenon of the times: the devaluation of the college degree at the precise moment the children of workers were given the chance to earn it. Indeed, it suggests a gloomy explanation for that development: the degree was devalued *because,* in a society of limited and rigid roles, the children of workers were permitted to earn it.

In conventional economic theory, Thurow shows, there are three main interpretations of how people get jobs. The microeconomists of the mainstream see wages as tending toward an equilibrium price which will clear the market by employing everyone. The Keynesians hold that wages are rigid and that demand for labor is determined by the overall level of output, not by the willingness of people to bid for work at a cheap price. And the labor economists focus on the interindustry, or interskill, differentials—on the structure of the labor market—and do not have a theory of average wages. Each of these views cancels out the other two and all of them have problems dealing with critical realities, e.g., the microeconomists have to bring in Ptolemaic epicycles (monopoly, discrimination) to explain the patent fact of unemployment.

Thurow proposes a radically new model to deal with all of these anomalies. It is not the skill and training of the worker which determine the job which he or she gets; it is the job which determines the skill and training of the worker. "Thus the labor market is not primarily a bidding market for selling existing skills but a training market where training slots must be allocated to different workers." How does an employer decide which workers will get one of those slots? It depends in part on their "background characteristics." Those who will be least expensive to train are obviously preferable and since, in a mass society, that can't normally be determined by face-to-face contact with every applicant, generalizations are used: males who have gone through high school are more likely to be dependable than those who have not, or than women.

Clearly, this is one of the mechanisms for transmitting racial and sexual prejudices.

But, Thurow continues, those background characteristics change with the circumstances. "When labor is plentiful, hiring characteristics escalate; when labor is in short supply, hiring characteristics relax." A survey of the Chicago labor market in the mid-sixties—long before Thurow developed his ideas—confirms this proposition. When the market was loose, newspaper ads specified that job applicants had to be high-school graduates; when it tightened up, that requirement was simply dropped. So the chief training school of the American economy is the job itself. And formal education can be an entrance ticket to the real schools in the plants and offices. This explains why wages tend to be rigid. If there were wage competition, people with jobs would be motivated to conceal their skills from new workers. They would hardly want to train their own replacements. Therefore, Thurow concludes, the importance of on-the-job training requires the employer to banish wage competition. Here again, Thurow's insight has been corroborated by an important independent researcher, Arthur Okun.

This analysis leads to some rather depressing notions about the economic value of education, and of college education in particular. In his model, Thurow writes, "education . . . becomes a defensive necessity. As the supply of more highly educated labor increases, individuals find that they must improve their own education qualifications simply to defend their current income position. If they do not go to college, others will, and they will not find their current job open to them. Education becomes a good investment, not because it would raise an individual's income above what it would have been if no others increased their education but because it raises this income above what it will be if others acquire an education and he does not."

The result is a Catch-22: "Each individual faces incentives to undertake activities that will help him if he, and he alone, responds to the incentives but will hurt him and his fellows if everyone responds to them." Moreover, Thurow sees this process as affecting everyone in the labor market. As the college-educated labor supply increases, that escalates the background characteristics for jobs; college graduates displace high-school graduates who displace grade-school graduates. At every level, higher—and largely irrelevant—qualifications are required in order to get the jobs which will really qualify the worker through on-the-job training.

Thurow's theory offers one explanation of an extremely significant phenomenon of the seventies—and eighties: the economic devaluation of the college degree (another analysis, we will see, reaches much the same conclusion by way of a more sociological approach). It is possible, as already noted, that 80 percent of college graduates are currently underemployed. That fact has impressed itself upon the minds of potential students. In the sixties, the expansion of higher education did not flood the market with bachelor's degrees in considerable measure because so many went on to postgraduate work. But then, in the early seventies, the number of college-educated workers rose and the "premium" received by a degree fell from 39 percent in 1969 to 15 percent in 1974. So college attendance went down (the end of the draft was another factor in this outcome).

In some corporate theories, all of these problems will be solved by the demographic shift of the next generation. In the mid-eighties, the American labor market will begin to feel the effect of the "baby bust" of the sixties. The "baby boom" generation will yield to the children of zero population growth. That, some business ideologists say, will make full employment easy to attain; indeed, it will pose a problem of labor shortage, not oversupply. Ironically, that might well be the case for "entry-level and low-status jobs." But there is no reason to believe that it will hold at the top of the class structure, where there will still be a surplus of degree holders fighting for scarce jobs. In 1980, for instance, between 20 percent and 21 percent of the labor force will hold degrees, but the share of professional and technical workers (the classic place for the middle class) in the economy will be between 14.9 percent and 15.4 percent (in 1960, 10 percent of the labor force had finished college and professional and technical workers were 11 percent). Another projection estimates that, in 1985, 2.5 college graduates will be competing for every "choice" job, thus generating a "surplus" of two hundred thousand degree holders.

So it is that one scholar, Stephen Dresch, makes this gloomy prediction: "In a traumatic reversal of historical experience, children born to persons entering adulthood in the 1950s and 1960s will, on average, experience relatively lower status than their parents." Before turning to the possibilities of dealing with that ominous development, the third major explanation of our plight will be outlined. It parallels Thurow's theory but it offers new insights into the common reality which both describe.

The late Fred Hirsch's remarkable book, *Social Limits to Growth,* is the best statement of the theme that we have entered a new era and that this is why education, among many other things, no longer has the meaning it once did. For Hirsch, that new area is defined socially; for others, it is a technological phenomenon. But in all these theories, it is the time factor which is crucial. It is not so much capitalism or the labor market, in and of themselves, which is the problem; it is capitalism at a specific and unprecedented stage in its evolution.

"Growth," Hirsch writes, "is a substitute for redistribution of goods for the worse off only in its early stages, for so long as unmet biological needs retain their primacy. Beyond that point, the political consensus behind an a-distributorial policy of economic expansion is weakened. In one key sector—the positional sector—there is no such thing as a leveling up." It is possible through growth to make huge increases in the number of people who have enough food, clothes and housing; but there is a limit on how many exclusive neighborhoods there can be. Exclusive neighborhoods are "positional" goods. They depend on being first, or in the top ten or the top hundred. When the majority seeks after things which are defined by their elite character, frustration, waste and social meanness are bound to result.

There is, for example, the paradox of the tourist: "The tourist, in his search for something different, inevitably erodes and destroys that difference by his very enjoyment of it." The first, rich people to buy a car enjoy many advantages; by the time the masses get their autos, there is congestion. Perhaps Hirsch's most illuminating image of this process is found in his description of how people get on tiptoe. There is a parade; the people in the second rank along the way want to see better. They stand on tiptoe. Then those behind them, in order to preserve their relative position, are forced to stand on tiptoe. The effect ripples back, through the crowd. Eventually, everyone not in the privileged front rank is standing on tiptoe—and no one sees better even though there has been a considerable expenditure of effort.

Apply that notion to the question of the economic value of education. Hirsch's concept of "tiptoe" might be taken as a summary statement of the process which Thurow described in which getting a college degree is a "defensive" maneuver without any real (or any great) economic value to either the society or the individual. But what Hirsch is saying is that this is inherent in the nature of the positional goods being sought, rather than in the competitive process within which they are sought. He quotes Alfred Marshall, the great synthesizer of neoclassical economics, that one must strive for a situation in which "by occupation, at least, every man is a gentleman."

But is that possible even with the qualification Marshall made ("by occupation, at least")? If there are gentlemen does that not require that there be other people— indeed, a majority of other people—who are not gentlemen and who will therefore defer to their betters? In his famous discussion of the master and the serf in the *Phenomenology of Spirit,* Hegel insisted, quite rightly, that "recognition" by inferiors is a precondition of proving, over and over, to superiors that they are indeed superior.

Therefore—and it should be noted that this is my own gloss on Hirsch, not Hirsch himself—would not a society in which everyone tries to be a gentleman be a place in which no one is a gentleman (not to mention gentlewomen)? Thus there are nonmaterial limits to growth.

At times, Hirsch makes those limits too purely social. He quotes the Marxist, J. H. Westergaard: "Contemporary capitalism generates a tension between aspirations increasingly widely shared and opportunities which, by the very nature of the class structure, remain restricted and unequally distributed." Hirsch then rewrites Westergaard's sentence to conform to his own theory: "Contemporary capitalism generates a tension between aspirations widely shared and opportunities which, by the very nature of *the things aspired to,* remain restricted and unequally distributed." In fact, Hirsch and Westergaard are, I think, talking about the same reality as seen from different perspectives. Westergaard focuses on the "objective" opportunities—the good jobs in occupational terms—and Hirsch concentrates on the "subjective" opportunities— the good jobs defined by their status. In both cases, analysts have understood that the capitalist class system, for all of the openness it may have manifested in the past, cannot accommodate the hopes which it has engendered in the present.

For Hirsch, the problem is one of the social limits of growth. For others, who also see a qualitatively new situation, the temporal change is defined more technologically or economically.

So, for instance, a Congressional study of long-term growth sees a "new era" in the eighties, characterized by a slowdown in labor force growth, reduced economic gains from higher education, rising raw materials costs, the maturing of postwar industries and cultural shifts inimical to expansion. An analysis made under the auspices of the Organization for Economic Cooperation and Development (OECD), an international advisory organization for sophisticated capitalism, warns of "jobless growth" in the medium term. The OECD study says, "The evidence we have is suggesting increasingly that the employment-displacing effects of automation, anticipated in the 1950s, are now beginning to arrive on a serious scale in the 1970s." And *Business Week* reports, "A grim mood prevails today among industrial research managers. America's vaunted technological superiority of the 1950s and 1960s is vanishing, they fear, the victim of wrongheaded federal policy, neglect, uncertain business conditions and short-sighted corporate management."

One could go on citing other projections of less real growth in the future. If that happens, then there could be severe material, as well as social, limits to growth. In either case, the problem which is central to this chapter —and which is already visible as a fact in some areas—is worsened: there will be a scarcity of good jobs at the top, a vast supply of overeducated workers (even if a labor shortage among the unskilled) and a ripple effect which would downgrade those with high-school and grade-school educations as well as the college graduates. As long as the economy and the social structure had a certain openness—and I do not want to go into the historic question of how open it was except to note that I think that mobility in the United States has often been exaggerated by scholars as well as citizens in the street—one could, as Hirsch says, dodge the redistribution question. But if a combination of reasons make it impossible for the society to fulfill the expectations it has provoked, then we are in deep trouble unless we are prepared to transform class structure consciously.

Before turning to ways to deal with this situation, it is important to look more closely at some of the negative possibilities in our situation. In Hirsch's view—and it is, I think, quite right—those have to do with the morality of economic and social life.

Adam Smith was the author of two great books, one of them widely celebrated (if not widely read), the other kept in print in the United States only because of the political dedication of a conservative group. The first volume is, of course, *The Wealth of Nations;* the second, *The Theory of*

Moral Sentiments. There is a dispute among scholars as to whether Smith changed his point of view between the *Theory,* which he wrote first, and the *Wealth of Nations.* That need not concern us here, for whatever the truth about Smith I think that the insights of his earlier volume are quite compelling. Men, Smith said, "could safely be trusted to pursue their self interest without undue harm to the community not only because of the restrictions imposed upon them by the law, but also because they were subject to built-in restraints derived from morals, religion, custom and education." That is, precapitalist values, derived from sources totally outside of the marketplace, were essential to the functioning of the market. To take but a simple and obvious instance, people felt under an obligation to tell the truth and keep their word, not simply because it was the "best policy," but also because it was right.

But now there is a certain "atrophy" of social ties. In a small community, God's commandments were silently enforced by one's neighbors, even if only passively, by means of wordless reproach directed at those who violated the mores. But now those small communities have been replaced by mass society, with its anonymity, and belief in God has declined. The external and internal restraints which were an essential part of social functioning were weakened at the same time.

If the social interconnections were thus frayed, and even broken, the individualistic drives remained, but now in an utterly new context. On the one hand, Keynesian governments found that it was necessary for the state to intervene in the economy. In the United States, in particular, this took the form of a "reluctant collectivism," i.e., a collectivist practice which took place in the name of Horatio Alger values. On the other hand, the competition for "positional goods" became all the more intense, but the demands were addressed to the visible hand of government rather than to the invisible hand of the Smithian marketplace. So groups organized to get their share of the scarce good jobs—but by definition there were not enough to go around. A new element of frustration and irritation thus came into the economy.

It is within this context that the country's schools have become a battleground at every level of education in recent years. One paradoxical way of putting this process is that every ethnic group in the United States decided to follow the Jewish path of social mobility at a time when that strategy could not possibly work for so many people. For a variety of historic and cultural reasons, but above all because of anti-Semitism, American Jews focused their hopes for economic progress on the liberal professions like medicine and law. For many years—and to this day—they were excluded from most of the top jobs in the corporate system because of vicious prejudice. A highly literate "people of the Book" in which many spoke several languages (Hebrew and Yiddish as well as the tongue of the area in which they lived), the Jews were quite successful in this undertaking.

Other ethnic groups took other routes: business, politics, athletics (*all* ethnic groups went through a criminal phase as far as I can tell). Then with the burst of post–World War II faith in education, everyone decided to follow the Jewish example. Blacks, Hispanics, women, the poor and all the hyphenated Americans saw the campus as the ticket office for admission to the middle, or even the upper, class. On the whole, those demands were quite just, i.e., blacks and Puerto Ricans were right to insist that the City University of New York serve them, too, by means of an open admissions policy. I do not in any way question the moral and judicial basis of those demanding to be allowed in; I support them. But I do argue that the effect they expected could not be achieved so long as only the schools were changed. And when that latter fact became apparent, the energies which were supposed to change everyone's relative position in the social structure were, too often, dissipated in group competition and hatred which changed little or nothing.

So it is not merely that the nation failed to honor its commitment to education and training in the sixties, though that is true enough. The entire strategy of relying primarily upon schooling to bring the poor into the working class and the working class into the middle class was fundamentally flawed. It suffered from the economic and labor market contradictions which Lester Thurow was particularly brilliant in describing; it faced the social limits which Hirsch illuminated. But what, then, are the economic and social changes which would allow education to make its full contribution—and even turn away from the totally utilitarian definitions of learning, permitting it to enrich the spirit as well as enhance a production function?[2]

II

There are a number of possible economic and social changes which at first glance have nothing to do with education. Yet they are absolutely essential to a rational, efficient school system at all levels. They are all characterized by the fact that they move, openly and directly, to change the class structure which frustrates the social potential of education in so many ways.

To begin with, one of the chief reasons for our current plight is that schooling is seen as the key to economic success but, as has been seen, can no longer function in that way. Some time ago, in the very midst of the sixties euphoria in this area, Christopher Jencks and David Riesman wrote with great perception, "Yet the heart of the problem is not, we think, in the educational system. So long as the distribution of power and privilege remains radically unequal, and so long as some children are raised by adults at the bottom while others are raised by adults at the top, the children will more often than not turn out unequal." And: "So long as American life is premised on dramatic inequalities of wealth and power, no system for allocating social roles will be very satisfactory." Precisely. And, conversely, egalitarian changes in the class structure will make it possible for the schools to participate much more effectively in a process of social change.[3]

In developing this basic thought in some detail there will be a necessary repetition of some of the themes treated in chapter 5. The concern with redistributionist policies in this context, however, is not with those policies in and of themselves, but with the way in which they open the road to a much better school system and indeed to the liberation of learning.

First, full employment, the precondition of all progressive change in the United States, would benefit every level of the society, but it would have the greatest consequence for those at the bottom. If, to use Lord Beveridge's excellent definition of full employment, there were more job opportunities than job seekers, and employers were forced to go out and look for workers, that would strike a tremendous blow against credentialism. We already know that the very inadequate approximations of full employment in the post–World War II period have resulted in a decline in irrelevant qualifications within the labor market. If that were to happen, then at least some of the waste involved in a "defensive" strategy of acquiring education, not to progress upward, but to avoid being pushed downward, could be done away with.

The very relative degree of full employment in the postwar period has been cited; the real full employment achieved during World War II is an even more persuasive case in point, though it involves a policy dimension that goes beyond macroeconomics. During the war, unemployment went down to a 1 percent level. It was in this period that black Americans made their most dramatic gains in relation to whites, and these were the years in which the income structure may have actually become somewhat more progressive. (These matters are documented in chapter 3.) In part, that was a result of the mere—and momentous—fact of war-induced full employment. In part, it was a consequence of conscious governmental policy.

There was in those days a strong feeling in the nation

that there should be "equality of sacrifice" in the war effort. The battle against fascism was, so to speak, a left-wing mobilization and it came right after the great surge of social consciousness in the thirties. In this political context, Lester Thurow points out, "the Federal government undertook to use its wage and labor controls to implement this consensus and equalize market wages." In the present situation, it will not be easy to persuade the nation to intervene directly so as to reduce the differentials between wages. As Christopher Jencks said in the early seventies, "Americans now tend to assume that incomes are determined by private decisions in a largely unregulated economy and that there is no realistic way to alter the resulting distribution." And even though there is clear evidence that those differentials are not functionally necessary—the Japanese have less of them, and have outcompeted the United States in a number of areas—that old belief will die hard.

But then Jencks added an extremely important point. Up until the New Deal, most people wrongly thought that the levels of investment and employment had to be left to the invisible hand of the market as it operated through the greed of private decision-makers. The nation got rid of that venerable myth under the pressure of the Great Depression. Perhaps the crisis of stagflation can force the society to realize that wage differentials were not handed down by God and chiseled on tablets of stone. If that is understood, there would be many happy results and one of them would be to lessen the pressure on the school system. If one wants to make a hardheaded statement of this theme, it would be well to follow Hirsch, who pointed out that a reduction in differentials will lower the value of credentials and therefore counter excess investment in education. More equality could actually help the nation save money!

There are related policies, detailed elsewhere in the book, which I will merely mention here. If the welfare state were extended so that there were a really adequate floor under every citizen, and if tax policy were truly progressive, then the extremes of poverty and wealth would be eliminated. People could then be somewhat more relaxed about the competitive race and more realistic about education. To get the full benefits from such a policy, however, a cultural shift would have to take place. It is not as preposterous as it might at first sound since at least some of the children of the upper middle class—and even of the corporate rich—have been acting on it for some time.

The status hysteria which often seizes young people striving for economic success is related to the contempt, and even fear, of the established society with regard to manual labor. It is well known, for instance, that there are men and women who will work for less money in a white-collar job because they know that is is "better" than a blue-collar occupation which pays more. The anxieties and hopes which motivate students to make "defensive" investments in education which do not improve them or the economy as far as we can tell are deeply involved in this psychology. But what if there were changes, not simply in the wages associated with various jobs, but with the status assigned to them as well?

There was, to be sure, much that was faddish and self-indulgent in the counterculture of the sixties. It was a product of the longest peacetime boom in American history, a time when young people could afford to be somewhat casual about "dropping out" of society. Put in the most pejorative light, there were rebels who were certain that they would be subsidized by the very bourgeoisie which they derided, i.e., by their own parents. But there was also something healthy in this reaction. The children of affluence, those who had known a freedom from serious want, rebelled against the competitiveness which, in most cases, had allowed their parents to give them a privileged life. Some of them went back to the land; others became artisans and acquired craft skills. Many, to be sure, dropped out of their own dropping out and came back to established society after an adventure or two.

It was, and still is, fashionable to sneer at these young people, not the least because they were radicals with incomes from home. And yet, for all that anomaly, their values were good and sound. They were objecting to the lockstep required of those who move up the normal income and status ladders. They rejected the cutthroat competition which demands that a person push his or her "inferiors" down. They looked for work lives that were enriching in personal, rather than merely monetary, terms. It is fair to object that such options should not be confined to the children of the upper middle class during an episode of full employment. But if there were to be permanent and planned full employment, then one result would be to increase vastly the numbers of those who could make such decisions. Indeed, the society might even act as rich parent to the children of all of its people, providing subsidies for anyone who wanted seriously to pursue a personal definition of work.

That obviously applies in the case of the arts, where the nation is already committed to placing some resources at the disposal of those with a talent which is recognized at a young age. But what about those who might want to become skilled workers in an economy in which the wages and status of such occupations would have been consciously raised? What of middle-aged or older people who, after a considerable time in one job, would want to strike out in another direction? The point is that, if the society were to "reduce the rewards of success and the punishments of failure" and thus make much more relaxed career decisions possible, it should also seek to provide practical ways in which people could act on those decisions. Work in America, as Harry Braverman pointed out in *Labor and Monopoly Capital,* has been designed according to a social and political, as well as a technological, calculus. Skills have been destroyed, decision making reserved to an increasingly tiny minority and the majority made into cogs in the wheel as far as that is possible.

Braverman's history of work must be read in conjunction with Bowles and Gintis's history of the schools, for they were, and are, interrelated. Technology was developed so as to require semirobots, and the schools were often designed to put a premium upon patient obedience and respect for authority. Indeed Bowles and Gintis rightly point out that working-class and minority preferences for types of schooling—for more discipline as compared to the middle-class interest in "open" schoolrooms and innovative curricula—reflect their own life experiences. Workers and the lower middle class are rewarded for following the routine without complaining; the middle and upper middle classes operate in a competitive atmosphere in which initiative and new ideas are often the way to success. I am suggesting that government policy could change the economic environment and in the process open up at least the possibilities of new values. The nation would no longer have to worship Mammon.

That, obviously, would have a profound effect upon the educational system. If the postwar period came to define schooling as an "input" in a production function, the partial failure of that approach and the new policy directions urged here could open the way to much greater diversity and even to a renewed emphasis upon schools as places where the human spirit is enriched and culture transmitted and developed. That ideal has historically been aristocratic because only aristocrats were able to indulge it. But if the social and economic changes advocated in this book were adopted in the United States, that excellent possibility could be democratized.

Let me outline one variant of such a development.* The society would provide free and open access to education for every citizen and would take special measures to see to it that the disadvantaged—minorities, women, the children of the poor—would have the opportunity to go to college. Those who find it preposterous to think that so many people could benefit from higher education might remember that in 1912 Professor Henry Goddard discovered that 83 percent of the Jews in the United States, 80 percent of the Hungarians, 79 percent of Italians and 87

---

* Many of these ideas were inspired by my friend, the late Robert M. Hutchins. I am, of course, solely responsible for the very brief formulation of them in this chapter.

percent of Russians were "feeble-minded." The grandchildren of those "feeble-minded" people probably constitute a majority of the college students in America today, or close to it. That is to say that the inferiority with which those groups were slandered was in the eye of the prejudiced beholder, not in the groups themselves. There is no reason to think that those who are at the social-economic bottom of American society today—and who are the victims of a similar ignorant contempt on the part of some of the supposedly educated—will be any different.

This is not to say that everyone will be *required* to go to college. The point I insist upon is for society to provide people with an *effective* right to make the best career choice for them. College would really be open to all—but so would the option of becoming a skilled worker, an artist or an artisan. And it would be possible to exercise that freedom more adventurously because the consequences of failure, in economic and social terms, would no longer be so terrible. But then the schools would be liberated in much the same way as the students who attended them.

College, for instance, would no longer be a training academy for business, not the least because the society would have understood the demonstrated irrelevance of most of the training. One could envision a broad core curriculum, beginning in what is today the junior year of high school and ending with a degree at what is now the completion of the second year of college. This would provide exposure to all of the basic intellectual disciplines. That education, we now know, is more than sufficient in terms of the economic needs of the society. It also could be much more concerned with the development of the mind and spirit than the present schools usually are. Those who wanted to specialize would become graduate students in their late teens; the others would enter the work force, but with the option of returning to some form of education at a later date.

One of the functions of this process would be to allow —and even encourage—people to study things which are not immediately "relevant." In the sixties, the Establishment and its radical critics often agreed on the essential proposition that the schools had to be relevant. They differed only as to what that relevance meant. The powers that be wanted learning to impart those skills which would make responsible, patient and contented workers; at least some of the Left wanted trade schools for the revolution. Both sides were wrong, I think. What is the relevance of poetry or music or philosophical studies pursued for their intrinsic value? From a "practical" point of view, it is often zero. From a human point of view, it can be enormous.

Education, in short, can play a crucial role in social change, but only on the condition that it gives up the sixties illusion, in both liberal and radical variants, that schools, and schools alone, are going to create a new social and economic order. If the unjust class sytem of American society—and of the world economic order, for that matter—were transformed, then, and only then, education could make the enormous contribution of which it is capable. For that reason, educators *as educators* must be concerned with society, i.e., with the context which determines what the school will be much more than its faculty does. And the champions of social change must see education, and sometimes education in and of itself, as one of the critical components for the enrichment of free men and women and children.

All well and good, someone could plausibly respond to this chapter. The abstractions are fine. But are they politically serious?

___ Notes _____

1. LBJ: Kearns, pp. 261 and 45. Nixon: Levitan and Taggart, *The Promise of Greatness,* pp. 135–36.

2. Output: Hitch and McKean, p. 33. Education increase: Thurow, *On Generating Inequality,* p. 65. Schultz: "Reflections on Investment in Man," p. 2. CEA, 1974: p. 141. Thurow: Op. cit., pp. 61–62. Aaron and

Vietnam shift: *Politics and the Professors,* pp. 27 and 126. Moynihan: *The Politics of the Guaranteed Annual Income,* p. 125. Levitan and Taggart: Op. cit., pp. 120 and 126. Aaron on tests: Op. cit., p. 94. Bowles and Gintis: *Schooling in Capitalist America,* p. 110 and fig. 4; pp. 120 ff. Aaron on Jencks: Op. cit., pp. 76 ff. Nixon on education: *A New Road for America,* pp. 202 ff. Thurow: Op. cit., p. 78. JEC study: U.S. Long-Term Economic Growth, p. 100. Jencks et al., passim. Thurow on labor market: Op. cit., p. 95. Chicago: Lamberton, ed., p. 112. Okun: *The Great Stagflation Swamp,* p. 2. Thurow on education and economic value: Op. cit., 96–97, 119; 184. College degree: JEC, *U.S. Long Term Economic Growth Prospects,* p. 40; pp. 105–8; p. 29; table III-2, p. 42; p. 100. Traumatic reversal: Ibid., p. 140. Hirsch: *Social Limits to Growth,* p. 176. Tourists: Ibid., p. 37. Marshall quoted: Ibid., p. 170. Congressional study: *U.S. Long Term Growth,* p. 1. OECD: Paul Lewis dispatch, *The New York Times,* July 5, 1978. *Business Week:* "Vanishing Innovation," July 5, 1978. Smith quote: Hirsch, p. 137. Values: Ibid., p. 138. Reluctant collectivism: Ibid., p. 175.

3. Riesman and Jencks: *The Academic Revolution,* pp. 147 and 156. Thurow on World War II; Op. cit., p. 59. Jencks: p. 264. Bowles and Gintis: Op. cit., pp. 133, 196.

9

To the Left,
Right and Center

Clearly, significant structural changes in American society are imperative if the nation is to solve its long-run problems. Such transformations are necessary. Are they politically possible?

I think so. Yet, I also think that it is not in the least necessary that the country respond in a progressive way to this crisis. It cannot go on for very long using the last generation's theories and practices to deal with this generation's unprecedented difficulties. There is no question that the stagflation analyzed in chapter 2, and the other structural contradictions explored subsequently, will provoke some basic new departures. Willy-nilly, the eighties are a decade of decision. The transformations, however, need not be benign. One can move out of this impasse in the direction of a sophisticated and modern Right as well as by turning to the democratic Left. Still, it is because our plight is both structural and profound that one is permitted even to hope that there will be a new political mobilization, as radical in its day as the New Deal was in the thirties.

I argue thus even though the popular wisdom of recent

years held that America is becoming more conservative. That conviction is relatively easy to refute, not the least because a number of academics from a broad political spectrum have assembled the data to show that it is not accurate. The countertruth, however, is hardly simple or even consoling. In the late seventies, the people of the United States were moving vigorously to the Left, the Right and the Center, all at the same time. There were clear signs that many traditional alignments were coming unstuck—and no clear sign as to a new realignment. So there was informed talk of party "decomposition," of "disalignment," of a situation in which people were "building coalitions in the sand."

I will first sort out some of the confusing trends since these portents of decadence are the necessary, but not the sufficient, condition for political hope. Then I will suggest the outline of a new alignment, a coalition not built in the sand. Its cement will be found in the interests of a number of social classes and strata. My perspective is a departure from most of the current scholarly literature, which sees these times characterized by a *decline* in the importance of class loyalties. My case will be presented in greater detail shortly, but its key assumption can, and should, be stated openly at the outset: that the structural crises analyzed in this book will once again place economic issues at the very center of the national agenda and that this development will, sooner or later, summon up new energies out of the exigencies of various class positions. I am not, of course, suggesting the return of the 1930s, which are dead and gone. There are social groups which may well play a very important role in the eighties and nineties which hardly existed during the New Deal. And yet, there still could be this important analogy to that bygone age: that economic issues will once again be center stage—even if the stage is quite new.

I will show how this could happen—and how it could not happen. On the latter count, I will imagine a scenario which is both plausible and abhorrent. In it, the Right, not the Left, will be the beneficiary of all of this tumult. I project the defeat of my own deepest hope in this way for two reasons. First, because it could well happen here and any analysis which claims to be serious should ponder that fact. Second, perhaps the very statement of the possibility of such a future will motivate people to act so that it never happens. As I explained in the first chapter, I study these matters as "objectively" as I can because that is profoundly in the interest of my intensively subjective commitment to a better America in a better world.

But even given this conditional optimism, this chapter does not pretend to present anything but a possibility: that the nation might actually take advantage of its myriad troubles and emerge so much the better for that fact.[1]

_____ **I** _____

In the late seventies there was a widespread belief among both politicians and average citizens that the nation was moving to the Right. In fact, that was not the case, and, in understanding why, one does more than show that a turn to the Left is possible. One also bears importantly on long-term analysis.

As the seventies ended, America was, and to a certain extent still is, moving Left, Right and Center at the same time. Two scholars, Lloyd A. Free and Hadley Cantril, wrote a study of *The Political Beliefs of Americans* in the mid-sixties which helps explicate that paradox. That book, and the distinction which it made between "ideological" and "operational" attitudes, was the basis of much of the scholarly work in the late seventies which discounted the notion that America was simply becoming more conservative. So it is worth looking back on their perceptive account of the past in order to understand the present and future.

Free and Cantril wrote that ". . . the majority of Americans remain conservative at the ideological level in the sense that they continue to accept the traditional ideology which advocates the curbing of Federal power. Yet, at the practical level of Governmental operations, there has been an apparently inexorable trend in a liberal direction since the days of the New Deal." This judgment, it is important to remember, was based on data gathered in 1964, i.e., in a period of declining unemployment, stable prices and popular governmental innovation. Even so, 30 percent of a national sample declared themselves to be "completely" conservative and another 20 percent said they were "predominantly" conservative. Only 4 percent identified themselves as "completely" liberal, and 12 percent as "predominantly" liberal. The rest—34 percent—said they were in the middle of the road. In short, even as Lyndon Johnson was building toward a landslide victory over a conservative, a majority of Americans said they were *ideologically* conservative. At the same time, 65 percent of the sample turned out to be *operationally* liberal while only 7 percent were "completely" conservative on operational questions. That operational liberalism was defined by support for specific federal programs whose very existence contradicted the principles of ideological conservatism.

Arthur Schlesinger, Jr., applied this critical distinction to 1939—one year before Franklin Roosevelt was elected to an unprecedented third term—when 52 percent of a representative sample of the American people told the Gallup poll that they were conservative. The liberal identifiers were 46 percent of the total and, at a time when more than ten million were still unemployed in the worst depression capitalism had ever known, a mere 2 percent said that they were radical.

In the late seventies, Everett Carl Ladd, Jr., used the Free-Cantril notion and discovered a similar schizophrenia in an America which was supposed to be moving to the right. The people, Ladd said, were "*institutional* conservatives and *operational* liberals." Thus, 72 percent thought the government was too strong *and* 61 percent favored mandatory wage and price controls, 67 percent were for national health insurance, 85 percent wanted the government to help people get low-cost medical care and 77 percent thought that Washington should "see to it that everyone who wants a job gets one." The federal government, 82 percent thought, was spending too much, but majorities, ranging from 73 percent to 90 percent, thought too little was being spent on the environment, health, aid to the cities, education and improving the condition of blacks. It was only when one mentioned "welfare" that support for further spending dropped to 39 percent. Yet, as chapter 7 documented, welfare spending is a relatively small part of public outlays. Incidentally, Ladd found that support for the "service state" existed at all income levels: people with incomes of under $10,000 were only marginally more enthusiastic about federal spending than those making over $25,000.

The conservative commentator James J. Kilpatrick responded to another poll, the results of which were similar to Ladd's (a *New York Times*–CBS survey in January 1978), with some shrewdness. When one takes such soundings, Kilpatrick said, the question asked invites an answer. Thus if you ask people, not whether "government" should do something, but whether "free enterprise" should, the same number will be positive. Herbert Stein, chairman of Nixon's Council of Economic Advisers, made a similar point while arguing for a tax cut. We have been asking, Stein said, how much should we spend on this or that program. Now, he continued, we are going to ask, how much should people pay in income taxes and then *derive* spending from the limit thus placed upon revenues.

In a survey, the pollsters—or those who pay them— decide on which questions to ask. But in politics, candidates, parties and the media determine that critical issue. If a movement succeeds in posing the question, Do you want lower property taxes, as Proposition 13 did in California in 1978, the answer is likely to be yes. But if the question is the one asked by Lyndon Johnson in 1964— should the federal government guarantee health care for people over sixty-five?—the answer is also yes. But then I exaggerate the indeterminacy of the situation. Questions can be asked according to the skill of politicians and influentials and answered according to the will of the people —but all answers are not equally possible in the real world.

Thus, many of the proponents of Proposition 13 were opponents of centralized governmental power and their attack on the property tax was, in part at least, motivated by that attitude. But by depriving municipalities of their most important single source of funds, they forced the state of California (and eventually the federal government) to play even more of a role. Still, it could be some time before that fact becomes apparent, or perhaps people will permanently delude themselves about it. So even though there are many unintended consequences in the process, it is still of enormous moment which questions are asked.

If ideologically conservative issues are the focus of attention, it will be obvious that America is Rightist; if operational liberal propositions are in the forefront, that same nation at the same time will seem to be leaning toward the moderate Left. Even the "social issue," to which the response is supposed to be inherently conservative, is much more complex than that. Responses in this area, Ladd said, show "a liberal drift. There has been a fairly dramatic growth of the pro-civil liberties and pro-civil rights positions; and there has been an erosion of many of the old codes of personal comportment, governing a range of such matters as pre-marital sex, abortion and the use of marijuana."

I do not, however, draw a complacent conclusion from all of this. It is not true that the democratic Left can stop worrying about ideology and concentrate on the operational issues which will come back into vogue sooner or later. These data suggest that America is an exceedingly confused nation and this has social, as well as individual psychological, significance. Because America still believes in a Horatio Alger idyll which it instinctively knows will not work in practice, its operational liberalism is truncated. Thus, the presence of a democratic socialist ideology in Europe is at least one of the reasons why unemployment there was half that of the American average during the post–World War II period—or why the United States is the only Western country without a national health system.

It is, in short, important to change America in *both* ideological and operational ways, for the two are not unrelated. The solace that one can draw from the evidence just presented is that it is at least possible that a political movement in the eighties could take the solid, long-established operational liberalism of this country as the point of departure for practical reforms *and* ideological education. However, if this analysis leads to a relatively optimistic conclusion—that it is at least possible to organize a progressive response to the challenges of the late twentieth century—it also emphasizes the complexity of the task.

There is no single, "natural" majority in the United States which can be mobilized behind a series of defined policies and programs. Rather, there are several potential majorities at any given time and which one will actually emerge depends on a whole range of factors. What political movements succeed in setting the agenda, in posing the questions? Which issues are pushed into the center of political discussion by events? Can government actually act upon the questions posed and the answers given or do sincere movements militantly undermine their deepest values when they are victorious?

In the past, political parties provided the answers to those questions. Thus, when the Depression posed the economic issue in a way which could not be ignored, Franklin Roosevelt and the Democratic party responded with the New Deal and thereby established the terms of debate, even for their opponents, and created the social base for a new majority coalition. Can one project a similar development in the eighties or the nineties? One group of sophisticated experts have their doubts. The party system, scholars and journalists have been saying for some time, is disintegrating and something unprecedented is happening. The old coalition is breaking down but there is no new coalition coming to take its place. Coalitions, Anthony King suggests, are assembled by putting together preexisting blocs: the workers, the minorities, the South and the middle-class liberals rally behind the New Deal. But is it possible that the society is now so atomized that there are no preexisting groups sufficiently cohesive to coalesce in a permanent and institutionalized majority? Are politics, then, to become highly indeterminate, personalized and mercurial?

In attempting to sketch an answer to these questions, I will not simply be dealing with the tactical considerations of a democratic Left majority. These matters have to do with the structural evolution of American society in an entire historic period.

The American Voter was an enormously influential study which appeared in 1960 and generalized the political experience of the fifties. The voters, if found, were not motivated by detailed knowledge or ideology or a knowledge about the policy positions of the parties. And yet, the parties played a crucial role. Party affiliation was handed on from generation to generation and most people voted the way their fathers did. Thus identification with a party was an emotional—even irrational—fact of life. And it was at the same time a major source of a critical value of (supposedly "value-free") social scientists in that period: stability. Given the fact that voters inherited strong party loyalties, most elections simply maintained basic patterns. Occasionally, there would be deviating elections in which special circumstances would momentarily upset, but not basically change, those patterns, e.g., the Republican split which brought Woodrow Wilson to power in 1912. And, very infrequently, there would be realigning elections in which a new dominant issue would energize a new majority coalition which would then persist for forty or fifty years, e.g., the emergence of modern capitalist Republicanism in 1896, Democratic welfareism in 1932.

There were many disputed points in this analysis. For instance, were the people who turned to the Democrats in the thirties new voters or old voters who changed their minds? Did "realigning elections" merely ratify decisions already made by an elite, as Gary Wills argues? But the basic interpretation provided a paradigm for academic discussion which totally dominated the mainstream. The countertrends, we now know, were clearly in motion in 1964, or before, yet as Jeanne Kirkpatrick rightly insists, no one knew that, or predicted it then. But as time went on events so obviously contradicted theory that the scholars had to go back to their drawing boards. In 1964, Lyndon Johnson received a landslide mandate; in 1968, he was effectively forced from office. In 1972, Richard Nixon received another landslide mandate; in 1974, he was driven out of the presidency. How could there be two counterposed landslides in eight years if voters' preferences were stable and inherited? And how could the electorates which put Johnson and Nixon in office help to push them out of it in a matter of a few years?

One of the most ambitious attempts to deal with these questions was the study of *The Changing American Voter* by Norman Nie, Sidney Verba and John R. Petrocik. It carefully went over the ground of *The American Voter* analysis in order to define the changes that had taken place. People in the seventies, it discovered, were much less partisan, more ideological, more coherent on issues than in the fifties. Between 1952 and 1964, the proportions of strong partisans, weak partisans and independents in the electorate were remarkably stable. A little more than a third of the people were strong partisans, a slightly larger group weak partisans and a fifth were independent. But between 1964 and 1974, there are marked changes: the independents are now 38 percent, the strong partisans only about 25 percent. Moreover the Democratic party becomes " more black, less Southern and has developed a larger 'silk-stocking' component," and the Republicans are more Southern, less black, more Catholic and less Protestant.

There was also a sharp drop in voter turnout and the Republican party, which in 1976 could count upon only about 20 percent of the electorate, seemed to become half a party. Alarm was expressed from every quarter of the political compass. Editing a volume for the conservative American Enterprise Institute, Anthony King commented, "The politics of the 1930s and 1940s resembled a nineteenth century battlefield, with two opposing armies arrayed against each other in more or less close formation; politics today is an altogether messier affair, with large numbers of small detachments engaged over a vast territory, and with individuals and groups frequently changing sides." The liberal Arthur Schlesinger, Jr., had earlier used a similar image: "We might then enter an era in which political leaders, like Chinese warlords, roam the countryside, organizing personal armies. . . . The crumbling away of the historic parties would leave political power in America concentrated in the warlords, the interest groups that financed their armies and the executive bureaucracy."

I will argue in the next section that the politics of the eighties could well revert to the forms (but not the content) of the thirties and forties. But if that is going to happen, it is imperative that one understand how the current interregnum, with all of its disintegrations, came into being. So I will accept these various descriptions of the immediate political past, present and future. Why are such things happening?

One popular answer is: The reformers did it. As analysts like Everett Ladd and Austin Ranney develop that theme, it was the "new class" of "college educated professionals and managers in the public sector" who forced the "opening up" of the energy system. That led to a decline in the power of institutionalized leadership, to a rise in the influence of (often ideological) activists and to much less attention being paid to the party's regular voters. McGovern's victory in 1972 at the Democratic party convention in Miami Beach would be a paradigmatic moment in this process. The "outsiders," Ranney would say, "captured" a party which had easily rebuffed mavericks like Estes Kefauver (who challenged Adlai Stevenson in 1956) and Eugene McCarthy (who fought Johnson and then Humphrey in 1968). One permanent and structural result of all of this well-intentioned reform, these people say, was the tremendous increase in the number of presidential primaries, a mode of selection which further weak-

ened the party regulars by turning decisions over to the
minority of activists who could dominate such events.

I find this theory most unconvincing—and an impediment to the development of a responsible party system in
the future. To begin with, the subversion of the old-style
"regular" political party began long before the reform efforts of the late sixties and early seventies. Political machines and bosses, the sociologists long ago recognized,
had an extremely important "welfare" function in the
United States: finding jobs, helping those in trouble with
the law, even providing food. When the New Deal came
into existence—in some considerable measure because
those machines and bosses supported Roosevelt—the
death knell for that political style sounded. The social-
work, community function of the clubhouse was taken
over by a governmental structure—and the clubhouses
would never again be the same.

At the same time as this process was set in motion the
voters became, as *The Changing American Voter* emphasized, more educated and sophisticated about issues. The
college-educated participate more than high-school graduates, who are, in turn, more active than those with less
than a high-school education. But it was precisely in the
post–World War II period, as the last chapter showed, that
educational attainment went up for the entire society.
This, too, made it more difficult to maintain a party system based on inherited, traditional loyalties.

Third, scholars like Ranney and Ladd are remarkably
careless when it comes to examining the specific events
which led to the reform movement in the late sixties.
When great masses of Democratic voters became—rightly
—disenchanted with Lyndon Johnson's Vietnam policy,
they discovered that the 1968 convention was controlled
from the top. Many of the delegates had been selected in
1967 and even if the antiwar forces won every primary
they could not have achieved a majority. It was this manifest *failure* of the party system to respond to popular sen-
timent which motivated the reformers. Moreover, the
reform movement was precisely committed to creating a

new and much more responsible party system based upon issues and ideology and they were frustrated at every turn by the regulars who were bent on maintaining institutional structures which were obviously obsolete. The Carter loyalists, for example, attempted to turn the 1978 Midterm Democratic Conference into a well-organized irrelevance.*

In short, there were profound economic and social forces at work, and the reform efforts refracted them much more than they caused them. And it should be emphasized, I have only mentioned a few of those "external" factors. I could also note that the atomization of politics was, after all, part of a process in which American life itself was becoming more atomized. Neighborhoods and neighborhood life were subverted by the migrations described in chapter 6. "We are beginning to learn," Norton Long wrote of these developments, "that the normative order on which our cities depended in the past was not the product of the formal governments but of the many informal governments of the ethnic neighborhoods." But it was precisely that normative order—which the political party had institutionalized in one of its important aspects—that was, and is, being destroyed by the unplanned, uncontrolled consequences of corporate decisions aided and abetted by federal subsidies.

And then there was the particular way in which the government intervention initiated by the New Deal proceeded. Secretary of HEW Joseph A. Califano outlined the situation to a Chicago audience in 1978: "Power is fragmented in Washington these days, not just within the executive branch, but by legislative mandates within HEW itself. . . . Political party discipline has been shattered by the rise of special interest politics in the nation's capital. Washington has become a city of political molecules, with fragmentation of power, and often authority and respon-

---

* I should "declare an interest" and identify a source. I was a participant in the reform effort from 1967 to the present. I was a delegate to the Democratic Midterm conventions of 1974 and 1978, and testified before the National Platform Committee in 1968 and 1976. At the 1978 Midterm Convention, I was one of the floor leaders of the reform caucus.

sibility, among increasingly narrow, what's-in-it-for-me interest groups. . . ." And this, of course, has led to a tremendous increase in outlays for lobbying.

On a more subtle—ideological—level there are similar developments. Charles Lindblom suggests that the "old indoctrination of class and leadership are losing effect. Although the old indoctrinations have muted demands for many long decades, acquiescence, deference and compliance are now waning." And he concludes, "In the decline of that indoctrination looms the possibility of the renewal of the war of all against all." Ironically, that tendency has probably been exacerbated by the delusions described in chapter 7. As many nonblack and nonpoor people came to believe that prodigies were being done on behalf of the blacks and the poor, they began to organize for their own proper entitlement. More often than not, this pitted them against the blacks, the poor and each other rather than against the united front of corporate and governmental power which was, and is, their real enemy.

There is a related phenomenon. Walter Dean Burnham, one of the most astute observers of the American political process, calls it the "hole" in the American electorate. The legions of nonvoters in the seventies are not randomly selected. They are disproportionately poor and working class, and indeed, as Burnham shrewdly points out, they are exactly the constituency which is mobilized in Europe behind socialist and labor parties. These people may have instinctively, but quite rationally, perceived an important truth: that an America which cannot even debate democratic and radical transformations cannot really provide solutions for those whom this society more and more marginalizes.

One could go on and cite many other factors at work in this disintegrative process, yet I think the central point has been made. Deep-going trends within the economy and social structure are much more important solvents of the traditional (since Roosevelt) party system than reformers. Indeed, one can say that the current problems in the political order are complex refractions of the problems and failures described in this book, that they are one more unintended consequence of running an increasingly social system on the basis of corporate priorities. And that means that a successful program to deal with our crisis must in some measure create its own constituency by giving people solid, rational reasons for participating in party life and developing new, and different, loyalties.

And finally, it is at least possible that the negatives which have just been examined may clear the way for new, and positive, developments. In the twenties, there were low election turnouts: only about 44 percent of the electorate went to the polls in 1920 and 1924. That, the theorists of *The Changing American Voter* suggest, might have helped create the basis for the Roosevelt surge, for it meant that there were a large number of uncommitted people in the society who were ready and waiting for a new loyalty when the proper moment came. Such moments, clearly, cannot be arranged in advance—and, yet, one can prepare for them. If the crisis of the late seventies and eighties is indeed analogous to, though quite different from, that of the thirties, it is important that some thought be devoted to the possibility. Which is why I now turn to some speculations on new alignments, for both good and bad, that might be in the American future.[2]

II

Social class and class interests are the key concepts of my analysis of the possibility of the emergence of a new party system capable of coping with the crises described in this book. That, of course, means that my approach is intellectually unfashionable, at least among the political scientists cited in the last section, all of whom insist upon the declining influence of class in American politics. But then, to cite Jeanne Kirkpatrick again, those experts did not anticipate the crisis which they now depict with such confidence—and perhaps they have overlooked its resolution as well.

There is, I will suggest, a working class in this country, the notices of its lingering, impending death to the contrary notwithstanding. That class has enormous potential for progressive change. There is also a vastly expanded middle class—or perhaps a "new" class—which, *under specific circumstances*, could discover an identity of interest with the working class. Those specific circumstances are at least one possible result of the economic contradictions which have been described in this book. If, however, such economic events do not have a unifying impact, there could be a war of each against all in American society which would be even more destructive than the gloomy essayists of *The New American Political System* imagine. Indeed, I outlined precisely such a possibility more than ten years ago in *Toward a Democratic Left*.

Finally, there is a reactionary, as well as a progressive, solution to these political woes, i.e., a new party system which would shore up, and provide a revived legitimacy for, the corporate power system which is the mainspring of this economy and society. We could, so to speak, socialize our miseries—and nothing else. That outcome, as will be seen, has little or nothing to do with the nostalgic conservatism which wants to retreat back into the nineteenth or even the eighteenth century. Those idylls might provide a myth which would hide the reality of corporate domination through the agony of a state which theoretically—but only theoretically—is dedicated to the common good. But that is all. The reactionary solution will be sophisticated and statist even if it is decked out with quotations from Adam Smith. I will, then, attempt a most realistic analysis of all possibilities, one in which my fears are argued as carefully as my hopes.

I begin with the hopes, first and foremost with the reality and potential of the American working class.

The data do indeed show a decline in the Democratic party identification of the white, traditional (last-generation) working class—but that is, as I will show in a moment, a more ambiguous proposition than many of its proponents realize. It is, however, an important half-truth. In the aftermath of the 1978 elections, for instance, a poll commissioned by the United Automobile Workers (UAW) showed that its members under fifty years of age were less likely to follow the union's political lead than those over fifty. Roughly speaking, that meant that the generation which had experienced the Great Depression was more likely to act on a class political base than the post–World War II generation. It is a reality clearly associated with *relative* affluence in the auto plants during the last several decades and to the fact that the UAW won Supplementary Unemployment Benefits (SUB) which maintained a jobless worker at 90 percent of straight time wage during the massive layoffs of 1974 (the SUB funds ran out in some instances, but on the whole, the system worked).

Does that mean that "much of the American working class has become bourgeois and is therefore anxious to protect a status gained at considerable effort and only temporarily held?" That judgment of Everett Ladd is a serious exaggeration of the half-truth. Part of the problem has to do with basic concepts, for this is an area in which the official government categories have caused endless confusion. Thus Ladd and Charles Hadley note that there has been a significant drop in the Democratic loyalty of "blue-collar whites." But does that mean that the "working class" or even the "white working class" has become less Democratic? The Bureau of the Census puts "blue-collar" and "service" workers in different slots. Many think that the former category defines the workers while the latter does not.

In fact, the service category includes a huge number of people paid much less than blue-collar workers and employed in menial jobs. It also includes an industry—health care—in which unionization has made important gains. Further, when one excludes private household workers, where black participation has gone down dramatically since 1960, this is a group in which minorities are concentrated. If, Andrew Levinson has persuasively argued in *Working Class Majority*, one breaks through the misleading concepts used by the government, it turns out that over 50 percent of the American people are workers. This is not to suggest that no changes have taken place or to deny that better-off workers have less of a class-conscious attitude today than they, or their poorer counterparts, in the thirties. It is to insist that there is a massive objective basis for class politics in America today which *could* be actualized by political movements and economic events. The key is this: that a majority of the American people do not have enough, as measured by the standards of this society; that they labor at routine, intrinsically unrewarding tasks; and that if they are not a "proletariat" in a nineteenth-century, or even 1930s, sense, neither are they a middle class.

Here, as in the discussion of the various possible political majorities in the United States, there is considerable indeterminacy. The class situation of American workers will not necessarily and inevitably force them to play a leading role in the progressive coalition in this chapter. My proposition is much more open-ended even if it is not agnostic: there are significant class factors in American life, usually overlooked in conventional political as well as in academic analyses, which make it *possible* that American workers might play that role. And one element which bears upon that possibility is whether people become aware of it and movements organize to further it. That is why I now turn to a brief, but serious, consideration of the position of working people in the American society of the 1980s.

In doing this, there is no point to make a scholarly detour into all of the debates over social class. Let me simply assert a methodology which I have elaborated elsewhere (in *The Twilight of Capitalism*). Social classes are not first defined by their "economic" position and only then become politically or ideologically conscious of it. They are economic, social, political and cultural from the very beginning, i.e., attitudes toward child rearing and family life, cocktails and beer, tennis and bowling, Democrats and Republicans are part of a coherent whole whose most basic, but by no means all-determining, fact is the work people do. Incomes are obviously related to jobs and consumption is constrained by income, so a penchant for good French wine or bad fast food is more a function of social structure than of the taste buds.

Moreover, I agree with the sociologist Morris Janowitz that the development of the welfare state has made the notion of a one-to-one relation between occupation and political behavior even less tenable than it was before. "The political process and its manifested tension," Janowitz has observed, "are not based . . . on broad social strata and social classes which produce polarized political demands and action. Instead, the politics of an advanced industrial society is a reflection of its own system of inequality, which is characterized by intensive occupational and interest-group competition." "Each person," he writes a little later, "and each member of the household must confront an elaborate set of contradictory or competing and often ambiguous issues in the pursuit of his self-interest—immediate or long-term. . . . A person's linkage to the mode of production under these conditions is based both on his occupation and on the institutions of social welfare."

A worker, in other words, is not simply a worker, but a member of a race, an ethnic group, a sex, a geographic community, a generation, etc. Each one of those attributes is the basis for various welfare state policies, and as a result there is much more volatility than in days of simpler social class structure and more conflicts within the working class. And yet, at certain periods, the basic economic interest may assert itself as an overwhelming and integrating factor. That happened in the thirties. It could happen in the eighties.

Having thus insisted upon the complexity of class formation—that it is simultaneously political and cultural as well as economic—I will now take a shortcut which will be clearly labeled as such. Income is only one of the "indices of the unobservable" which is social class. In other contexts, it would be utterly inadequate for defining class reality. But in this instance, a provisional definition of classes in terms of income serves to focus upon the essential variables of the analysis: that the majority of Americans do not have enough and that, because of this fact, they are particularly vulnerable to the structural crisis of stagflation in which we are now living. It is at least possible that events and political movements will help them to become much more conscious of this fact in the future and that this will provide the basis for the new politics projected in this chapter.

In 1977, 12.9 percent of the families in the United States had incomes of $6000 or less. These are essentially the people who are poor, and their characteristics have been described at length in chapter 7. Another 37 percent of the families were between $6000 and $16,000. Most, but not all, of these people were in routine, repetitive jobs requiring no decision making. Roughly half of the blue-collar workers had family incomes less than $16,000; so did well over half of service employees and almost all farm laborers. Clerical and sales people are a more ambiguous category (they are, for example, much less likely to be in unions than blue-collar workers), but they are less than a quarter of the population with $16,000 or less.

The group with family incomes between $16,000 and $25,000 is less easy to define. It includes millions of better-paid blue-collar workers and a good number of professionals. In this range, then, one finds the upper working class (working class because of the nature of work done —"blue collar") and the beginnings of the middle class. There is also the impact of working wives: the wages of two unionized blue-collar jobs equal the salary of a middling professional. But in general, the families in the $25,000 to $50,000 range mainly derive their income from professional and technical work and constitute the heart of the middle class proper. Finally, there is a small group (less than 2 percent of the families) making more than $50,000 a year. They are the upper middle class. Somewhere around $200,000 a year, as chapter 4 documented, the wealthy appear.

The Bureau of Labor Statistics periodically updates an "urban family budget" for a four-person family (an employed husband, age thirty-eight; a wife not employed outside the home; an eight-year-old girl and a thirteen-year-old boy). It is clear that this benchmark will have to be corrected to take into account the enormous increase in working wives, but it is good enough for our present purpose. In the autumn of 1977, the "intermediate budget" was $17,106. It did not provide for luxury living or even for "affluence." The family, for instance, was assumed to spend $671 during the course of the year on food eaten away from home and $377 on personal care. Yet this modest target was more than a majority of Americans could afford. It obviously did not represent poverty; it did mean that people had to think long and hard before going out for dinner and a movie.

Finally, the working people who are the focus of this section have been on an income roller coaster during the seventies. Between 1970 and 1977, their real buying power went down in three years (1970, 1974, 1975) and up in five (1971–73; 1976–77). For the eight-year period the decrease in bad years totaled slightly more than the increase in good years. Measured in constant dollars, the real buying power of industrial workers in 1977 was $5 a week less than in 1973. And even a bit less than in 1969. Indeed, a comparison with the sixties is quite instructive in many ways. During that decade, real buying power increased in every year and in 1969, average gross weekly earnings, measured in constant dollars, were 15 percent higher than in 1960.

These figures, it must be emphasized once again, describe indices of the existence of a working class, not that class itself, and they do not predetermine any particular politics, though they make some developments more likely than others. Having once again acknowledged this indeterminacy, it is important to outline the positive content of this analysis.

The majority of Americans know that they are neither rich nor poor. So if you give them only one other choice for self-classification—that everyone in between the rich and poor is therefore part of the middle class—that is how they will identify themselves. That is a perfect example of how the way a question is asked can guarantee the answer which will be given. But, the data have shown, that model of an America with only three classes leads to absurd conclusions. For one must distinguish between two middle classes. Middle Class A is college educated, professional and in 1976 had a mean income of $25,404. Middle Class B is without a college degree, mainly works at manual and/or routine jobs and had a 1976 mean income of $15,928 (blue collar), $11,999 (service), $8754 (farm laborers) and rather ambiguously includes the lower-paid clerical and sales workers. The point is obvious: "Middle Class B" is the working class.

But is that class conscious of itself? If one defines class consciousness to mean an antagonistic self-definition in opposition to other "superior" classes, the answer is obviously no. But there is certainly a class "awareness" in the United States, an understanding of the difference between "us" and "them" which is communicated in manners and speech as well as in politics. Moreover, the various studies which focus on a *decline* in working-class loyalty to the Democratic party demonstrate that there is still an important social class factor in American politics. It is true that "only" 46 percent of the blue-collar whites identified with the Democrats in 1974 as compared with 57 percent in 1960 and 51 percent in 1940; but that 46 percent also represents a continuing, disproportionate leaning toward the Democrats which can only be explained on the basis of a common class political behavior. In class-conscious England (as differentiated from Scotland and Wales), the Labour party itself does not command such loyalty.

In short, not only is there an "objective" working class defined by occupation, income and many other observable commonalities; that class situation leads to distinctive political attitudes. Indeed, without being too paradoxical, I think that it is at least possible that there was a class factor, and moreover a potentially Left and radical class factor, in the turn toward the "Right" discussed earlier. The working-class and lower-middle-class voters who supported Proposition 13 believed that they were paying too high taxes. They were absolutely right, as the chapter on wealth distribution showed. They vented their justifiable anger, not against the reactionary way in which public services are financed, but against the services themselves. It is, I believe, quite possible that a vigorous movement of the democratic Left could direct that anger toward its proper object: the tax slackers and dodgers of the corporate rich.

Indeed, this analysis suggests that one of the elements which will decide whether the possibility of a new, class-based coalition is actualized will be the ability of a democratic Left movement to capture the lead of the tax revolt. But even if that were done, even if the roller-coaster economic conditions of the era of stagflation put economics back on the agenda, the mobilization of the working class would not, in and of itself, make it possible to transform the country. For, as Walter Burnham has emphasized, this is precisely the class with a high number of non-voters. It may be a majority of the labor force; it is not a majority of the active electorate. It must, therefore, be a part of a coalition if it is going to prevail. That is why I now turn to the "New Class."[3]

———— III ————————————————————————

The discussion of a new class has been going on for some time now.* At first, the phenomenon tended to be seen positively and from the democratic Left. Writers like

* Whether the new class is truly a class or merely an enlargement of the "new middle class" of employed educated people (as compared to the "old middle class" of doctors, lawyers and medium-sized-property owners) is a fascinating question which I will not explore here. I have developed my views on this issue in some detail in *The New Class*, edited by B. Bruce-Briggs.

Galbraith, Bazelon and this author all expressed this attitude. But then, as some of the important manifestations
of the youthful idealism of the sixties, like Students for
a Democratic Society, soured, another perspective
emerged. Kevin Phillips, whose *Emerging Republican
Majority* was reputed to be the key to Nixon's 1968 strategy, argued that the success of well-educated young people in the Democratic party opened up the possibility for
the conservatives to capture a working class which stood
by traditional cultural values. William Rusher, a theorist
of the New Right, took much the same line.

Everett Ladd is one of the most important of contemporary analysts developing this concept. American politics, he argues, have been turned upside down. "Whereas
once upon a time it was the lower economic group that
provided liberalism with its bedrock strength, especially
in the Presidential arena, now it is increasingly the intellectual and professional groups from the upper economic
spheres who do." So in a reversal of traditional patterns, a
bourgeoisified working class, angry over the tax squeeze
and no longer benefiting from the New Deal, will be pitted
against the radicalized affluent.

This development, these thinkers feel, creates a crisis
in the Democratic party which currently contains both the
new class and the old, presumably conservatized working
class. Thus, in 1956, the Democratic party had a massive
center of 41 percent, with 15 percent on the Left and 11
percent on the Right, 22 percent on the moderate Left and
13 percent on the moderate Right. (Rounded fractions result in a total of more than 100 percent.) That was, to use
a favored fifties term, a configuration which favored "stability." But in 1972, the Democratic center had dropped to
26 percent and both the Right and Left had grown propor-
tionately. Now the party was an organized faction fight.
And, these theories held, the left wing was based on an
affluent elite—the New Class.

These generalizations are, I think, flawed, deceptive
half-truths. They are all based on the sixties (which ended
with the election of 1972) and developments within the
antiwar movement and the campus Left. In political

terms, they describe the battle between the Kennedy-McCarthy-McGovern and the Humphrey-Johnson wings of the Democratic party. Yet they do not prove one of the most critical determinants of that period: its relative affluence. In the sixties, there was a continuous rise in the living standards of Americans, the growth of mass higher education, a vast expansion of middle-class (New Class) jobs in the information sector. When the New Left emerged at the beginning of the decade, it was moved by noneconomic issues: by the struggle against capital punishment and the House Un-American Activities Committee and, above all, by the civil rights battle. Moreover, it is unquestionable that the first organizing efforts took place in elite colleges: at Berkeley, Ann Arbor, Harvard and Yale rather than at community colleges. Later on in the decade, when the central issue was the war in Vietnam, the emphasis was once again noneconomic.

But in the seventies, the economic issue reasserted itself, and not simply for working people. College, as we have seen, turned out to be something less than a passport to affluence. There was a "surplus" of Ph.D.s as well as of the black and brown young. And there were signs that the New Class was responding to the change. In many instances, environmentalists had taken an elite, and even aesthetic, attitude toward the pollution issue. They were outraged by a sulfurous factory—but failed to notice the workers who would lose their jobs if it were closed down. As a result, there were the topsy-turvy alliances that Ladd evokes. Unions made united fronts with corporate executives against well-educated professionals.

Some of the neoconservative critics of the New Class seized upon these trends to attack the college-educated idealists as people pursuing their own narrow self-interest in the guise of fighting for humanity. Thus Aaron Wildavsky argued that in an age of the "social limits of growth" the better off need the government to clean up the air and regulate politics in order to further their own privileged happiness. That is a typically determinist, Beardian and unidimensional reading of a complex cultural reality, a vulgar Marxist explanation by a "sophisticated" anti-Marxist. For example, Wildavsky did not even note the contrary evidence which was at hand when he was writing his simplistic condemnation.

In the mid- and late seventies there were significant "New Class" stirrings in the opposite direction from the one described by Wildavsky. There were groups like Environmentalists for Full Employment which publicly backed both the full employment and labor law reform bills. In analyzing the 1972 election, the conservative critics of the New Class had considerable fun with the fact that 29 percent of the delegates to that McGovern-dominated event held graduate degrees (compared with 4 percent of the population in general). But they did not note that at the 1976 convention, which nominated Jimmy Carter, fully 50 percent of the delegates had graduate degrees.

More generally, the New Class has contradictory political tendencies. Insofar as it is educated and relatively well off, it can take elitist positions and look down on the workers. The self-absorbed theatricality of some of the antiwar militants, who showed contempt for all traditional values in a way which probably made many Americans more prowar, would be a case in point. But insofar as the New Class now finds itself facing the problems of a stagflation economy, that class has a self-interest in making a common cause with the workers in a campaign for full employment through planned social investments. Finally, in college the New Class has become aware of the structural inadequacies of American society.

One of the New Left victories of the sixties which survived through the seventies had to do with college curricula. In the 1950s, radical critiques of this country, even when made by non-Communists, were seen as giving aid and comfort to a foreign enemy. With the exception of a few elite campuses there were no serious courses in Marxism, socialist history or left-wing perspectives in any of the social sciences. Then the surge of social consciousness and involvement of the sixties legitimated such subjects.

There were, to be sure, absurdities at times. Militants opposed to universities being treated as trade schools for a corporate cadre thought they should be turned into trade schools for a revolutionary cadre instead. But after all of the turmoil, there was a significant gain and higher education in America became more socially conscious.

So it is not just a narrow class interest, but an educated concern as well, which could motivate this generation to join in a new coalition with the trade unionists. Indeed—and here I rely on my own experience as an activist rather than on published data—many of the graduates of the sixties are now found on municipal councils, state legislatures and the Congress. For some journalists, the end of the confrontations meant that the Left generation of the sixties had vanished into thin air. In fact, many of its members had become less visible because they were more serious.

There is, then, another stratum in the society, not part of the working class, but with a basis for making an alliance with the working class. That possible coalition is the basis for political hope on the democratic Left during the next ten to twenty years.[4]

IV

There is, however, another possibility—on the Right. What would a modern reactionary program fit for the eighties and nineties look like?

One of its political preconditions would be to destroy the potential coalition described in the last section. To do that, it would be necessary to set the various constituencies within those broad categories against one another, to pit poor blacks against organized workers, women against men, New Class environmentalists against trade unionists fighting for their jobs, etc. Indeed, that is precisely the strategy of some of the theorists of the New Right like Kevin Phillips and William Rusher. But, they try to develop that tactic within the framework of an old-fashioned economic conservatism. And that conservatism cannot possibly appeal to labor over any long period of time no matter how angry the workers might get at the irreverence and countercultural values of the New Class.

So the program of modern reaction would have to advocate governmental policies which would maintain the living standard of some of the workers and the middle class, and even provide benefits for them, but which would pay for their security by attacking the poorly organized and the unorganized. Traditional conservatism—which is, as Free and Cantril rightly said, a philosophy without a program—cannot possibly do that since it is programmatically hostile to working people. And the nostrums of traditional conservatism, as we have seen, are utterly incapable of dealing with the crisis of stagflation in any case.

A truly up-to-date reactionary, then, has to come up with a means of dealing with the current contradictions of inflation-recession in such a way as to pit the potential constituents of a mass democratic Left against one another. That, alas, is at least conceivable, though it will be difficult to do, primarily because of the schizophrenia of business in America.

Business, as chapter 4 showed, is torn by ideological allegiance to free enterprise principles which must be systematically violated if late capitalism is going to work. As Herbert Stein, the conservative economist, so well put it: "Many people, including businessmen, are confused about the meaning of the free enterprise system. They think the critical, and sufficient, thing is that the system should be 'private'—meaning that the highest-paid people are not on the public payroll. They do not regard the free competitive-market aspects of the system as crucial or necessarily as constructive." To which we may simply add that these same businessmen are constantly trying to get subsidies from Washington.[5]

There will, then, be ideological resistance in the corporate sector to a modern reactionary program. The American rich, after all, furiously tried to stop Franklin Roosevelt from saving them from the Great Depression. And they are perfectly capable of fighting tooth and nail against any serious—and sophisticated conservative— measures to do with the crisis of stagflation. However, there is a wing of big business which is practical about these matters. Felix Rohatyn is a prime example (but a very sophisticated, New York example) of the breed.

Rohatyn, as chapter 7 documented, is in favor of solving the urban crisis by having the federal government hire the private sector to deal with social woes. That concept is one key to modern reaction. In the overtly statist sixties, when many a businessman joined Lyndon Johnson's Great Society, that was to be done by a direct partnership between federal and corporate planners. In the seventies, a somewhat more conservative ideology assigned a distinctly junior role to Washington: it was to create the conditions, and provide the subsidies, for the companies which would then resolve all of our difficulties. But in both cases—and in any sophisticated reactionary strategy —the intertwining of government and corporate power is essential.

The businessmen, Rohatyn said in 1978, should become much more openly and aggressively political. They are "usually timid . . . about getting involved in 'politics' and, through the media, in taking public positions on a variety of issues." But now, he continued, "statesmanship must come from the private sector since it seems incapable of flourishing in government." Rohatyn was not alone in this attitude. In 1979, *Business Week* reported that corporations were stung by the polls which showed only 22 percent of the people with confidence in the executives (down from 55 percent in 1970). In responding, one public relations expert said, "The corporation is being politicized and has assumed another dimension in our society that it did not have as recently as ten years ago." So it was, for instance, that Mobil Oil spent $21 million in 1978 taking a position in favor of mass transit as well as against proposals to break up concentrated power in the oil industry itself.

But why was Mobil advocating mass transit, a traditional liberal demand? That is because shrewd reactionaries have understood that old-fashioned conservatism will not work. It is, they realize, necessary to make concessions with regard to details in order to preserve the essential. Take Peter Drucker, whose speculations about "pension fund socialism" were discussed earlier. First, he is bent on proving that contemporary capitalism *is* socialism, i.e., he gives a leftist argument for the status quo. That is because he realizes that the system is losing the ideological hold it once had upon the people. "Pension fund socialism," Drucker writes, "should make it possible *for management to regain legitimacy* precisely because it reestablished a genuine socially anchored ownership." That, not so incidentally, was also the program of Charles de Gaulle.

Drucker even goes so far as to advocate worker representation on the corporate board of directors (so, for much more liberal reasons, does George Cabot Lodge of the Harvard Business School). But if that is the case, what is the democratic Left's objection to businessmen who adopt progressive values? It is that they do so only in order to maintain the basically unfair relations of dominance and subordination in the society as well as the antisocial allo cations they bring. Drucker, for instance, makes it quite clear that his leftist rationale for contemporary capitalism, and even his advocacy of a seat on the board of directors for the workers, is designed to allow the boardroom to get on with its work, not to change any power relationships.

In the 1960s, there were some on the New Left who called such tactics "corporate liberalism." Sometimes the term became a mere insult without any serious content (as when Dwight Eisenhower was characterized as part of a liberal cabal). It was also used to counterpose an essentially white, middle-class and college-educated Left against a mass democratic Left which was seen as merely "liberal" and therefore in cahoots with the corporate leadership. In this guise the concept was not only politically useless; it was a rationalization of the righteous self-alienation of the New Left, a phenomenon which eventually played a major role in destroying the movement.

But if one prescinds from the origins and ambiguities of the term, corporate liberalism is a good description of modernized reaction. Here, again, Rohatyn is an illuminating figure. In the same commentary in which he advocated a militancy in the boardroom, he congratulated himself and his corporate colleagues for having solved the New York City fiscal crisis. But that "solution" was accomplished by laying off thousands of workers, imposing tuition at the City University of New York, cutting back on services, passing state tax laws which provided new subsidies for corporations (and therefore a higher relative burden for the average citizen), etc. Rohatyn and company were "liberal" in the sense that they were interventionist and concerned; but they were profoundly conservative in that they imposed the costs of dealing with the fiscal crisis on those least able to bear the burden, i.e., upon the black and Spanish poor, the white poor, the municipal workers and other vulnerable people.

This analysis helps to understand a phenomenon which puzzled many observers in the late seventies. In those years many corporations followed Rohatyn's advice and, taking advantage of a change in the law, formed their own Political Action Committees (PACs). It was widely assumed that this would work in favor of conservatives in general and Republicans in particular. In fact, it turned out that most of the money went to Democrats, incuding liberal Democrats. That, most people understood, was because the Democrats were incumbents and likely to remain so. In such matters, the corporations were being quite pragmatic. But they were also being corporate liberals, I would add. That is, they had understood that some minimal concessions were required if the essentials of the status quo were to be maintained. In this perspective, they did not give money to the Democrats, and even to the liberals, simply because they were practical, but because some of them at least were acting on the basis of a corporate liberal policy.

That may be, someone might say; however, it doesn't explain how a modern reactionary program will deal with the structural crisis of stagflation which is so central to the analysis in this book. The answer here is a risky one since it asserts that the quintessential corporate position is one now vigorously opposed by almost all corporate leaders.* Still, that is my response. The big business program for stagflation is—or rather, would be if the executives were clear about their own interest—a regressive incomes policy.

The most obvious form of such a policy would be wage and price controls which would not affect the concentration of wealth of the top one-half of 1 percent nor really limit the incomes of the upper middle class. It would, if it followed the specifications suggested here, guarantee a relatively decent, even slightly improved, living standard for the middle class and the upper working class. And it would fight inflation by maintaining a chronic recession for those in the bottom third. That would take the form of unemployment, underemployment and declining social services. In essence, the top of the society would try to bribe the middle, splitting them off from those below them who would then be forced to pay the cost of fighting stagflation.

I am, of course, perfectly aware of the fact that big business is opposed to mandatory controls, even though the last time they were applied, under Richard Nixon, they had something like the impact I have just projected into the future. I do not for a moment exclude the possibility that the schizophrenia of the corporate sector, plus its resentment when the federal government issues complex regulations, might keep it from adopting the program

---

* I am also laboring under the difficulties of an extremely fluid situation. In what follows, I am talking about trends toward the future, not the prediction of events, and I am sure that reality will turn out to be much more complex and sloppy than an analysis focusing on just a few crucial variables suggests. I suspect, for instance, that President Carter may well have imposed mandatory wage and price controls by the time this book appears.

which actually suits its interest. Indeed, I devoutly hope
that this will be the case, since that will leave no alternative but the one on the Left.

And yet, it is important to think about this reactionary
possibility. For that focuses attention on a key to a progressive alternative: unity between the various constituencies of the democratic Left.

I will not describe the program of that coalition in this
chapter. Suffice it to say that I have outlined the conditions in which a democratic Left alternative is politically
possible: the convergence of the working class and the
New Class in a movement which would emphasize the
common interest of both constituencies in challenging
and transforming the corporate power which is the source
of the crisis of stagflation and of most of the other social
ills in the United States. Strangely enough, one of the
leading conservative political analysts in the United
States, Kevin Phillips, ruefully came to conclusions which
gave aid and comfort to my hopes in May of 1979.

There is, Phillips wrote at that time, "a possible 1970s
context for a major anti-business shift in U.S. opinion and
politics. . . . New polls now routinely contain sour news
for business; economic populist politics is gaining
strength at the local level; and even stalwart GOP Sena-
tors like Howard Baker, Ted Stevens and Paul Laxalt are
criticizing oil companies or raising the prospect of public
outrage and punitive legislation." "Business," Phillips
continued, "is losing ground with public opinion" and
"Left liberal activists are shifting from social issues to
economics." So "the populist thrust of the 1980s," unlike
that of George Wallace and Proposition 13 in California,
"could be economic in nature and left-tinted."

So it is, one of the political opponents concedes, *possible* that the positive perspective outlined in this chapter
could become a reality. In the final, and summary, chapter of this book, to which I now turn, I will sketch, not so
much the program for such a movement, which has already been detailed in numerous specifics, but rather a
sense of its informing vision.

____ Notes _____

1. Decomposition: King, ed. passim and chapter 100.
2. Free and Cantril: *The Political Beliefs of Americans*, pp. 5–6, 30–32. Schlesinger: "Is the Swing to the Right Real?" *The Wall Street Journal*, February 21, 1978. Ladd: "What the Voters Really Want." Kilpatrick: *St. Louis Globe-Democrat*, August 8, 1978. Stein: "The Real Reason for a Tax Cut," *The Wall Street Journal*, King: in King, ed., pp. 392 ff. Changing American voter: p. 241. Wills: *Confessions of a Conservative*, p. 157. Republican identification: King, ed., fig. 7–2, p. 271. King: King, ed., p. 372. Schlesinger in Schlesinger, ed., vol. I, liii. Reformers: Ranney, chap. VI, in King, ed; Ladd, *Where Have All the Voters Gone?* p. 37. Ranney: King, ed., p. 246. New Deal and parties: Merton, pp. 126 ff. Education and politics: parties: Nie et al., *The Changing American Voter*, fig. 15–5, p. 276. Long: In *Toward a National Urban Policy*, p. 49. Califano: Remarks, April 20, 1978 (HEW). Lobbying increase: King, ed., p. 97. Lindblom: pp. 352–53. Voter turnout: Nie et al., op. cit., p. 77.
3. UAW: Communication from Douglas Fraser, president, UAW, to author, January 3, 1979. Bourgeois working class: Ladd, *Where Have All the Voters Gone?* p. 38. Ladd and Hadley: *Transformation of the American Political System*, p. 231. Service workers: *Statistical Abstract*, pp. 395 ff. Janowitz: *Social Control of the Welfare State*, pp. 75 and 83. Incomes: *Money Incomes and Poverty Status of Persons in the United States*, 1977, p. 2; *Money Incomes in 1976*, pp. 138–39. Bureau of Labor Statistics: "Autumn 1977 Urban Family Budgets," Release, April 26, 1978. Living standards: CEA, 1978, p. 279. Democrats and workers: King, ed., p. 262.
4. New Class and Right: King, ed., p. 281. Ladd: *Where Have All the Voters Gone?* p. 44. Convention delegates: King, ed., p. 232.
5. Stein: "Businessmen of the World Unite," *The Wall Street Journal*, June 12, 1978. Rohatyn: "Statesmanship from the Private Sector," *The New York Times*, July 12, 1978. *Business Week:* "The Corporate Image," January 22, 1979. Drucker: *The Unseen Revolution*, p. 92. Phillips: *The American Political Report*, May 25, 1979.

10

Turning Point

The United States, then, is at a critical turning point. The outcome will not be decided quickly and dramatically, in a year or even in one four-year presidential term. What is involved is a structural transformation of the system and that is certain to require a considerable time.

The New Deal, which eventually became the de facto philosophy even of its opponents, is no longer minimally adequate to deal with the problems defined in this book. The most obvious case in point, we have seen, is the collapse of the theory and practice of the Phillips Curve. Once upon a time it was axiomatic that employment and prices varied inversely. Entire academic theories were based upon that irrefutable truth. But now Henry Aaron, himself a former member of the Brookings Institution, comments wryly on the Phillips Curve, "The succession of articles amending previous estimates in the Brookings Papers on Economic Activity forms the most accessible compendium of such revisions." Like the epicycles of a decadent Ptolemaic astronomy, ingenious calculations are necessary to give even the semblance of life to a concept which was once taken as established beyond doubt.

America could survive a period of confusion among academic economists, of course. The problem is, the policy based upon the Phillips Curve was essential to the functioning of the federal government in the recent past. Excessive unemployment was to be dealt with by mild inflation; high prices were to be brought down by mild unemployment. Now there is stagflation and that once sovereign remedy simply does not work. That is the most obvious index of the turning point in the national life. It ramifies, as we have seen, throughout the entire economy, affecting the aging, the workers, the minorities, the young, the environment, the Third World, the prospects for peace, and on and on.

But stagflation, if the analysis of this book is right, is only a symptom of a deeper problem. The New Deal, I argued in *Toward a Democratic Left*, was based upon Adam Smith's John Maynard Keynes, i.e., on a liberal tactic for preserving conservative values. It saw the basic economic infrastructure, and above all the domination of the investment process by profit-maximizing corporations, as sound. Government was to provide a safety net for those who could not participate in a private economy, which would function well because of Washington's fiscal and monetary policies. That was our very individualistic version of the welfare state.

That strategy did not work during the Great Depression since full employment had to wait for a war; it functioned fairly well during the boom of 1945–69; and it has been in a shambles during the decade of the seventies. It may be that the recent failures are related to a Kondratiev downturn and that we have entered a period of chronic recessions and weak recoveries. That, I have suggested, is a subject for speculation. I am much more positive about the structural sources of our current woes. Whether Kondratiev (and Schumpeter) are right or wrong, there is no doubt that the corporate domination of the economy and the attendant ideological assumption that private control of investment yields a maximum public happiness are basic causes of the current crisis.

In thus focusing upon the corporate control of investment I have not urged a monocausal explanation of our problems. Corporate domination, this analysis has made quite clear, is not to be found in some single "factor." It is expressed through a complex structure. For instance, the corporate leadership is often deluded as to its real position in the society, torn between a sentimental *laisser-faire* and a practical collectivism, capable of believing in myths like "crowding out" and the "capital shortage." Indeed, if business had really run the system on its own during the last half century, it probably would have destroyed it.

Corporate power, both economic and political, thus operates in convoluted, and even unconscious, ways. Yet because the sophisticated profit maximizers in the boardroom are left in control of the critical economic function in the society—investment—the society follows their priorities even when their enemies, or critics, occupy the White House. And that leads to a fundamental contradiction of the system, one which the New Deal (and its successor liberalisms) sometimes ameliorated but never challenged. The structural tendencies toward periodic overproduction and underconsumption are the inevitable consequence of that corporate domination of the investment process.

So it is that the central policy conclusion of this book is that there must be a structural transformation of corporate power. And the key to that development is the democratization of the investment function.

I have, as I stated at the outset, no illusion that this country is suddenly going to leap from a backward liberalism (relative to the Western European welfare states) to a militant socialism. The United States will, for the foreseeable future, continue to pay a terrible price for its historic, and often fanatic, antisocialism. The national consciousness and subconscious are both permeated by an individualistic libido, a survival from simpler times that keeps us from facing up to the complexities of the present and the immediate future.

The next step, then, will not be revolution or even a

sudden and dramatic lurch to the socialist Left. It will be the emergence of a revived liberalism—taking that term to mean the reform of the system within the system—which will, of necessity, be much more socialistic even though it will not, in all probability, be socialist. To be sure, there is the possibility posed in the last chapter: that a truly modern and innovative Right will triumph in political struggle and lead the country toward a socially cruel, but economically functional, future. I will leave the further exploration of that scenario to its partisans. In the few pages remaining I will summarize the alternatives to it.

In the course of this book there have been literally dozens of proposals which specified the program of a more socialistic liberalism. Let me recall just a few of them: price controls on oligopolies; sectoral changes, like national health and a farm program based on family producers and maximum output, as part of a struggle against inflation; social allocation of resources, paid for by social sources of finance like pensions, retained profits and the like, in order to achieve full employment by meeting human needs; the redistribution of income and wealth *and* of the power which their maldistribution brings; making America one nation with a single, and decent, standard of well-being; freeing education from the production functions by reducing the rewards of success and the punishments of failure.

In developing these themes it was shown that the particular problems were part of a larger mosaic and that the basic framework, the dominant fact, the pervasive lightning of that mosaic, was corporate power. Each one of the specific reforms, however valuable it might be in and of itself, was part of a larger program: to gain democratic control of the investment process. Some of these ideas, like national health, have been on the liberal agenda for a generation and may even seem stodgy to some. Others, like winning democratic and social control of pension funds or introducing democracy from the shop floor to the boardroom are more recent in origin. But what is distinctive—what must be the basis of judging the worth of this analysis and these proposals—is the insistence that the problems and the solutions are structural in nature.

Grant all these points and a huge question still remains: Is there some coherent vision which informs all of these specifics? In this torrent of analysis and prescription is there a new "public philosophy" which might be grasped by the citizen in the street?

During the waning days of the sixties counterculture there was a book, *The Greening of America,* which developed some ideas which might provide a point of departure for answering those questions. There were, said Charles Reich, three forms of contemporary consciousness: Consciousness I, the mind-set of the traditional conservative, was clearly obsolete; Consciousness II, the perspective of the liberal, the social planner and engineer, had triumphed in the New Deal but was now somewhat bewildered; and Consciousness III, the view from the counterculture, was decentralist, personalist, relaxed and spontaneous. Reich's book had a brief, meteoric life and then disappeared. The attitudes it expressed did not.

There is a suspicion of "Consciousness II," of technocratic planning, which can be found on both the Right and the Left. Some of the idylls proposed in the name of that critique—on the Right as well as the Left—are simply silly. The enormous increase in the use of marijuana in America over the last generation has hardly made the society a better place as Reich suggested. Put more strongly: the hedonism and fixation with the sovereign self which have so often characterized the counterculture are signs of the breakdown of the old order, not creative sources of energy for building alternatives to it. So there is a temptation to dismiss this entire ideology as a tantrum of the pampered, affluent young.

That is wrong. If the flower children were woefully short on analysis and completely vague as to the future, they, among many others, sensed the crisis of the society. Much more profoundly, an E. F. Schumacher argued for face-to-face, human-scaled solutions to our problems. And

Harry Braverman developed an extraordinary analytic history of work under capitalism which is particularly relevant to this last chapter. Technology, Braverman said, does not evolve technologically. That is, there are political, social, even philosophic, considerations which enter into the design of a machine or a factory. For instance, practically every innovation under capitalism involved reducing the skill and decision making for the vast majority of immediate producers. That was not the expression of an engineering necessity but of a political-economic value system.

Therefore, Braverman went on, many of the well-intentioned proposals for "workers' control" as a means of overcoming the alienation of work are doomed to failure. You cannot impose socialist values upon a capitalist technology, workers' control upon a system designed for top-down control by the technocratic representatives of wealth. To get a genuine participation, it is necessary to redesign the factory and the work process. That, of course, is not something done overnight, although immediate, partial realizations of that principle may well be worth fighting for here and now. But one must realize that the system is of a piece and that limiting social movements to partial reforms all but guarantees that they will eventually be co-opted by their enemies.

I take this point as emblematic of a larger theme: that what is needed in the United States in the eighties and nineties is not simply a rearrangement of a few of the political and economic elements of the New Deal but a creation of new institutions and attitudes, a striving toward the elaboration of a new context. For if I have some chastened sense of the limitations placed upon social movements in these decades, they must be at least as radical as the times if they are going to be minimally effective. And the times are structural; it is now the long run.

But then, cannot one fairly say that I am suggesting that this country square a circle, that it return to the scale and spontaneity of precapitalist society, so marvelously celebrated by the Romantics, and press forward to a planned social justice based upon the postcapitalist use and redesign of capitalist technology? How can such an impossible synthesis of *Gemeinschaft* and *Gesellschaft* take place?

Let me begin with a paradox: that conscious centralization is a precondition for decentralization. An example should make this point precise. If the response to the energy crisis is designed by the oil corporations, handsomely subsidized by the government to solve the unnecessary catastrophe which they themselves made—which is what President Carter proposed in 1979, even though his anticorporate rhetoric may have obscured the fact—the broad lines of that "solution" can be predicted even if the details cannot. Those multinationals will erect a concentrated, bureaucratic, huge system, e.g., they will do something like buying the Arizona desert, covering it with a reflector and plugging every energy user in the nation into their grid. If the past is any guide in this case—and it is—they will certainly impose tragic social costs, like cancer, upon the society and they could even create a doomsday potential.

Clearly, almost everyone would prefer a solar technology on a human scale, adapted to individual and community use, with a potential for bringing cheap energy to the poor people of the globe's south who are blessed with an abundance of sun and little else. If, however, the decision in this case is left up to the spontaneous and unplanned workings of this society, i.e., to the hidden corporate dominated planning process, the outcome can hardly be in doubt. The inhuman technology will triumph. Therefore the political precondition for decentralization is a nationwide political movement; the economic precondition is a government capable of planning for smallness and human scale.

But, then, haven't I simply reproduced my paradox in the form of an example? I think not. It is possible for a planning process to decentralize power. Rural electrification under Roosevelt is a case in point. Washington provided cheap, subsidized credit to locally controlled cooperatives which then generated their own power. The results were far from perfect, since those cooperatives have sometimes made cozy arrangements with the private sector and have been insensitive to the environment. But if the new public philosophy insisted, not simply upon planning, but upon planning with genuine popular participation and, above all, if the dominance of the entire private sector was being challenged, then one could go beyond rural electrification. Far beyond it.

As I have already noted, planning exercised by technocrats with a monopoly of the computers will obviously lead to some kind of authoritarian result. Of course, public bureaucracies are a threat to freedom as well as private bureaucracies. But what if there were legal provision of funds for any significant group of citizens who wanted to hire their own experts in order to put together a counter plan? What if the ritualistic, and normally empty, requirements of public hearings were taken seriously? Would it not then be possible to introduce a third term into our present discussion: Not *either* cancerous growth or no growth, but *also*, planned growth on a human scale?

That notion relates to one of the pervasive themes of this book. In a good number of cases, it was necessary to point out that official statistics were value judgments masquerading as facts. The Council of Economic Advisers' figures on the decline in mining productivity only make sense if one assumes that saving miners' lives has no economic value. The Congressional Budget Office's revision of the poverty estimates requires that one accept the idea that the poor receive health care equal to the monies paid to the Medicaid mill. The new definition of the full employment unemployment rates makes a Marxist point for a conservative purpose: it is recognized that a "reserve army of the unemployed," particularly of the black, brown, female and young unemployed, is necessary to the functioning of the system, and this "necessity" then becomes a reason for ignoring human suffering.

Even as I was completing this study, the events at Three Mile Island, and related cases, reinforced this point.

In the 1950s, the government told American soldiers that it was completely safe for them to move into an area immediately after a nuclear weapon had been exploded. I assume that the scientists, officers and chaplains who said these things believed them (though there is evidence that Dwight Eisenhower consciously wanted to fool the American people with regard to some of the dangers). They *thought* they knew the facts. Then, some twenty to twenty-five years later a pattern of premature deaths suggested that they were tragically ignorant.

Similarly, all of the elaborate discussions of how an accident might take place at a nuclear power plant failed to discuss even the possibility of the accident that did take place at Three Mile Island. In that case, and in the probable deaths resulting from atomic testing in the fifties, a particularly fearful structural problem of these times is obviously present. Technology has become so intricate and complex, so incredibly powerful, that our planning ingenuity regularly produces unforeseen—and perhaps unforeseeable—consequences. People die twenty or twenty-five years after the fact. So it is that in 1979, no one really knows for sure what the eventual toll will be in the Three Mile Island accident.

These reflections point to a very important idea. It is indeed true that knowledge is power in these times. Therefore the democratization of information, of expertise, of statistical definitions, is as important as the democratization of the corporate boardroom. Or rather, the one cannot take place without the other. Unless every significant opposition in the United States is provided by society with the means of challenging the society's official experts, then those experts turn into priests in the worst sense of that word: a caste charged with the interpretation of awesome secrets which, not so incidentally, shore up and preserve all of the established relations of power.

And this point relates to an even larger problem. Government, for many Americans, is "them," a distant labyrinth run by technocrats contemptuous of ordinary people. George Wallace built a very effective, and reactionary, populist movement on the basis of that proposition plus racism. Wallace twisted, and exaggerated, and manipulated a truth—but there was a truth there. What, then, should one do? Reduce government intervention into the society, i.e., move, not toward anarchism, but in the direction of the total and unchallenged control of private, corporate bureaucracies? Obviously not.

The challenge to the economic power of corporations derived from their control of the investment process will only succeed if it is accomplished by means of a genuine democratization. And that, in turn, requires that every single proposal urged here be designed, not simply to carry out this or that function, but to involve people in carrying it out as well. That, clearly, is the work of a generation at least and it is part of a process, of a transformation of the social and economic conditions of life on this planet, that will last many generations. I have outlined the beginning of a staggering task, in a time when many Americans are bewildered and uncertain and nostalgic for a past that never existed. I do so, fully conscious of all the risks, because it is now the long run, because there is no alternative to structural change. If new institutions are not created democratically they will be created undemocratically. We have entered a decade of decision, a crisis of the system, whether we like it or not.

But perhaps if this nation faces up to that fact it will not simply achieve full employment and the redistribution of wealth, the elimination of poverty and racism at home and the possibility of eliminating it around the globe, decent health and respect for the environment, disarmament and the participation of the people in the decisions that shape their lives, and all the rest. Perhaps in the struggle for democratic alternatives to corporate domination, the country will find, not simply answers to various problems, but its humanity, its generosity, its purpose. In a bewildered America in which public woes have given rise to private confusions, that possibility is not simply programmatic. It offers the hope of a new vision as well.

____ Notes _____

1. Aaron: *Politics and the Professors,* p. 142, n. 24. Reich: *The Greening of America,* passim. E. F. Schumacher: *Small Is Beautiful,* passim. Harry Braverman: *Labor and Monopoly Capital,* passim.

Bibliography

Aaron, Henry. *Politics and the Professors: The Great Society in Perspective.* Washington, D.C.: Brookings, 1978.

Adams, Walter. "Merging Sick Steel Giants." *The New York Times,* August 8, 1978.

Advisory Commission on Intra-Governmental Relations. *Significant Features of Fiscal Federalism,* 1966–1976. Vol II. Washington, D.C.: Government Printing Office, 1978.

Anderson, Martin. *Welfare: The Political Economy of Welfare Reform in the United States.* Palo Alto: Hoover Institution, 1978.

Atkinson, A. B. *Unequal Shares: Wealth in Britain,* 1972.

Attali, Jacques. *La Nouvelle Economie Française.* Paris: Flammiron, 1978.

Auletta, Ken. *The Streets Were Paved with Gold.* New York: Random House, 1979.

Belden, Joe, with Forte, Gregg. *Towards a National Food Policy.* Washington, D.C.: Exploratory Project for Economic Alternatives, 1976.

Bellmon, Senator Henry. Speech, May 17, 1977. *Congressional Record,* June 28, 1977.

Bensman, David, and Carpenter, Luther. "Steel Industry Woes." *Newsletter of the Democratic Left,* November 1977.

Blinder, Alan S., et al., eds. *The Economics of Public Finance.* Washington, D.C.: Brookings, 1974.

Bogdanich, George. "Steel Mill Blues." Unpublished manuscript, 1978.

Bowles, Samuel, and Gintis, Herbert. *Schooling in Capitalist America.* New York: Basic Books, 1977.

Brittain, John A. *Inheritance and the Inequality of Material Wealth.* Washington, D.C.: Brookings, 1978.

Braverman, Harry. *Labor and Monopoly Capital.* New York: Monthly Review Press, 1974.

Bureau of Labor Statistics. *The New York Market: An Update.* New York, May 25, 1978.

Burns, Arthur. Speech to the American Enterprise Institute. Reprinted in *John Herling's Labor Letter,* December 23, 1978.

Byung Yoo Hong. "Inflation Under Cost Pass-Along Management." Ph.D. dissertation, Columbia University, 1978.

Campbell, Angus, et al. *The American Voter.* New York: John Wiley, 1960.

Caro, Robert. *The Power Broker.* New York: Random House, Vintage Books, 1975.

Castells, Manuel. *The Urban Question.* Cambridge, Mass.: The M.I.T. Press, 1979.

Chapman, Stephen. "Poor Laws." *The New Republic,* December 2, 1978.

Characteristics of the Population Below the Poverty Level: 1976 Current Population Reports, p-60. July 1978.

Clark, Kenneth B. "The Negro and the Urban Crisis." In *Agenda for the Nation.* Washington, D.C.: Brookings, 1968.

Clark, Peter K., "Investment in the 1970s." Brookings Papers on Economic Activity, 1979.

Congressional Budget Office. *The Disappointing Recovery.* Washington, D.C.: Government Printing Office, June 11, 1977.

———. *Income Disparities Between Black and White Americans.* Washington, D.C.: Government Printing Office, December 1977.

———. *Poverty Status of Families Under Alternate Definitions of Income.* Rev. ed. Washington, D.C.: Government Printing Office, June 1977.

Council of Economic Advisers. Economic Report of the President Together with the Annual Report of the Council of Economic Advisers. Annual, 1946–.

Data on the Distribution of Wealth in the United States. Hearings, Task Force on Distributive Impacts of Budget and Economic Policies, House Committee on Budget, September 26 and 29, 1977.

Day, Richard. "Trotsky versus Kondratiev." *New Left Review* (London), September–October 1976.

Drucker, Peter. *The Age of Discontinuity.* New York: Harper and Row, 1969.

———. *The Unseen Revolution.* New York: Harper and Row, 1976.

Eisenhower, Dwight D. "To Ensure Domestic Tranquillity." *Reader's Digest,* May 1968.

Emergency Future, Report of the Energy Project at the Harvard Business School, Robert Stobaugh and Daniel Yergin, eds. New York: Random House, 1979.

Feldstein, Martin. "Inflation and Capital Formation." *The Wall Street Journal*, July 22, 1978.

———. "Social Security and the Distribution of Wealth." *Journal of the American Statistical Association*, December 1976.

———, and Summers, Lawrence. "Is the Rate of Profit Falling?" Brookings Papers on Economic Activity, vol. I. Washington, D.C.: Brookings, 1976.

Forrester, Jay. "Are We Headed for Another Depression?" *Fortune*, January 16, 1978.

———. "Overlooked Reasons for Our Social Troubles." *Fortune*, December 1969.

Free, Lloyd A., and Cantril, Hadley. *The Political Beliefs of Americans*. New Brunswick, N.J.: Rutgers University Press, 1967.

Furniss, Norman, and Tilton, Timothy. *The Case for the Welfare State*. Bloomington: Indiana University Press, 1977.

Galbraith, James K. "Why We Have No Full Employment Policy." *Working Papers*, March–April 1978.

Goldschmid, Harvey J.; Mann, H. Michael; and Weston, J. Fred, eds. *Industrial Concentration: The New Learning*. Boston: Little, Brown, 1974.

Gough, Robert, and Siegel, Robin. "Why Inflation Became Worse." Data Resources, *U.S. Review*, January 1979.

Hacker, Andrew. "Who Rules America?" *New York Review*, May 1, 1975.

Harrington, Michael. *The Twilight of Capitalism*. New York: Simon and Schuster, 1976.

———. *The Vast Majority*. New York: Simon and Schuster, 1977.

———. "Full Employment: The Issue and the Movement." New York: Institute for Democratic Socialism, 1977.

———. "Hiding the Other America." *The New Republic*, February 26, 1977.

———. "How to Run a Railroad." *Harper's*, December 1975.

———. "The South Bronx Shall Rise Again." *New York*, April 3, 1978.

Health, Education and Welfare, Department of. *The Measure of Poverty*. Washington, D.C.: Government Printing Office, Mass.: April 1976.

Heller, Walter. *New Dimensions of Political Economy*. Cambridge, Mass.: Harvard University Press, 1966.

———. "The Realities of Inflation." *The Wall Street Journal*, January 19, 1979.

Hirsch, Fred. *Social Limits to Growth*. Cambridge, Mass.: Harvard University Press, 1976.

Hitch, Charles J., and McKean, Roland N. *The Economics of Defense in the Nuclear Age*. Cambridge, Mass.: Harvard University Press, 1960.

Howard, Robert. "Going Bust in Youngstown." *Commonweal*, May 25, 1979.

Huxtable, Ada Louise. "The New French Towns." *The New York Times Magazine*, August 13, 1978.

Jacobs, Jane. *The Death and Life of Great American Cities.* New York: Random House, 1961.

Janowitz, Morris. *Social Control of the Welfare State.* Chicago: University of Chicago Press, 1976.

Jencks, Christopher. *Inequality.* New York: Basic Books, 1972.

———, et al. *Who Gets Ahead?* New York: Basic Books, 1979.

Joint Economic Committee. *The 1978 Economic Report of the President.* Hearings, pt. I. Washington, D.C.: Government Printing Office, 1978.

———. *The 1979 Economic Report of the President.* Hearing, pt. I. Washington, D.C.: Government Printing Office, 1979.

———. *Economic Stabilization Policies: The Historical Record, 1962–1976.* Washington, D.C.: Government Printing Office, 1977.

———. *Employment and Unemployment.* Hearings, pt. 12. Washington, D.C.: Government Printing Office, 1978.

———. *The Federal Trade Commission and Inflation.* Hearings. Washington, D.C.: Government Printing Office, 1974.

———. *Midyear Review of the Economy.* Hearings, pt. 3. Washington, D.C.: Government Printing Office, 1978.

———. *Midyear Review of the Economy.* Washington, D.C.: Government Printing Office, 1977. *Midyear Review of the Economy,* 1979. Washington: Government Printing Office, 1979. *The Role of Federal Tax Policy in Stimulating Capital Formation and Economic Growth.* Hearings, July 1977. Washington, D.C.: Government Printing Office, 1977.

———. *Special Study on Economic Change.* Hearings, 1978. Washington, D.C.: Government Printing Office, 1978.

———. Subcommittee on Energy. Hearings. Washington, D.C.: Government Printing Office, 1978.

———. *U.S. Long Term Economic Growth Prospects: Entering a New Era.* Staff study. Washington, D.C.: Government Printing Office, 1978.

Juster, F. Thomas, ed. *The Distribution of Economic Well Being.* Studies in Income and Wealth, vol. 41. Cambridge, Mass.: Balinger, 1977.

Kain, John F. "A Computer Version of How a City Works." *Fortune,* November 1969.

Kearns, Doris. *Lyndon Johnson and the American Dream.* New York: New American Library, 1976.

Kelman, Steven. "Regulation That Works." *The New Republic,* November 25, 1978.

Keynes, John Maynard. *The Collected Writings.* Edited by Donald Moggridge. Cambridge: At the University Press; New York: Macmillan, 1978.

———. *The General Theory.* New York: Harcourt Brace, 1964.

King, Anthony, ed. *The New American Political System.* Washington, D.C.: American Enterprise Institute, 1978.

Kinsley, Michael. "Alms for the Rich." *The New Republic,* August 19, 1978.

Kolm, Serge-Christophe. *La Transition Socialiste.* Paris: Cerf, 1977.
———. *Solutions Socialistes.* Paris: Editions Ramsay, 1978.
Kotz, Nick. "Feeding the Hungry." *The New Republic,* November 25, 1978.
Ladd, Everett C. "What the Voters Really Want." *Fortune,* December 18, 1978.
———. *Where Have All the Voters Gone?* New York: Norton, 1978.
———, and Hadley, Charles. *Transformation of the American Political System.* New York: Norton, 1976.
Lamberton, D. M., ed. *Economics of Information and Knowledge.* Baltimore: Penguin, 1971.
Lasch, Christopher. *The Culture of Narcissism.* New York: Norton, 1979.
Levenson, Charles. *Capital, Inflation and the Multinationals.* New York: Macmillan, 1971.
Levitan, Sar, and Taggart, Robert. *The Promise of Greatness.* Cambridge, Mass.: Harvard University Press, 1976.
Lindblom, Charles E. *Politics and Markets.* New York: Basic Books, 1978.
Lowenthal, Richard, ed. *Demokratische Sozialismus in den Achtziger Jahren.* Frankfurt: Europaische Verlagsanstalt, 1979.
Lubell, Samuel. *The Future of American Politics.* New York: Harper and Row, Colophon Books, 1965.
Magdoff, Harry, and Sweezy, Paul. *The End of Prosperity: The American Economy in the 1970s.* New York: Monthly Review Press, 1977.
Mandel, Ernest. *The Second Slump.* London: New Left Books, 1978.
Martindale, Don. "Prefatory Remarks." In *The City,* by Max Weber. New York: Free Press, 1958.
Melman, Seymour. *The Permanent War Economy.* New York: Simon and Schuster, 1974.
Merton, Robert K. *Social Theory and Social Structure.* 1968. ed. New York: Free Press, 1968.
The Metropolitan Enigma: Inquiries into the Nature and Dimensions of America's "Urban Crisis." Edited by James Q. Wilson. Washington, D.C.: Chamber of Commerce, 1967.
Money Incomes in 1976 of Families and Persons in the United States. Current Population Studies P-60, 114, July 1978.
Money Incomes and Poverty Status of Families and Persons in the United States (Advance Report), 1977. Current Population Studies, P-60, 116, 1978.
Money Incomes and Poverty Status of Persons in the United States. Current Population Studies, P-60, 116, 1977.
Moore, Barrington. *The Social Bases of Obedience and Revolt.* White Plains: Sharpe, 1978.
Moynihan, Daniel P. *Maximum Feasible Misunderstanding.* New York: Free Press, 1969.

————. *The Politics of the Guaranteed Annual Income.* New York: Random House, 1973.

National Bureau of Economic Research. *The Business Cycle Today.* Edited by Victor Zarnowitz. New York: NBER, 1972.

————. 56th Annual Report, September 1976.

National Commission on the Causes and Prevention and Violence. *To Establish Justice.* Final Report. Washington, D.C.: Government Printing Office, 1969.

National Commission on Employment and Unemployment Statistics. Public Hearings. Washington, D.C.: Joint Economic Committee (GPO), 1978.

National Commission on Technology, Automation and Economic Progress. Report. Washington, D.C.: Government Printing Office, 1966.

National Commission on Urban Problems. *Building the American City.* Washington, D.C.: Government Printing Office, 1968.

National Urban Coalition. *City Neighborhoods in Transition.* Washington: 1978.

New York Stock Exchange. *The Capital Needs and Savings Potential of the U.S. Economy.* New York: NYSE, 1974.

Nie, Norman; Verba, Sidney; and Petrocik, John R. *The Changing American Voter.* Cambridge: Harvard University Press, 1976.

Nixon, Richard. *A New Road for America.* New York: Doubleday, 1972.

Nordhaus, William. "The Falling Share of Profit." *Brookings Papers on Economic Activity,* vol. I. 1974. Washington, D.C.: Brookings, 1974.

Nulty, Leslie. Testimony for the International Association of Machinists. Joint Economic Committee. Mimeographed. May 7, 1979.

————. *Understanding the New Inflation.* Washington, D.C.: Exploratory Project for Economic Alternatives, 1977.

O'Connor, James. *The Fiscal Crisis of the State.* New York: St. Martin's Press, 1973.

Okun, Arthur. *Equality and Efficiency.* Washington, D.C.: Brookings, 1975.

————. *The Great Stagflation Swamp.* Brookings bulletin, Fall, 1977.

Owen, Henry, and Schultze, Charles. *Setting National Priorities: The Next Ten Years.* Washington, D.C.: Brookings, 1976.

Pechman, Joseph, ed. *Comprehensive Income Taxation.* Washington, D.C.: Brookings, 1977.

————. *Setting National Priorities: the 1980 Budget.* Washington, D.C.: Brookings, 1979.

————. *Setting National Priorities: the 1978 Budget.* Washington, D.C.: Brookings, 1977.

Pechman, Joseph, and Okner, Benjamin. *Who Bears the Tax Burden?* Washington, D.C.: Brookings, 1974.

Perry, George L. "Potential Output and Productivity." *Brookings Papers on Economic Activity,* vol. I. Washington, D.C.: Brookings, 1977.

Plattner, Marc. "The Welfare State versus the Redistributive State." *Public Interest,* Spring, 1979.

Ratner, Ronnie Steinberg, ed. *Equal Employment Strategies for Women*. Philadelphia: University of Pennsylvania Press, forthcoming.

Rawls, John. *A Theory of Justice*. Cambridge, Mass.: Harvard University Press, Belknap Press, 1971.

Reich, Charles. *The Greening of America*. New York: Random House, 1970.

Revitalizing the Northeast Economy: General Summary and Recommendations. New York: The Academy for Contemporary Problems, n.d. (1977).

Riesman, David, and Jencks, Christopher. *The Academic Revolution*. New York: Doubleday, Anchor Books, 1969.

Rivlin, Alice. "Income Distribution, Can Economists Help?" *American Economic Review*, May 1974.

The Roots of Inflation. New York: Burt Franklin, 1975.

Rostow, Walt. "It Will Take Skill to Avoid a Boom." *The New York Times*, May 21, 1978.

Royal Commission on the Distribution of Income and Wealth. *Report*. 2 vols. London. Her Majesty's Stationer's Office, 1975.

Schlesinger, Arthur, Jr., ed. *History of U.S. Political Parties*. New York: Chelsea House, 1973.

———. *The Politics of Upheaval*. Boston, Mass.: Houghton Mifflin, 1960.

Schmidt, Helmut. Interview. *Business Week*, June 28, 1978.

Schultz, Theodore W. "Reflections on Investment in Man." *Journal of Political Economy*, October 1962 (Supplement).

Schultze, Charles. *The Public Use of Private Interest*. Washington D.C.: Brookings, 1977.

———. Study Paper #1, JEC Study of Employment, Growth and Price Levels, JEC. Washington, D.C.. Government Printing Office, 1959.

———, et al. *Setting National Priorities, the 1972 Budget*. Washington D.C.: Brookings, 1971.

Schumpeter, Joseph. *Business Cycles*. 2 vols. New York: McGraw-Hill, 1939.

Shapiro, Eli, and White, William L., eds. *Capital for Productivity and Jobs*. Englewood Cliffs, N.J.: Prentice-Hall, 1977.

Sidel, Victor, and Sidel, Ruth. *A Healthy State*. New York: Pantheon, 1977.

Seligman, Ben. *Main Currents in Modern Economics*. New York: Free Press, 1963.

Smith, James D., and Franklin, Steven. "The Concentration of Personal Wealth in America." *Review of Income and Wealth*, Series 20, #2.

"Steel Troubles." *The New Republic*, editorial, July 22, 1978.

Tait, Alain. *The Taxation of Personal Wealth*. Champaign-Urbana: The University of Illinois Press, 1967.

Tawney, R. H. *Equality*. 4th ed. New York: Allen and Unwin, 1964.

Thurow, Lester. *On Generating Inequality*. New York: Basic Books, 1977.

————, and Lucas, Robert. *The American Distribution of Income: A Structural Problem*. Joint Economic Committee, May 17, 1972.

Toward a National Urban Policy, Subcommittee on Banking and Finance. Hearings. September 28, 1977.

Transportation, Department of. *A Prospectus for Change in the Freight Railroad Industry*. Washington, D.C.: Government Printing Office, October 1978.

Tufte, Edward. *Political Control of the Economy*. Princeton, N.J.: Princeton University Press, 1978.

U.S., Senate, Committee on Government Operations. *Corporate Ownership and Control*, November 1975.

U.S., Senate, Special Committee on Aging. Report. *Developments in Aging*. Washington: Government Printing Office, 1976.

U.S., Senate, Subcommittee on Anti-Trust and Monopoly. Hearings, May 12, July 27 and 28, September 21, 1978.

Vaughan, Robert J. *The Urban Impact of Federal Policies*. Vol II: *Economic Development*. Santa Monica, Calif.: Rand Corporation, 1977.

Wachtel, Michael, and Adelsheim, Peter. *The Inflationary Impact of Unemployment*. Joint Economic Committee, November 1976.

Ways, Max. "Creative Federalism." *Fortune*, January 1966.

————. "The Road to 1977." *Fortune*, January 1967.

Weidenbaum, Murray. *The Costs of Government Regulation of Business*. Joint Economic Committee, April 10, 1978.

Wills, Gary. *Confessions of a Conservative*. New York: Doubleday, 1979.

Wynn, George, ed. *Survival Strategies, Paris and New York*. New Brunswick, N.J.: Transaction Books, 1979.

Index

Aaron, Henry, 65, 113, 224, 242, 259, 262, 264, 318
Academy for Contemporary Problems, 201
Ackley, Gardner, 29
Adelsheim, Peter, 67–68
Administered price theory, 67–68
AFL-CIO, 259
Aged
poverty among, 253
Social Security crisis and, 85
Agribusiness, subsidies to, 75–76
Aid to Families of Dependent Children, 229, 241–42
Air pollution, 102, see also Pollution
Allende, Salvador, 171
American crisis, internal dimensions of, 30
American Economic Association, 166
American economic system, structural foundation of, 33
American economy
global nature of, 30–31
"Great Divide" in, 55–57
inputs and outputs in, 259–60
"scrapping and rearranging" of, 26
American Enterprise Institute, 54, 97, 293
American Iron and Steel Institute, 24

American society
ideological limits of, 106
structural changes in, 285–87
American Voter, The, 292
American welfare state
structural limitations of, 247
underpinnings of, 245
American workers
class situation of, 301
multilevel definition of, 302
see also New Class; Social class; Workers; Working class
Anderson, Martin, 236
Antiegalitarianism, 168
Anti-inflation program, Carter and, 24
Anti-Marxists, 309
Antipoverty program, 246, 250
see also War on Poverty
Appalachia, government programs for, 184
Appalachian pattern, 178–220
Apparel industry, pricing in, 69
Armament expenditures, 31–32
Atkinson, A. B., 157, 163
Attali, Jacques, 134, 140, 164
Auletta, Ken, 181

Baby boom, of fifties, 269
Baby bust, of sixties, 269
"Background characteristics," in labor market, 267–68
Baker, Howard, 316

Bank of America, 110
Barrett, Nancy Smith, 95
Basic oxygen furnace, 20, 23
Bazelon, David T., 307
Bedford-Stuyvesant section
  (Brooklyn), urban crisis in,
  213–14
Beer, Samuel, 37
Beeridge, Sir William, 90
Bellmon, Henry, 73
Big business, wage/price controls
  and, 315
Big cities
  deterioration of, 181–82, 191
  joblessness in, 182
  Nixon's victimizing of, 198–99
Black Congressional Caucus,
  234
Black family, income of, 95
Black household workers, decline
  of, 300
Blacks
  full employment of, 277
  joblessness of, 87
  poverty and, 225, 231–35
  progress of, 233
  social mobility of, 275
  as stereotype of "poor," 226
  urban crisis and, 217–18
Black/white income ratios, 234
"Blue-collar whites," Democratic
  loyalty of, 300
Blue-collar workers, family
  income of, 303
Blumenthal, W. Michael, 60
Book profits, in corporate returns,
  124
Boom-and-bust cycle
  New Deal and, 54
  structural transformations and,
  136
  welfare state and, 43
  see also Business cycle
Bosworth, Barry, 135
Bowles, Samuel, 264, 280
Brannon Plan, 76
Braverman, Harry, 280, 323
Break, George F., 165
British Labour Party, 160, 170,
  305
British upper class, 170
Brittain, John A., 158–59, 162

Bronx, New York, see South
  Bronx
Brookings Institution, 24, 58, 65,
  92, 129, 136, 162, 166, 318
Brookings Papers in Economic
  Activity, 318
Brooklyn Heights, 213
Brooklyn Navy Yard, 212
Brown, Jerry, 55, 66
Brown, Sam, 144
Browning, Edgar K., 235
Bruce-Briggs, B., 306 n.
Built-in stabilizers, deficit and, 84
Bureau of Labor Statistics, 90, 95,
  133, 248, 304
Burnham, Walter Dean, 297, 306
Burns, Arthur F., 47, 54, 61, 66,
  92, 97, 120, 124
Business
  "big," 315
  free enterprise and, 311
  "schizophrenia" of, 311, 315–16
  see also Corporation
Business cycle
  as "dinosaur," 96–97, 135
  poverty and, 228
  of seventies, 30
  of sixties, 46
  structural factors other than,
  137
  see also Boom-and-bust cycle
Business Cycles (Schumpeter), 96
Business/government
  "partnership," 114
Business investment, in corporate
  ideology, 121–22
  see also Investment
Business Week, 13, 18, 24–25, 48,
  52, 87, 104, 122, 125, 199–
  200, 273, 312
Buying power, of working class,
  304–05

Califano, Joseph A., 296
Campus Left, 307–08
Cantril, Hadley, 287, 311
Capital gains tax
  progressive nature of, 172
  reduction of, 130–31
Capital goods boom, 113
Capitalism
  cycles in, 15

government/business coalition in, 170
Capitalist ideology, religion in, 109
  see also Corporate ideology
Capital shortage
  "impossibility" of, 123
  of seventies, 121
Caro, Robert, 181
Carter, Jimmy, 24, 40, 52, 67, 98, 103, 223, 241, 324
  and business/government "partnership," 116–17
  "doomed strategy" of, 99
  on full employment bill, 248
  on wage/price controls, 315 n.
Carter administration
  business confidence as goal of, 111
  Keynesian theory and, 100
  1980 budget of, 98
  symbolic attacks on inflation by, 77
  tax reductions under, 59–60, 105
Cash glut, of large corporations, 122–23
CBO, *see* Congressional Budget Office
Center, movement toward, 287
Central cities
  deterioration of, 184–91
  Nixon's victimizing of, 198–99
CETA, *see* Comprehensive Employment and Training Act
Changing American Voter, The (Nie et al.), 293, 295, 298
Chase Manhattan Bank, 21
Chemical Bank and Trust Co., 21
Chronic unemployment, stagflation and, 83–84
  see also Unemployment
Citibank (N.Y.), 21
Cities, problems of, *see* Big cities; Urban crisis
City University of New York, 275, 314
Civil Rights Act (1964), 232
Clark, Kenneth B., 218
Clark, Peter K., 136

Classes, *see* Middle class; New Class; Working class
Class formation, complexity of, 301
Class interests, new party system and, 298
Class loyalties, decreased importance of, 286
Class structure
  education and, 262
  egalitarian changes in, 276–77
  revolution of, 256–83
Class struggle, vs. education, 263–64
Clinch River breeder reactor, 102
Coalition Organized Against the Inflation of Necessities, 72
Coalitions, of eighties and nineties, 291, 316
Cognitive skills, social class and, 264
Colby, William E., 249–50
Cold War, 31, 197
  Marshall Plan and, 205
  productivity of West and, 12
Coleman Report, 265
Collectivism, "reluctant," 274
College
  broader curricula for, 282
  job competition and, 168, 270
  middle-class jobs and, 169
  New Class and, 308
  New Left and, 307–08
  relevancy of studies in, 282–83
  see also Education
Columbia Broadcasting System, 213
Common Cause, 151
Common Market, 23
Compensation, wealth maldistribution and, 152
Comprehensive Employment and Training Act (1973), 250
Conference Board, 151
Congressional Budget Office, 48, 166, 224, 235–37, 325
Congressional Joint Economic Committee, 44–45
Conscious centralization, 324
Consciousness II and III, 322
Conservatism
  vs. federal power, 287–88

Conservatism (*cont.*)
  growth of, 286
  ideological, 288
  institutional, 288
  majority in, 288
Conservative issues, vs. liberal
    propositions, 290
Consumer Price Index, 241
"Controlled inflation," in
    Keynesian theory, 45
Coolidge, Calvin, 84
Corporate costs, payment of by
    workers and consumers, 62–
    63
Corporate elite, power of, 27–28
Corporate ideology, 108–45
  business investment in, 121–22
  laisser-faire in, 123
  New Frontier in, 111
  social conscience version of,
    118
Corporate liberalism, 313
Corporate power
  stagflation and, 68–71
  structural transformation of,
    320
Corporate stock
  pension-fund ownership of, 138
  worker ownership of, 141–42
Corporation
  cash flow of, 122
  economic power of, 27–28, 68–
    71, 320, 327
  public interest and, 29
  urban planning and, 212
Corporation salaries, as share of
    profits, 152
Cost of entry, to major industries,
    68–69
"Cost-pass-along management,"
    69–70
Council of Economic Advisers, 11,
    13, 16, 18, 20, 42, 46, 58, 64,
    68, 72, 91, 93, 99–100, 113,
    122, 124, 126, 130–31, 187,
    189, 191, 224, 233, 235, 261,
    289, 325
Council on Wage and Price
    Stability, 73, 135
Counterculture, significance of,
    322
Crash of 1929, 45–46

"Creative Federalism," 117
Credit rating, inflation and, 143–
    144
Culture of Narcissism, The
    (Lasch), 31
Cycle, *see also* Business cycle

Debt financing, Keynesian
    policies and, 44
"Decade of decision," 11–38
Decentralization, 324
Declining productivity,
    investment and, 127
Deficit spending
  inflation and, 54–56
  in New Deal, 56–57
Dellums, Ronald, 74
Demand, reduction of, 99
Demand-pull inflation, 46, 55, 70,
    72–74, 89
  see also Inflation
Democratic Left, as "liberal," 313
Democratic party
  changes in, 293
  crisis in, 307
  working-class loyalty to, 305
Democratic Study Group, 105
Democratic welfareism, 292
Determinist rationales, for urban
    disaster, 180
Dietrich, Kate, 257
"Dinosaur," business cycle as,
    82–83, 96, 135
Disarmament, as unattainable
    ideal, 327
Dividends, "double taxation" of,
    121
Douglas, Paul, 211
Dresch, Stephen, 270
Drucker, Peter, 18, 128–29, 138–
    140, 142, 157, 313
"Dumping," by foreign
    steelmakers, 22

Earned income, as percentage of
    national income, 152
Economic Development
    Administration, 24
Economic success, status and,
    279–80
Economic system, *see* American
    economic system

Economist, see London Economist
Education
adult income and, 261
antiegalitarianism and, 261
as antipoverty measure, 259, 262
vs. class struggle, 263–64
"defensive" investment in, 279
democratization of, 281–82
economic and social changes relating to, 276–83
economic value of, 268
growth of, 260
income and, 261, 268
as "input in production function," 258
as "investment" in job market, 268, 279
number benefiting from, 281
productivity and, 260
racial discrimination and, 258
in Thurow model of labor market, 268
"tiptoe" concept in, 271
yields from, 137
Eighties
coalitions of, 291–92
as "decade of decision," 11–38
growth slowdowns in, 272–73
job competition in, 270
"new era" in, 272
populist threat in, 316
structural crisis of, 30
see also Sixties; Seventies
Eisenhower, Dwight D., 51, 197, 217–18, 240, 313, 326
Eisner, Robert, 63, 127
Elementary and Secondary Education Act (1965), 256
Elite, as New Class, 307
Elitism, vs. education, 270–71
Emerging Republican Majority (Phillips), 307
Employee Stock Ownership Plan, 142
Employment
energy crisis and, 103
"invisible hand" and, 278
public-service, 100–01
see also Full employment; Unemployment

Employment Act (1946), 82–83, 234
Employment program, stagflation and, 32–33
Energy, alternate sources of, 103
Energy crisis (1979), 13–14
employment aspect of, 103
energy policy and, 103
federal highway program and, 51
OPEC price rise and, 76
Energy policy
energy crisis as opportunity for, 103
urban crisis and, 203
Energy shifts, 1850–70, 18
England
equality in, 166
redistribution reform in, 170
see also British (*adj.*); Great Britain
Enlightenment, capitalist ideology and, 109
Environment, stagflation and, 88
Environmental Protection Agency, 62–63, 102
"pollution cost" and, 62–66
Equality
education and, 261
in England, 166
ESOP, *see* Employee Stock Ownership Plan
Ethnic groups, social mobility and, 275
Executive salaries, as share of profits, 152
Exploratory Project for Economic Alternatives, 71
Exxon Corp., 52
cash glut of, 123

Fabricant, Solomon, 80, 122
Family, female-headed, 252
Family Assistance Plan, 208, 223
Family budget, 304
Family income, 95, 154, 303
Farben, I.G., Company, 52
Farmers, nonproduction payments to, 75
Farming, as industrial activity, 137

Federal expenditures, urban crisis and, 184–203
Federal Highway Administration, 194–95
Federal highway program, 51
  urban crisis and, 193–95
Federal policy, big cities and, 191–92
Federal regulation, cost of, 62
Federal Reserve System, 60, 98, 143
  "new economic policy" and, 47–48
  Regulation Q of, 143–44
Federal subsidies, 75, 193–95
  rail system and, 195–96
Feldstein, Martin, 121, 124, 141, 156–58
Females, see Women
Fifties, wastefulness of, 51, 67
  see also Sixties; Seventies; Eighties; Nineties
First National City Bank, 213
Fiscal crisis
  corporate ideology and, 111
  social cost of profits and, 85
Fiscal Crisis of the State, The (O'Connor), 84
Fiscal drag, GNP and, 42
Food budget, as poverty index, 237
Food exports, inflation and, 48–49
Food industry, markup in, 76
Food stamp program, 157, 252
Ford, Gerald R., 52, 75–76, 84, 86, 100, 103, 131, 223, 235, 241
Ford, William, 210
Forrester, Jay W., 16–17, 217, 219
Fortune, 117
Fortunes, devolution of, 155–56, 162
France
  city planning in, 219
  planned decentralization in, 218
Franklin, Stephen, 154–55
Free, Lloyd A., 287, 311
Free enterprise, vs. federal subsidies, 311
Freud, Sigmund, 148
Friedman, Milton, 223
Full employment
  antipoverty program and, 247, 250
  blacks and, 277

class structure and, 276–77
defined, 90
education and, 277
failure of, 45
Humphrey on, 248
inflation and, 223
institutional limits and, 101
planned, 138
post-World War II, 277
as precondition for progressive programs, 246
public ventures and, 101–02
social happiness and, 82
as unattainable ideal, 327
"Full employment" GNP, 240
"Full employment unemployment," 100
  new definition of, 325
Full employment unemployment rate, 35, 90
Furniss, Norman, 245

Galbraith, James, 103
Galbraith, John Kenneth, 113, 307
Garment Workers Union, 167
Gary, Elbert Henry, 20
Gary dinners, 20
Gasoline shortages, 13–14
Gemeinschaft, synthesis with Gesellschaft, 324
General Theory of Employment, Interest and Money (Keynes), 41, 165
  see also Keynesian theory
Georgetown section, Washington, D.C., 215–16
George Washington Bridge, 181
Ghetto population, voluntary redistribution of, 218
Gibson, Kenneth, 181
Gintis, Herbert, 264, 280
GNP, see Gross National Product
God, belief in, 274
Goddard, Henry, 281
Goldwater, Barry, 110, 117
Goldman, Sachs Company, 70
Goods and services, production of, 132–33
Government, as "them," 326
  see also Federal (adj.)
Government agencies, cost of, 62–63

Government/industry partnership, 214

Government spending
budget deficit and, 54–55
federally mandated, 55

Government subsidies, 75, 195–196, 311
harmful effects of, 193–94

Great Britain, relocation in, 218
see also British (adj.); England; United Kingdom

Great Depression, 14–15, 28, 34, 66–67, 156, 170, 212, 278, 291, 319

Great Society, 29, 112, 114, 117, 120, 126, 214, 240, 245, 257, 312
corporate ideology and, 111
destruction of, 12
New Deal and, 37

Great Society in Perspective, The (Aaron), 262

Greening of America, The (Reich), 332

Greenspan, Alan, 131

Greenwich Village, 213

Gross National Product
education and, 258–60
federal percentage of, 242–43
fiscal drag and, 42
"full employment" and, 240
growth of, 58, 81, 130
health care and, 73
increased productivity and, 130
inflation and, 48
investment rate and, 115
public debt and, 60

Growth
eighties' slowdowns in, 272
as "substitute for goods distribution," 270

Growth cycles, vs. recessions, 80–81

Guaranteed income
Family Assistance Program and, 223
welfare system and, 252

Hadley, Charles, 300

Harvard Business School, 53, 140, 313

Harvard University, 121, 189

Haussmann, Baron Georges, 214

Head Start program, 263

Health, Education and Welfare Department, U.S., 133, 246, 296

Health care, inflation and, 72–74
see also Medicaid; Medicare

Hegel, George Wilhelm, 271

Heller, Walter, 42, 61, 69

Highway program
"free will" and, 197
urban crisis and, 193–97

Hirsch, Fred, 168, 270, 272–73, 278

Hispanics, poverty of, 225–26, 232–35

Hoadley, Walter E., 110

Hoover, Herbert C., 28, 51, 77, 126

Hoover Institution, 236

Horatio Alger myth, 138, 163–64, 274, 290

Homer, Garnett D., 120, 239

House Budget Committee, 58

House Committee on Population, 249

House Steel Caucus, 19

House Ways and Means Committee, 130

Housing, inflation in, 74–75

Houthakker, Henrick, 20–21

Hughes, James A., 185, 193

Human resources, federal expenditures on (1961–76), 243

Humphrey, Hubert H., 114, 116, 167, 248, 294
on business/government "partnership," 114–15

Humphrey-Hawkins Bill, 82–83, 99, 101, 105, 234

Hutchins, Robert M., 281 n.

Huxtable, Ada Louise, 218

Ickes, Harold L., 50

"Ideological limits," 106

Ideology, corporate, see Corporate ideology

Income
black percentage, 233
education, 261, 268

Income (*cont.*)
  family, 95, 303–04
  "in-kind," 238
  pre-tax, 165
  as "score," 165
Income distribution, 148–51
Income maldistribution, 149–76
Income redistribution, 111
  defined, 171
  of eighties, 273
Income tax, progressive, 208
  see also Taxation; Tax cuts
Indoctrinations, decline of, 297
Industry
  cost of entering, 68–69
  expansion plans for, 57–58
  social costs of, 61
  see also Business; Corporation
Inequality, rationalization for, 165
  see also Income maldistribution
Inequality (Jencks), 163
Inflation
  administered price and, 67–68
  as Carter challenge, 40
  in Chile, 171
  controlled, 45
  credit rationing in, 143–44
  "demand-pull," 46, 55, 70, 72–74, 89
  federal deficits and, 55–56, 61
  food prices and, 75–76
  vs. full employment, 223
  health care and, 72–74
  housing and, 74–75
  Nixon and, 54, 58, 78, 143
  price index and, 71
  and reduction of demand, 99
  "tight" money and, 143
  unemployment and, 40, 99, 223
  Vietnam War and, 46
Inheritance tax, 174–75
In-kind transfers, 159, 238
Intellectual coherence, decline of, 37
Internal Revenue Service, 124
International Association of Machinists, 88, 103
International Business Machines Corp., 213
Interstate Commerce Commission, 62, 195

Investment
  corporate control of, 320
  declining productivity and, 127–128
  multinational companies and, 27
Investment funds, profits and, 169
Investment tax credit, 200
IQ, socioeconomic class and, 264–265
Iran, Shah of, 53

Jackson, Henry, 103
Jacobs, Jane, 212, 219
Janeway, Eliot, 122
Janowitz, Morris, 302
Japan, income/wealth distribution in, 166
Japanese steel companies, U.S. investments in, 22
Japanese steelworkers
  American jobs and, 26
  production by, 20
  rising wages of, 21
Jencks, Christopher, 265, 276, 278
Jewish social mobility, 275
Jim Crowism, of sixties, 112
Job competition, higher education and, 168, 270
Job Corps, 257, 262–63
Joblessness
  in big cities, 182
  in Kennedy-Johnson years, 229–230
  "necessary," 35, 92
  in New York City, 182
  of 1974, 66
  as price curb, 56
  during World War II, 251
  see also Unemployment
Job market
  education in, 268
  prejudices in, 267–68
  Thurow's model of, 267–68
  women in, 92–93, 303
Johnson, Lyndon B., 13, 41–42, 112, 114, 118, 184, 206, 214, 222, 240, 244, 256–57, 262–263, 289, 294–95, 312
  landslide mandate and failed presidency of, 293
  stagflation and, 53, 78

Joint Economic Committee, 13, 20, 25, 70, 132, 134, 165, 185
Joint Economic Committee Midyear Review of the Economy, 125-27
Jones and Laughlin Steel Co., 21
"Junctures," theory of, 15-16
Justice Department, U.S., 21

Kahn, Alfred, 67, 70
Kefauver, Estes, 294
Kelly, Edward, 21
Kelman, Steven, 63
Kelso, Louis, 142
Kemp, Jack, 130-31
Kemp-Roth Bill, 131
Kennedy, Edward, 21, 74, 103-05, 123, 195
Kennedy, John F., 13, 67, 112, 116, 184, 222
Kennedy, Robert, 212
Keynes, John Maynard, 34, 41, 45, 57, 100, 165, 319
Keynesian theory, 13, 45, 77
  conservatism and, 119
  "controlled inflation" in, 45
  failure of, 100
  New Deal and, 38
  Nixon and, 41
  overproduction and, 97, 140
  prosperity and, 109-10
  "replacement" of, 34
  of sixties, 17
  tax cuts in, 112-13
Keyserling, Leon, 113
"Key to executive washroom" theme, 166
Kilpatrick, James J., 289
King, Anthony, 293
King, Martin Luther, Jr., 112, 222
Kinsley, Michael, 112
Kirkpatrick, Jeanne, 293, 298
Knight, Frank, 149
Kolm, Serge-Christopher, 152, 169
Kondratiev, N. D., 15-16, 319
Kondratiev-Schumpeter theory, 15-17
Korean War, 56

Labor and Monopoly Capital (Braverman), 280

Labor force
  composition of, 92-93
  eighties slowdown in, 272
  expansion of in sixties, 57-58
  male predominance in, 93
  women in, 92-93, 303
  see also Job market
Labor/management relations, "equal sacrifice" in, 142
Ladd, Everett Carl, Jr., 288, 294-295, 300, 307-08
Laffer, Arthur B., 111
Laisser-faire ideology, corporate ideology and, 110, 123, 138
Lampman, Robert, 156
Lance, Bert, 116
Land, Ewin, 163
Lasch, Christopher, 31
Laxalt, Paul, 316
Laziness, poverty linked with, 226-27
Left
  democratic, 308-10, 313
  movement toward, 287
  new, see New Left
Lehman Brothers, 116
Leveson, Irving, 134-35
Levinson, Andrew, 300
Levinson, Charles, 68, 142
Levitan, Sar, 90-91, 262-63
Liberalism, operational, 288
Liberal propositions, vs. conservative issues, 290
Liberal society, moral premise of, 161
Lindblom, Charles E., 165, 170, 297
Lodge, George Cabot, 140, 313
London Economist, 20, 22, 64, 127, 139, 189-90, 192-93
Long, Norton, 296
Long, Russell, 142
LTV (Ling-Temco Voght), 21
Lubell, Samuel, 118
Lucas, Robert, 165
Lustgarten, Steven, 67
Lykes Shipbuilding Co., 21-22

McCarthy, Eugene, 294
McGovern, George, 54, 105, 167, 223, 294, 309

Mahoning River Valley, industrial growth in, 19
Maldistribution, of income and wealth, 148-76
Management, legitimacy of, 313
Mandel, Ernest, 60-61
Manpower Development and Training program, 263
Marijuana, increased use of, 322
Markets
   function of, 188
   urban crisis and, 185-89
Market system, inequality of income and, 150
Marshall, Alfred, 271
Marshall, Ray, 105
Marshall Plan, 205-06
Marx, Karl, 15, 96, 100
Marxist determinism, 180
Massachusetts Institute of Technology, 16, 189, 217
Mass transit, Mobil Oil Corp. and, 312-13
Means, Gardiner, 67
Medical care, deductions for, 172-173
Medicaid, 159, 235-38, 242-43, 325
Medicare, 236-38, 241-42
Meidner Plan (Sweden), 141
Mellon, Andrew, 116
Mellon Bank, 11
Melman, Seymour, 31
Merit wants, federal expenditures on, 242-43
Merrill Lynch Pierce Fenner & Smith, Inc., 20
Metropolitan areas, shrinkage of, 33
Metropolitan Enigma, The (Wilson), 189
Mexico, "invasion" from, 249-50
Middle class
   income of, 305
   two ranges in, 305
   working class and, 299, 305
Middle East, Communist threat in, 50
Middle East oil, in World War II, 50
Midwest cities, urban crisis in, 198-99, 205-06, 208, 215, 251
Mills, C. Wright, 186

Mining productivity, mine deaths and, 64-65
Minsky, Hyman, 13
Mitchell, Parren J., 125
Mobil Oil Corp., mass transit advocacy by, 312-13
Mondale, Walter F., 210
Mondale-Ford Bill, 210
Monopoly policy, pricing and, 68-69
Moore, George, 213
Morgan Guarantee Trust Company, 116
Moses, Robert, 181
Mothers, support of children by, 94-95
   see also Working wives
Moynihan, Daniel Patrick, 42, 114-16, 124, 127-28, 198-99, 202, 223-24, 252, 262
   on urban crisis and federal expenditures, 198-201
Mueller, Willard, 67
Multinational companies
   bureaucracy of, 324
   public policy making and, 27
Murtha, John, 19
Myrdal, Gunnar, 197

National Bureau of Economic Research, 80, 96
National Commission on Employment and Unemployment Statistics, 90, 95
National Commission on Technology, Automation and Economic Progress, 92
National Commission on the Causes and Prevention of Violence, 183
National Commission on Urban Problems, 211
National energy plan, employment and, 103
National health, urban crisis and, 209
National health system, 74, 291, 321
National income, land income as percentage of, 152
   see also Income
National poverty policy, 207-08

National Urban Coalition, 215
Neighborhood Youth Corps, 262
Netherlands, capital growth
    sharing in, 141
New American Ideology, The
    (Lodge), 140
New American Political System,
    The, 299
New class, 306–10
    as affluent elite, 307
    contradictory tendencies of, 309
    middle class as, 299
    working class and, 316
New Class, The (Bruce-Briggs),
    306 n.
New Deal, 12, 28, 54, 109, 111,
    126, 222, 278, 285–86, 288,
    291–92, 295–96, 307, 318–19,
    322–23
    as ad hoc response to problems,
        38
    "ambiguity" of, 28–29
    deficit spending in, 56–57
    failure of, 45, 57
    full employment and, 45
    Keynesian policies and, 45
    as purpose or vision, 37
New Frontier, 111, 240, 245
New Left, 308
    college curricula and, 309
    self-alienation of, 313–14
New party system, social class and
    class interests in, 298–300
New Right, 310–11
New York City
    bankruptcy threat to, 180–81
    budget crisis of, 251, 314
    decay in, 181–85, 190
    job loss in, 182
    muggings and vandalism in,
        183
    "shrinking size" of, 190, 217
New York State, federal taxes
    paid by, 198
New York Stock Exchange, 120–
    123
New York Times, 13, 97, 102, 116,
    128, 208, 218, 235, 239, 249
New York University, 212
Nie, Norman, 293
Nineteen eighties, see Eighties
Nixon, Richard M., 20, 41, 46–47,
    115, 223, 307

big cities and, 198–99
dollar devaluation and, 47–48
"economic Watergate" of, 54
Family Assistance Plan of, 208
on Great Society educational
    programs, 265–66
ideological reversal by, 119–20
inflation and, 54, 58, 78, 143
"jawboning" of, 67
as Keynesian liberal, 118–19
landslide mandate and flawed
    presidency of, 293
manpower programs of, 256–57
and "new economic policy," 47
on New Frontier and Great
    Society spending, 239–40
poverty programs and, 224,
    230–31
stagflation and, 53
on "throwing money at
    problems," 224, 240, 244, 252
Nordhaus, William, 124
Norfolk and Western Railway, 195
Northeast cities, urban crisis in,
    198–200, 205–06, 208, 215,
    251
Nuclear power, Three Mile Island
    accident and, 325–26
Nulty, Leslie, 71

O'Connor, James, 84
OECD, see Organization for
    Economic Cooperation and
    Development
Office of Technology Assessment,
    104
Oil companies
    antitrust actions of, 49–50
    cash glut of, 122–23
Oil import quotas, 51
Oil industry, alternate energy
    sources and, 103
Okun, Arthur, 48, 161, 166, 268
Oligopolies, price controls on, 321
OPEC, see Organization of
    Petroleum Exporting
    Countries
Oppenheimer Fund, 116
Organization of Petroleum
    Exporting Countries, 18, 51,
    68
    boycott of (1973–74), 49
    inflation and, 48

Organization of Petroleum (*cont.*)
1973 price increase by, 43, 48,
76
"Organization of Wheat Exporting
Countries," 75
Organization for Economic
Compensation and
Development, 272
Orshansky, Molly, 237
Other America, The (Harrington),
217, 228
Overproduction, maldistributed
wealth and, 97, 149
Oxygen furnace, first use of, 20

PACs, *see* Political action
committees
Paley, William, 213
Palme, Olaf, 128
Penn Central Railroad, 101, 196,
247
Pension funds, 129
"Social Security wealth" and,
156
stock ownership by, 138
"Pension fund socialism," 138–39
Perry, David, 247
Perry, George L., 58, 92–93
Personal productive capacity,
factors in, 149
Peru, "military socialism" of, 141
Petrocik, John R., 293
Petroleum Reserve Corp., 50
Phenomenology of Spirit (Hegel),
271
Phillips, Kevin, 307, 310, 316
Phillips Curve, 42, 46, 56, 318–19
Plattner, Marc, 161
Polaroid Corp. shares, rise in,
163–64
Political action committees, 151,
314
*Political Beliefs of Americans,
The* (Free and Cantril), 287–
288
Politics and the Professions
(Aaron), 262
Pollution
as "cost," 62–66
federal subsidies for, 65
TVA and, 102

Poor
blacks and Hispanics as
stereotypes of, 226
defined, 225–27
nonexistent "wealth" of, 155
number of in U.S., 228–29
as permanent underclass, 228
stereotypes of, 226
tax policy and, 171–72
typical, 227–28
see also Poverty
Population, redistribution of, 178–
179, 218
Populist thrust, of eighties, 316
"Positional" goods, exclusive
neighborhoods as, 270
Postindustrial society, 132–34
Poverty
of aged, 253
blacks and, 225–26, 231–35
business cycle and, 228
defined, 225–26
education and, 259, 262
Family Assistance Program
and, 223
food budget as index of, 237–38
government definition of, 225–
226
Hispanics and, 225, 232–35
laziness equated with, 226–27
national policy on, 207–08
in Nixon-Ford years, 230–31
prejudices and, 253
racial aspects of, 225, 231–35,
246–47
rightist critique of, 236–39
stereotypes of, 225–26, 253
undercount in, 237–38
see also Poor
Poverty programs, federal, 210
Power Broker, The (Caro), 181
Price controls, 47
repeal of, 119–20
Price rise, giant corporations and,
67
Prices
administered, 67–68
monopoly policy and, 68–69
stagflation and, 64
tax expenditures and, 70
Private property, economic
rewards from, 161

Productivity
 education and, 260
 factors affecting, 149
 fall of, 132–34
 investment rate and, 127
 rise in, 132
Productivity crisis, 145
Profits, investment funds and, 169
Profit sharing, following capital formation, 142
Progressive income tax, as only tax, 208
 see also Income tax; Taxation
Promise of Greatness, The (Levitan and Taggart), 262
Property taxes, 289–90
Proposition 13 (California), 289–290, 306, 316
Prosperity
 government role in, 109
 as "normal state," 11
 profit margin and, 97
Protestantism, capitalist ideology and, 109
Proxmire, William, 13
"Prudent man rule," 140
Public debt, GNP and, 60
Public funds, "necessary" expenditure of, 42
Public interest, business and, 29
Public Interest, 115, 235
Public pension fund reserve, Sweden, 140–41
 see also Pension funds
Public philosophy, new form of, 322
Public projects, vs. tax cut, 105
Public-service employment, 100
Public ventures, full employment and, 101

Railroad industry, wrecking of, 195–96
Rand Corporation, 185, 192, 265
Ranney, Austin, 294–95
Rawls, John, 161
Reactionary individuals, inflation-recession problems and, 311
Reader's Digest, 217
Real buying power, of working class, 304–05

Real output, federal portion of, 241
Real wages, unemployment and, 85
Recessions
 in capitalist society, 15
 "growth cycle" and, 80–81
 number of (1954–64), 41–45
 vs. "reduced rate of growth," 97
"Recovery"
 of seventies, 98
 unemployment and, 81
Redistribution of income, see Income redistribution; Wealth redistribution
Redistributive tax program, 172–173
"Redlining" practice, 144
Reich, Charles, 322
Religion, in capitalist ideology, 109
Relocation program, vs. ghetto redistribution, 218
"Reluctant collectivism," 274
Republican capitalism, 292
Republican party, changes in, 293
Restoration Corp., 213–14
Retirement Income Security for Employees Act (1972), 158
Ricardo, David, 162
Rich, tax laws favoring, 108, 130–132, 148–49
Riches
 changed definition of, 35
 as "dirty little secret," 153
Riesman, David, 276
Right
 movement toward, 287
 triumph of, 321
Rinfret, Pierre, 122
Risk capital, tax subsidies and, 126
Rivlin, Alice, 166
Robin Hood, government role of, 148–49
Rockefeller, Nelson A., 52
Rohatyn, Felix, 312, 314
Roosevelt, Franklin D., 28–29, 38, 50, 109, 111, 126, 245, 288, 291, 295, 297, 312, 324
Rostow, Walt W., 16
Rural electrification, cooperatives in, 324
Rusher, William, 307, 310

Salomon Brothers and Hutzler, 129
Samuelson, Paul, 42, 80–81
Saudi Arabian oil, Petroleum Reserve Corp. and, 50
Schlesinger, Arthur, Jr., 28, 288, 294
Schmidt, Benno, 213
Schmidt, Helmut, 18
Schultz, Theodore W., 260
Schultze, Charles, 67, 99, 101, 150, 241–42
Schumacher, E. F., 322
Schumpeter, Joseph, 15–16, 21, 96, 110, 319
Schumpeter-Kondratiev theory, 56
Schwartz, Harry, 235
Sectoral changes, 321
Securities and Exchange Commission, 144, 196
Senate Budget Committee, 60
Senate Finance Subcomittee, 122
Service workers, vs. blue-collar workers, 300
Services, provision of, 132–33
Seventies
    black/white income ratio in, 234
    business cycle of, 30
    "capital shortage" theme of, 121
    corporate ideology of, 109–11
    deficits of, 59
    educational expenditures in, 263
    falsifications and half-truths of, 120–21
    Keynesian liberalism in, 119–20
    "military socialism" of Peru in, 141
    "recovery" in, 98
    steel industry crisis of, 17
    structural crisis of, 30, 36
    welfare state and, 245
Sex analogy, poverty as, 148
Shah of Iran, overthrow of, 53
Shriver, Sargent, 206
Silk, Leonard, 97
Simon, William, 16, 120–23, 136
Sixties
    boom of, 46
    educational expenditures of, 263

Equal Educational Opportunity Study of, 265
Jim Crowism of, 112
Keynesianism of, 17
liberal reform of, 112
social revolution of, 30
"throwing money at problems" in, 224, 240, 244, 252
Smith, Adam, 44, 50, 71, 123–24, 155, 186, 273–74, 299, 319
Smith, James D., 154, 156, 233
Snow Belt, poverty of, 201
Social class
    "economic" position of, 301
    IQ and, 264–65
    multilevel definition of, 301–02
    new levels of, 299–300
    new party system and, 298
Social irresponsibility, in urban crisis, 187
Socialism
    vs. capitalism, 28–29
    militant, 320
    pension funds and, 138–40
Socialism (Harrington), 26
Social Limits to Growth (Hirsch), 168, 270
Social mobility
    higher education and, 168–70
    Jewish, 275
Social Security benefits
    "comprehensive" taxation and, 173
    higher payments in, 58, 241, 253
    husband's pension and, 93–94
    New Deal and, 28
    1977 expenditures on, 241–42
    and recession of 1973–74, 158
    "Social security stage," 245–46
Social Security system
    seventies' crisis in, 86
    short-term deficit in, 85–86
    strains on, 85–86
Social Security tax
    regressive nature of, 209
    rise in, 208–09
"Social Security wealth," 35, 156–159, 238
Social ties, atrophy of, 274
Social welfare state, 246
Solar power, potential of, 104
Solar technology, 324

Solarz, Stephen, 172, 209
Solow, Robert, 28
South Bronx (New York City), as
    disaster area, 183–85, 190,
    204, 211, 219, 247, 249
    see also Urban crisis
Soviet Union
    American food exports to, 48–49
    grain imports of, 75–76
    U.S. poverty and, 222
Spending, government, see
    Government spending
Stagflation, 40–78
    corporate power and, 69–71
    defined, 13
    investment during, 128
    Johnson and, 53
    of 1973–74, 42–43
    Nixon and, 53
    "one-time shocks" and, 53
    overproduction and, 150
    pricing administration and, 64
    seventies' deficits and, 59
    statistical problem in, 90
    steel industry and, 17–18
    as symptom of deeper problem,
        319
    Third World and, 87–88
    unemployment and, 32, 83–84
    wage differentials and, 278
    wage-price spiral and, 70–71
Stalin, Joseph, 157, 170, 190
Stalinist collectivization, 178, 219
State taxes, regressive nature of,
    172
Status, education as investment
    in, 279–80
Steel industry
    "dumping" in, 22–23
    growth of, 18
    "insidious liquidation" of, 18
    Joint Economic Committee
        study of, 25
    overstimulation in, 25
    protectionism plea by, 22–23
    "trigger prices" in, 23
    worldwide crisis of, 17
Steel prices, rise in, 1953–57, 67
Steiger, William, 129–30
Stein, Herbert, 13, 89–91, 209,
    311
Sternlieb, George, 182, 185, 193
Stevens, Ted, 316

Stevenson, Adlai, 294
Stock Exchange, see New York
    Stock Exchange
Stock issues, new, 129
Structural crisis
    history of, 43–54
    intellectual coherence and, 37
    of seventies and eighties, 19,
        30, 32, 36
Students for a Democratic
    Society, 307
SUB, see Supplementary
    Unemployment Benefits
Suburbia, as "federal creation,"
    202
Subsidies, see Government
    subsidies
Subways, mugging and
    vandalism in, 183
Summers, Lawrence, 124
Sun Belt, 33, 205–06, 208
    exodus to, 248
    ghetto population of, 201
Supplemental Security Income,
    242
Supplementary Unemployment
    Benefits, 300
Sweden
    Meidner Plan in, 141
    public pension fund reserve in,
        140–41
    as social welfare state, 246
Swedish socialists, wage
    bargaining by, 167
Synthetic fuel industry, 52
Synthetic rubber program, 52

Taft Ellender Wagner Act (1949),
    214
Taggart, Robert, 262–63
Tawney, R. H., 166
Taxation
    "comprehensive," 173
    on "economic income," 173–74
    inheritance, 174–75
    redistributive, 171–73
    structural reform and, 175–76
Tax cuts
    Carter and, 59–60, 105, 129–30
    demand and, 171
    in Keynesian theory, 112–13
    poor and, 171–72
    vs. public works projects, 105

Tax expenditures
  government decisions on, 60
  prices and, 70
Tax laws
  exemptions in, 172
  homeowners vs. renters in, 172–
  173
  income redistribution and, 171–
  173
  rich favored by, 108, 130–32,
  145, 148–49
Tax policy, urban crisis and, 208
Tax profits, in IRS returns, 124
Tax reductions, see Tax cuts
Tax revenues, "built-in
  stabilizers" and, 84
Tax subsidies, risk capital and,
  126
Tax system, federal, 172
Taylor, Gen. Maxwell, 249–50
Technology, urban crisis and,
  184–88, 323–24
Tennessee Valley Authority, 102,
  247
Theory of Justice, A (Rawls), 161
Theory of Moral Sentiments, The
  (Smith), 273–74
Thermonuclear war, threat of, 31
Third World, 32, 319
  steel industry and, 19
  Western stagflation and, 87–88
Thomas, Franklin, 213
Three Mile Island, nuclear
  accident at, 325–26
Thurow, Lester, 163–65, 261,
  266–67, 269, 271, 276, 278
"Tight" money, inflation control
  through, 143
Tilton, Timothy, 245
Tourist paradox, 271
Toward a Democratic Left
  (Harrington), 26, 299, 319
Transportation decisions,
  structural character of, 196–
  197
Treasury Department, U.S., 24
"Trickle-down" theory of wealth,
  101, 161, 214
"Trigger prices," in steel industry,
  23
Trotsky, Leon, 15
Truman, Harry S., 76, 83

Truman administration,
  agricultural crisis of, 78
TVA, see Tennessee Valley
  Authority
Twilight of Capitalism, The
  (Harrington), 26, 49, 96, 240,
  301

UAW, see United Automobile
  Workers
Uncounted people, poverty
  among, 237–38
Unemployment
  aging and, 85
  chronic, 83–84
  "necessary" amount of, 35
  false reasoning about, 81
  full employment, see "Full
  employment unemployment"
  inflation and, 40, 99
  inflation as "cure" for, 319
  price rise and, 66–67
  real wages and, 85
  stagflation and, 32–33
  structural, 99
  World War II and, 137–38
United Kingdom, maldistribution
  of wealth in, 160
  see also England; Great Britain
United Automobile Workers, 300
United States
  coalitions in, 291–92
  compared to Japan on income/
  wealth distribution, 166
  concentration of wealth in, 154–
  155
  as "confused nation," 290
  conservatism vs. liberalism in,
  290–92
  as corporate collectivist nation,
  26
  family income in, 95, 154, 303
  as major steel producer, 18
  maldistribution of income and
  wealth in, 148–76
  net worth percentages owned by
  richest in, 154
  "new economic policy" of 1971
  for, 47
  potential majorities in, 291
  poverty statistics for, 228–29

structural history of, 44–53
at turning point, 318–27
United States Railway
Association, 196
Unseen Revolution, The
(Drucker), 138
"Upbringing money," for women,
93
Urban crisis
blacks and, 217–18
corporation's responsibility in,
209–10
denial of, 189
in Europe, 218
federal highway program and,
193–95
government role in, 191–203
sectionalism and, 201
social irresponsibility in, 187
market analysis of, 185–87
national health and, 200
pro-urban legislation and, 203
remedial program for, 216–17
strategy for, 206–07
tax policy and, 208
Urban decay
"benevolent" effects of, 185–86
determinist rationale for, 180–
184
"inevitability" of, 183–85
Urban family budget, 304
Urban planning, "spontaneity" of
corporations in, 212
"Urban war zone," in South
Bronx, 183–85

Vast Majority, The (Harrington),
31, 250
Verba, Sidney, 293
Vietnam War, 12, 42, 118–19, 295
inflation and, 46, 56, 78
steel industry during, 18
and War on Poverty, 262
Violence, in South Bronx, 183
Voter turnout, decrease in, 293,
298

Wachtel, Michael, 67–68
Wage increases, prices and, 70
Wage-price controls, profit
sharing and, 142–43

Wage-price spiral, 70
see also Inflation
Wallace, George, 316, 326–27
Wall Street Journal, 28, 52, 89–
90, 98, 118, 131, 162, 164,
175, 193, 195, 214–15
War on Poverty, 206, 242, 244
beginnings of, 262
Vietnam War and, 262
see also Antipoverty program
Washington, D.C., fragmentation
of power in, 296–97
Washington Star, 239
Wastefulness, of fifties, 51
Watergate affair, 47
Watkins, Alfred, 247
Watson, Thomas, 213
Ways, Max, 116
Wealth
' as "dirty little secret," 153
concentration of, 154, 175–70
devolution of, 156
inflation-proof nature of, 156
property and mortgages as, 155
"random walk" nature of, 164–
165
self-duplicating nature of, 155–
156
share of top one percent of, 157
transfer of, 156
"trickle-down" theory of, 101,
161, 211
Wealth maldistribution, 97, 148–
176
Wealth of Nations (Smith), 273
Wealth redistribution, 111, 327
Weidenbaum, Murray, 62–64
Welch, Finis R., 233
*Welfare: The Political Economy
of Welfare Reform in the
United States* (Anderson), 236
Welfare capitalism, emergence of,
14
Welfare state
basis of, 245
boom-and-bust cycle and, 43
extension of, 278–79
laisser-faire and, 110
structural crisis and, 44
Welfare system
changes in, 251–52
guaranteed income and, 252

Wenglowski, Gary M., 70
West, productivity of, 12
Westergaard, J. H., 272
West Germany, "upbringing money" in, 93
Weston, J. Fred, 67
West Virginia, poverty in, 184
White family, average income of, 95
Whitney, J. H., 213
Wildavsky, Aaron, 308
Wills, Gary, 292
Wilson, James Q., 189
Wilson, Woodrow, 292
Winpisinger, William, 103–04
Winter, Ralph, 98
Women
  as heads of families, 252
  in labor force, 92–93, 303
  "upbringing money" for, 93
  as working wives, 303
Wood, Robert, 199
Worker(s)
  "background characteristics" of, 267–68
  education for, 280–81
  multilevel definition of, 302
  ownership of means of production by, 157
  real wages of, 85
  as stockholders, 141–42
  in Thurow's labor market model, 267–68

Worker's control, work alienation and, 323
Working class
  "bourgeoisified," 307
  buying power of, 304–05
  loyalty of to Democratic party, 305
  middle class as, 305
  New Class and, 316
  "objective," 305
  potential for change in, 299–300
Working Class Majority (Levinson), 300
Working wives, middle class and, 303
World War II
  education following, 260, 264
  fluctuations in wealth following, 154–55
  industrial expansion during, 137
  unemployment and, 137, 251

Xerox shares, rise in, 163–64

Yoo Hong, Byung, 70
Youngstown Sheet and Tube Co., 21, 24–25
Yugoslavia, employee stock ownership in, 142

Zanowitz, Victor, 96